CHAPTERS

IN THE

HISTORY OF YORKSHIRE:

BEING A COLLECTION OF

ORIGINAL LETTERS, PAPERS, AND PUBLIC DOCUMENTS,

ILLUSTRATING THE STATE OF THAT COUNTY IN THE REIGNS OF
ELIZABETH, JAMES I., AND CHARLES I.

With Introductions, Notes and Index,

BY

JAMES J. CARTWRIGHT, M.A., CANTAB.,

OF THE PUBLIC RECORD OFFICE.

SUBSCRIBER'S COPY.

WAKEFIELD: B. W. ALLEN.
—
1872.

𝕯𝖊𝖉𝖎𝖈𝖆𝖙𝖊𝖉,

WITH PERMISSION,

TO THE

RIGHT HONOURABLE

LORD ROMILLY,

MASTER OF THE ROLLS,

KEEPER OF THE RECORDS,

&c., &c., &c.

LIST OF SUBSCRIBERS.

(*) *denotes Large Paper Copies.*

*Abbott, Robert, Esq., Ealing, Middlesex. (Five copies.)
Abbot, Jabez, Esq., Alford, Lincolnshire.
*Akroyd, Edward, Esq., M.P., F.S.A., Bank Field, Halifax.
*Alder, George W., Esq., Wakefield.
Allen, B. Willoughby, Wakefield.
Armytage, G. J., Esq., F.S.A., Clifton, Brighouse.
*Ash, Alfred, Esq., Agbrigg, Wakefield.
Ash, John S., Esq., Wakefield.
Ash, William, Esq., Wakefield.
*Ashlin, Mrs., Firsby, Lincolnshire.
*Atkinson, James, Esq., Clee, Grimsby.

Baines, Edward, Esq., M.P., Burley, Leeds.
Balme, E. B. Wheatley, Esq., J.P., Cote Wall, Mirfield.
Banks, W. Stott, Esq., Wakefield.
Barber, Fairless, Esq., F.S.A., Castle-hill, Rastrick.
*Barker, Major, J.P., Holme Field, Wakefield.
*Battersby, Miss, Scothern, Lincolnshire.
Belton, William, Esq., Chevet, Wakefield.
Briggs, Archibald, Esq., Stanley Hall, Wakefield.
Brooke, Colonel, J.P., F.S.A., Armitage-bridge, Huddersfield.
Brooke, Rev. J. Ingham, Thornhill Rectory.
Brown, B., Esq., Wakefield.
Bruce, Samuel, Esq., LL.B., J.P., Barrister-at-Law, Wakefield.
Buckton, George, Esq., Roundhay, Leeds.
Burkill, Miss, Scarborough.
Burrell, Mrs., Scarborough.
Burrell, Henry, Esq., Harwood House, Scarborough.
Burrell, Rev. R., Stanley, near Wakefield.

Cadman, J. Heaton, Esq., Ackworth.
Carr, ——, Esq., Barton-le-Street, Malton.
Carter, Henry M., Esq., Wakefield.
*Cartwright, Miss, West Rasen, Lincolnshire.
Cartwright, Miss F. A., Limber Hill, Lincolnshire.
Cartwright, George, Esq., Kirmington, Lincolnshire.
Cartwright, Thomas, Esq., Durham-on-Trent, Notts.
*Clarkson, Mrs., Beech House, Sandal, Wakefield.
Clay, Charles, Esq., Walton, Wakefield.

CLAYTON, WILLIAM, Esq., Sandal, Wakefield.
CROSSLEY, JOHN, Esq., Manor Heath, Halifax.

*DEVONSHIRE, His Grace the DUKE of, K.G., Devonshire House, Piccadilly, W.
DALE, Mrs., Florence Villa, Scarborough.
DAVIES, ROBERT, Esq., F.S.A., The Mount, York.
DANIEL, Rev. W.C., M.A., The Parsonage, Dewsbury Moor.
DEAN, THOMAS, Esq., Batley.
DIBB, JOHN E., Esq. (*the late*), Barrister-at-Law, Wakefield.
DICKONS, J. NORTON, Esq., Market-street, Bradford.
DYKES, FRED., Esq., South Parade, Wakefield.
DUGDALE, Mrs., Rose-hill, Burnley.
EDWARDS, Sir HENRY, Bart., late High Sheriff of Yorkshire, Pye Nest, Halifax.
EDWARDS, JOHN, Esq., Secretary of the Public Record Office, London.
EMMERSON, GEORGE, Esq., Wakefield.

*FAIRBAIRN, Sir ANDREW, Woodsley House, Leeds.
FARRAR, Mrs., Park House, Halifax.
FAWCETT, JOHN, Esq., Greenfield, Luddenden Foot.
FERNANDES, NOWELL L., Esq., The Grove, High Ackworth.
*FERNANDES, J. L., Esq., South Villa, Wakefield.
FERNANDES, GUY D. L., Esq., Wakefield.
FERNANDES, C. B. L., Esq., Egremont House, Wakefield.
FENNELL, WILLIAM, Esq., Wakefield.
*FOSTER, Mrs., Lindum-terrace, Lincoln.
FOWLER, JAMES, Esq., F.S.A., Wakefield.
*FRANK, F. BACON, Esq., High Sheriff of Yorkshire, Campsall Hall, Doncaster.
*FRANKISH, JOHN, Esq., Temple House, Anlaby-road, Hull.
FRANKISH, Mrs. HENRY, Normanby-on-the-Wold, Lincolnshire.
FURBISHER, RICHARD, Esq., Crofton, Wakefield.

*GASKELL, DANIEL, Esq., Lupset Hall, Wakefield.
GATRILL, Rev. J. M., Horbury, Wakefield.
GILL, W. H., Esq., Solicitor, Wakefield.
*GREEN, EDWARD, Esq., Heath Old Hall, Wakefield.
GRIFFITH, HENRY, Esq., 30, Prince's-gardens, W.

*HAGUE, J., Esq., Many-gates House, Sandal, Wakefield.
HAIGH, GEORGE, Esq., Beechfield, Sandal, Wakefield.
*HAILSTONE, EDWARD, Esq., F.S.A., Walton Hall, Wakefield (one large and one small copy).
HALIFAX, The Right Hon. VISCOUNT, G.C.B., Hickleton, Doncaster.
HALL, JOHN, Esq.

*HAMER, CHARLES M., Esq., Snitterfield, Stratford-on-Avon.
HANDSON, Miss, West Rasen, Lincolnshire.
HARDY, Sir T. DUFFUS, D.C.L., the Deputy Keeper of the Public
    Records.
HART, ROBERT W., Esq., Sandal, Wakefield.
*HARTLEY, Captain, J.P., Horbury, Wakefield.
HASLEGRAVE, JOSEPH, Esq., Dirtcar House, Wakefield.
*HAWORTH, FRED., Esq., Wakefield.
HAWORTH, JOSEPH W., Esq., The Cliffe, Wakefield.
HEMINGWAY, C. A., Esq., The Elms, Dewsbury.
HICK, M. B., Esq., Chald House, Wakefield.
HOLDSWORTH, RICHARD, Esq., Castle Lodge, Sandal, Wakefield.
HOLDSWORTH, S., Esq., M.D., J.P., Wakefield.
HOLME, Rev. ROBERT, M.A., Compton House, Brighton.
HOLMES, JOHN, Esq., Holmeville, Methley.
HORSFALL, HENRY, Esq., Wakefield.
*HOUGHTON, The Right Hon. LORD, D.C.L., F.S.A., Fryston Hall,
    Ferrybridge.
HOWDEN, JOE, Esq., Wakefield.
HOWDEN, THOMAS, Esq., Wakefield.

IANSON, JOHN M., Esq., Wakefield.
IKIN, Miss, Scarborough.
IVESON, W. B., Esq., Heckmondwike.

JACKSON, JOHN, Esq., Milnthorpe House, Wakefield.
JACKSON, Rev. PETER, Newstead Hall, Wakefield.
JOHNSON, T. C., Esq., Chevet, Wakefield.
JOHNSON, T. C., Esq., Tothby, Alford, Lincolnshire.
JONES, Rev. HENRY, St. Mark's, Myddelton-square, E.C.

*KAYE, JOHN, Esq., J.P., Clayton West, Huddersfield (one large
    and one small copy).
KAYE, JOHN, Esq., Bretton, Wakefield.
*KENDELL, D. B., Esq., M.B, Heath House, Wakefield.
*KIRK, Mrs., Woodside, Halifax.

*LEEDS, His Grace the DUKE of (*the late*), Gogmagog-hills, Cambridge.
*LANGHORNE, J. BAILEY, Esq., Outwood Hall, Wakefield.
LEATHAM, W. H., Esq., J.P., Hemsworth Hall, Pontefract.
LEE, HENRY, Esq., Thornes, Wakefield.
LINDLEY, J. E., Esq., Wakefield.
LISTER, JOHN L., Esq., J.P., Shibden Hall, near Halifax.
LOCKWOOD, Mrs. CHARLES, Moorcroft, New Mill, Huddersfield.
LOCKWOOD, BEN., Esq., Huddersfield.

*MACKIE, R. BOWNAS, Esq., J.P., St. John's, Wakefield.
    (One large copy and two small copies.)

*MACKIE, Colonel, The Manor House, Heath, Wakefield.
*MACKIE, JOHN, Esq., Crigglestone Cliff, Wakefield.
*MARCH, GEORGE, Esq., Scarcroft, near Leeds.
MARCH, J. O., Esq., Beech Grove House, Leeds.
*MARRIOTT, W. T., Esq., Sandal Grange, Wakefield.
  (Two large and two small copies.)
MARRIOTT, Mrs., Hopton.
MARSDEN, JOHN, Esq., Walton House, Wakefield.
MARSDEN, J. E., Esq., St. John's, Wakefield.
MASTERMAN, JOHN, Esq., Wakefield.
MICKLETHWAIT, Rev. J. H., Painthorpe, Wakefield.
MICKLETHWAITE, Miss, Wakefield.
MICKLETHWAITE, Mrs. W., Wakefield.
MILTHORP, GEORGE, Esq., Wakefield.
MOREHOUSE, H. J., Esq., F.S.A., Stoney Bank, Huddersfield.

*NORFOLK, His Grace the DUKE of, Hereditary Earl Marshal.
*NORTON, The Hon. G. C., Kettlethorpe Hall, Wakefield.
NORTH, Mrs., Scarborough.
NORTH, J. W., Esq., Wakefield.

ORMEROD, THOMAS, Esq., Woodfield, Brighouse.

*POLLINGTON, The VISCOUNT, 8, John-street, Berkeley-square, London.
PHILIPS, Rev. GILBERT H., M.A., Rural Dean, Brodsworth Vicarage,
  Doncaster.
*PILKINGTON, Sir LIONEL M. S., Bart., Chevet Hall, Wakefield.

RIPON, The Most Hon. the MARQUESS of, K.G., D.C.L., Studley
  Royal, near Ripon.
*RAMSDEN, Sir JOHN W., Bart., M.P., Byram, Ferrybridge.
  (Two copies.)
RAINE, Rev. Canon, York.
RAYNER, R. LEE, Esq., Ings Grove, Mirfield.
*ROBERTS, G. H., Esq., South Parade, Wakefield.
ROBERTS, C., Esq., Wakefield.
*ROBINSON, Mrs., The Priory, St. Leonard's-on-Sea.
ROBINSON, FRED., Esq., Wakefield.
RILEY, H., Esq., Edwood Hall.

SAGAR, H., Esq., Whitefield House, Nelson, near Burnley.
*SALT, Sir TITUS, Bart., Crow Nest, Halifax.
  (One large and one small copy.)
*SALT, EDWARD, Esq., J.P., Ferniehurst, Shipley, near Leeds.
SANDERSON, MICHAEL, Esq., Scarborough.
*SANDERSON, T. K., Esq., South Parade, Wakefield.
SCHOLEFIELD, Mrs., Boyne Hill, Wall Green, Wakefield.
SCHOFIELD, PHILIP, Esq., Maltby Hall, Rotherham.

SCHOLEFIELD, MATTHEW S., Esq., Batley.

SENIOR, THOMAS, Esq., Solicitor, Ash Grove, Bradford.

SHARP, Rev. JOHN, Horbury Vicarage, Wakefield.

*SHAW, JOSEPH, Esq., Woodlands, Sandal, Wakefield.

SHAW, E. P., Esq., Wakefield.

SHEARD, MICHAEL, Esq., Batley.

*SIMPSON, Mrs., Walton, Wakefield. (Two copies.)

*SIMPSON, E. T., Esq., Walton, Wakefield. (Two copies.)

*SIMPSON, EDWARD, Esq., Crofton Hall, Wakefield.

*SIMPSON, CHARLES H., Esq., Ackworth, Pontefract.

SKAIFE, ROBERT H., Esq., The Mount, York.

*SMEATHAM, Mrs., Clinton House, Harrogate. (One large copy and two small copies.)

SMIRTHWAITE, J. S., Esq., Grove House, Wakefield.

SMITH, Mrs., Bank House.

SMITH, ALFRED, Esq., Wakefield.

STANSFELD, THOS. WOLRYCHE, Esq., Weetwood Grove, near Leeds.

STEWART, W. H., Esq., Wakefield.

STEWART, MARTIN, Esq., Wakefield.

SURTEES, Rev. SCOTT F., Rectory, Sprotbro', Doncaster.

SUTCLIFFE, Mrs., 17, Dover-street, Manchester.

SUTCLIFFE, W., Esq., Bacup, Lancashire. (Two copies.)

*SYKES, CHRISTOPHER, Esq., M.P., Brantingham Park, Brough.

SYKES, JOHN, Esq., M.D., F.S.A., Doncaster.

*TAYLOR, THOS., Esq., Coroner, Wakefield.

TEW, PERCY, Esq., J.P., Wakefield.

THEAKSTON, S. W., Esq., Scarborough.

*THOMPSON, Mrs., Rue Vineuse, Passy, Paris.

THOMPSON, JOHN, Esq., Cheadle, near Manchester.

*THOMPSON, FRED., Esq., Wakefield.

THOMPSON, ROBT., Esq., Carr Field, Luddenden.

THOMPSON, TOM, Esq., 42, St. Domingo Grove, Liverpool.

*THOMPSON, GEORGE. Esq., Bank House.

*THOMPSON, W. H., Esq., Stansfeld Hall.

*THOMPSON, WILLIAM, Esq., Scarcroft, Leeds.

*TOMLINSON, W. H. B., Esq., Mayor of Wakefield.

TOMLINSON, Rev. ROUTH, Kirkthorp Vicarage, Wakefield.

TOMLINSON, G. W., Esq., Ramsden-street, Huddersfield.

TOOTAL, CHARLES, Esq., Wakefield.

TOWNSEND, H., Esq., Stubbing House.

*VARLEY, J., Esq., Edgerton House, Huddersfield.

* WHARNCLIFFE, The Right Hon. LORD, Wortley Hall, Sheffield.

WALKER, —, Esq., Scarborough.

WARD, JOHN, Esq., Wakefield.

WATSON, WILLIAM, Esq., Wakefield.

*WESTERMAN, G. H., Esq., J.P., Sandal, Wakefield.

*WHITE, J. TOLSON, Esq., Halesfield, Altofts, Normanton.

WHITEHEAD, F. F., Esq., Beech Hill, Saddleworth.

WIGGLESWORTH, JAMES, Esq., Wakefield.

WILKINSON, Mrs., Trinity-street, Huddersfield.   (Two copies.)

WILKINSON, JOHNSON, Esq., Trinity-street, Huddersfield.   (Two copies.)

WILKINSON, JOSEPH, Esq., Barnsley.

WILKINSON, J., Esq., Austhorpe Lodge.

WILSON, EDMUND, Esq., Red Hall, Leeds.

WILSON, J., Esq., Gainsborough.

WILSON, H. S. L., Esq., Crofton, Wakefield.

*WILSON, J. W. RIMINGTON, Esq., J.P., Broomhead Hall, Sheffield.

WILSON, MATTHEW, Esq., J.P., Eshton Hall, Gargrave.

WILSON, W. R., Esq., Wakefield.

*WINN, CHARLES, Esq., J.P., Nostel Priory,. Wakefield.

WOOD, Rev. J. S., D.D., President of St. John's College, Cambridge.

WOOD, Miss, Alford, Lincolnshire.

*WOODHEAD, Captain, Wakefield.

*WORMALD, Major, Dewsbury.

WORMALD, HENRY, Esq., Wakefield.

WRIGHT, S. M., Esq., Solicitor, Bacup.

THE LIBRARY OF ST. JOHN'S COLLEGE, CAMBRIDGE.

THE LIBRARY OF THE PUBLIC RECORD OFFICE.

*THE PUBLIC LIBRARY, LEEDS.

PREFACE.

THE materials for the following pages have been derived for the most part from the State Papers preserved in the Public Record Office; the manuscript collections in the British Museum have been of great service in the preparation of the explanatory notes; and the ordinary sources of historical information have been occasionally employed to complete a narrative which might otherwise appear disjointed. It has been my object to illustrate Yorkshire history and biography, as far as possible, in the very words of the principal actors in the events described.

I have to express my best acknowledgments to Lord Romilly for his liberal permission to take the facsimiles used in the volume; and to Sir Thomas Duffus Hardy, the Deputy Keeper of the Public Records, for his kind interest in the work, and his friendly advice on many points in connection with it. Mr. Alfred Kingston, of the Public Record Office, has rendered much help in my various researches.

To many who are more immediately interested in the subject I am under considerable obligations. To say that Lord Houghton encouraged my efforts is but to repeat the experience of many literary aspirants. Mr.

J. L. Fernandes and Mr. W. S. Banks, of Wakefield, have watched the progress of the work, and have made many useful suggestions. The services of these two gentlemen demand special recognition; but I hesitate to mention the names of other friends, lest an omission should give offence.

It remains for me to return my warm thanks to the numerous subscribers who have enabled me to issue the volume.

J. J. C.

London, 10th *October,* 1872.

TABLE OF CONTENTS.

CHAPTER III.—YORKSHIRE RECUSANTS.

CHAPTER IV.—YORKSHIRE REPRESENTATIVES AND THEIR CONTEMPORARIES, 1603-1628.

against them successful—again returned—Parliament immediately dissolved—Wentworth pricked for Sheriff—the forced loan—list of Yorkshire defaulters—Wentworth's disgrace—Sir John Savile, Comptroller of the Household—Wentworth joins the King's party, and is made President of the North—Wentworth and Savile created peers—death of Savile, and account of his estates—Wentworth's letter depicting the plague in Yorkshire—final characteristic letter.

CHAPTER V.—TOWNS AND THEIR TRADES.

A description of Scarborough in the time of Elizabeth—construction and repair of the pier there—report of the bailiffs—Seamer market—attempts to suppress it successful—report of mayor and corporation of Hull and of York—the York bakers—the corn-dealers of Hull—disputes between York and Hull merchants—Ripon ale-houses—petitions of Leeds, Halifax, and Wakefield against the imposition of shipmoney —the West Riding clothiers—petition of Leeds clothiers—reports of justices from Halifax, Doncaster, Bradford, Wakefield, Staincross, &c., on the stock of corn, the suppression of ale-houses, &c.—letter of Sir Henry Savile—note about tobacco-dealers—Assessment for shipmoney.

CHAPTER VI.—TRAVELLERS' NOTES IN 1634 AND 1639.

The three members of the Noble Military Company at Norwich set forth on their travels—enter Yorkshire—old knitting Doncaster—Robin Hood's Well—Pomfret and its Castle—their lodgings at York—the Minster—the Council of the North and the clerical dignitaries—Sir Arthur Ingram's house—another journey to York, and notes by the way —York ordinaries, &c.—Ripon, Bradford, and Halifax.

APPENDICES.

LIST OF FAC-SIMILES.

CHAPTERS

IN THE

HISTORY OF YORKSHIRE.

CHAPTER I.

SIR THOMAS GARGRAVE.

THE roll of Yorkshire Worthies is a long one, and
so rich is it in names distinguished in every kind of
knowledge and action, that it is easy to understand
how the claims of some men equally deserving of the
title may be overlooked. Surely the subject of this
First Chapter is fit to take his place amongst the best
of them; yet but little has been hitherto done to preserve him in our memories. An attempt to remedy
this defect will form a not unapt introduction to the
task we have undertaken.

The Gargraves were a family of some antiquity in
the neighbourhood of Wakefield, as a well-authen-
ticated pedigree of them shows. Sir John Gargrave, Knight, described as of Snapethorpe and Gargrave, was Master of the Ordnance, and a Governor in
France under King Henry the Fifth. He was tutor to
Richard, Duke of York, who was slain at the Battle

of Wakefield, in 1460.   Sir John Gargrave was buried
at Bayonne, in France.   From his second son, William,
was descended Thomas Gargrave, who married Elizabeth, daughter of William Levett, of Normanton.
The only issue of this marriage was the subject of the
present memoir.   Thomas, the father, owned some land
in the "Pear-tree* Acres, in Kirkgate," Wakefield, as
appears by an inquisition taken in the reign of Henry
the Eighth.   That the "Pear-tree Acres" was the site
of the son's birth-place, is touchingly evident to us by
his own words; for towards the close of his long life,
he prayed the Queen to be allowed to purchase from
her the Old Park at Wakefield, adding," I would build
me a dwelling-house therein, for that it adjoineth to
the place where I was born, and where my land lieth."†

   The date of his birth is very uncertain.   Lodge, in
his "Illustrations of British History," first published at
the end of the last century, speaks of a portrait, then in

---

   * In the Court-rolls of the Manor of Wakefield it is called
Pear Treen; the catalogue of the Earl of Strafford's sale describes it as the "Pear-Tree Meadow," containing 2 acres 1 rood
20 perches.
   † The Station of the Lancashire and Yorkshire Railway Company is built upon the Pear-tree Acres; and the fact of its
neighbourhood to the Old Park of Wakefield is preserved to us
by the Park Street, which forms the principal approach to it.
A survey of the manor of Wakefield, made about the year 1545,
says that "the Old Park is distant half-a mile from the town. The
Pale in a convenient state, about three miles in circuit, and
contains about four score fallow-deer. The new park distant
one mile, and contains in circuit four miles. The paling decayed, low and in some places down.   220 fallow-deer."

the possession of Levett Hanson, Esq., of Normanton, inscribed, " Thomas Gargrave, Miles, 1570, æt. 75 ;" which portrait, at the time Hunter wrote his " History of South Yorkshire "—about the year 1830—was in the hands of Viscount Galway. It is difficult to believe that Gargrave had attained so great an age in the year 1570. This year and the preceding one were precisely the most active periods of his career; he was then engaged, as we shall presently see, in the suppression of the Northern Rebellion.

Few particulars can be gleaned of his early life. Thus much, however, is clear, from his own letters, and from other sources, that he was educated for the profession of the law. He must have acquired some considerable reputation in his profession, otherwise he would hardly have been placed upon the Council of the North, as one of its learned members, very shortly after the establishment of that body. The Council was first instituted in 1537, and owed its origin to the very unsettled state of the Northern Counties, caused by the suppression of the lesser monasteries. King Henry thought it advisable, before proceeding with further reforms, that a body possessed of full ruling powers should be settled at York, and so should be able to check more promptly any future disturbances. It was in the year 1539 that Gargrave first appeared as a member of the Council, and in that capacity he continued throughout the remainder of life. The untiring energy with which he performed the duties assigned to him is sufficiently evident in the letters which he wrote at a later period of his life, and from which we shall hereafter quote; and there can be little doubt that this quality was equally prominent on his first appointment.

In 1547 he accompanied the Earl of Warwick into Scotland, acting as Treasurer of the expedition, and while there he received the honour of knighthood. Shortly after his return he made large purchases of land in Wakefield and the neighbourhood; and these acquisitions, together with the reputation he seems already to have gained as a man of marked vigour and ability, placed him in the first rank of the West Riding gentry. Kinsley Hall, near Hemsworth, was his principal residence for many years previous to his adding Nostel Priory and estate to his possessions. From the accession of Edward the Sixth down to the year 1580, no name is of more frequent occurrence in the affairs of the West Riding than that of Sir Thomas Gargrave.

It was just after his return from Scotland that the first Parliament of Edward was summoned, and the City of York honoured Gargrave by returning him as one of its representatives. In the succeeding Parliament, too, which began and ended its sittings in March, 1553, the like distinction was conferred upon him. A year or two later his reputation was sufficiently great to cause him to aspire to, and to obtain, the still higher dignity of a knight of the shire.

During the reign of Queen Mary, Gargrave was especially active on the Council of the North, and he had to make frequent journeys to Newcastle, Berwick, and other places. The Scots, about this time, were making great inroads on the Marches, driving away cattle, burning houses, and taking prisoners. The Council, in consequence, had their time well occupied in devising means to suppress this evil, and especially in raising troops in the Northern counties. This latter was by no means an easy task, from the unwillingness of people to serve so unpopular a government.

In the first Parliament of Queen Elizabeth, Sir Thomas Gargrave was again returned for the county. The journals of the House of Commons, under the date of 25th of January, 1558-59, tell us that " by the first motion and nomination of Mr. Treasurer of the Queen's House, the Worshipful Sir Thomas Gargrave, Knt., one of the Honourable Council in the North Parts, and learned in the laws of this Realm, was, with one voice of the whole House, chosen to be Speaker." It would appear that, in accordance with a time-honoured custom, Gargrave professed but a modest opinion of his own fitness for the office, and prayed the Queen that he might be excused; for in a speech addressed to him by the Lord Keeper, Sir Nicholas Bacon, the following passage occurs : " Her Majesty, being credibly informed of your approved fidelity, wisdom, and discretion, and of the long experience you have

had in Parliament matters, thinketh that if she should
consent to your desire, it would be prejudicial to the
service of Her Majesty and the Commonwealth of this
Realm."

Again, the journals recount that the Queen having
taken her seat upon the throne, Mr. Speaker made a
notable oration, touching partly the decays of the
Realm, with some remedies for the same; and also
made certain petitions for the ancient liberties, which
were granted by the Queen, to be used reverently and
decently. On the 6th of February the Speaker was
one of those deputed to demand an audience of Her
Majesty, and to request her, in the name of the nation,
to be pleased to take to herself a husband.

Parliaments had no long life in those days, and this
one was no exception to the rule, for it was dissolved on
the 8th May in the same year. On this occasion, we
are told, Mr. Speaker made another learned oration,
much praised by the Lord Keeper.

The Queen shortly afterwards gave another proof of
her appreciation of Gargrave's merits. The Duke of Norfolk was about this time appointed Lieutenant-General
of the North, and in the open instructions delivered to
him by Elizabeth, Sir Thomas Gargrave is specially
recommended in civil matters; the secret instructions
with which the Duke was also supplied direct that in
matters of war other Counsellors may be consulted,
but that in civil business no step was to be taken without
the assent being had of Sir Thomas Gargrave.

Francis, Earl of Shrewsbury, was Lord-Lieutenant of Yorkshire and President of the Council of the North at this time, and a letter of his dated from Ferry-bridge on the 17th of January, 1559-60, to Sir William Cecil, states that he was about to take some troops to Newcastle, and that he had appointed his "verie loving freend, Sir Thomas Gargrave, knight," Vice-President in his absence, "who I right well knowe bothe canne and will execute the same accordinglie, and in as willinge and painfull wise, as if myself werre present." In the following month Gargrave was commissioned to go into Holderness to raise as many soldiers there as he should think needful to furnish four ships then lying at Hull.

It was but a few months after this, that is, on the 21st of September, 1560, that the Earl died, and it was necessary to supply his place as President of the Council. Sir William Cecil thought this a likely opportunity for making some change in the constitution of the Board, or, at any rate, effecting some reduction of expenditure. He applied to Gargrave, as the man whose opinion was best worth having on the subject. The reply has great interest for us in the information given about the Council, so we append it at full length :—

SIR THOMAS GARGRAVE TO SIR WILLIAM CECIL.

"My deuty humbly remembryd to your mastershyppe. I receyvyd your mastershypps letter upon

Friday last, beyng in my iorney to kepe a sessyons
wyche I wyth others have apoyntyd to be kepte
throughe this shyre in every hundreth twyse for the
execution of certen necessary lawes, wyche at the
comon sessyons cannot be so well done, and therfore
yt was ohe day longer before I could answer your
mastershyppe.   I have herwyth sent your mastershyppe the copyes of the Commyssyons and the
warrant for this Counsaill, and also two copyes of our
Instructions, the one of them beyng a true copy, and
the other wyth suche additions as I have addyd, the
wyche may be usyd as shalbe thought mete.   I have
also in certen notes herwith declaryd myn openyon
or devise to certen poynts of your letter, the wyche I
beseche you to take in good parte, bot myn openyon
ys that yf yt be the quenes Majestie's pleasure to place
a noble man to be resydent in the offyce of Presydent
of her Majestie's Counsaill here, that his fee of one
thowsand pounds by yere for the dyett of the Counsaill
cannot be demynyshed, for that he shall here by all
things if the peny (*sic.*) without provission, so that
then the quenes Majestie, I think, cannot save any of
her highnes charges, onles yt shuld be in some tryfell
of some Counsalor's fee.   Surely moche cannot be
savyd, onles it were in the L. Pr. absens, and by
lessenyng the nombr of Counsailors, and with the
alteration of the estate thereof, I dare not take upon
me to intermedle, unles yt were by conference with
your mastershyppe or others, yet I have herwith sent

one note concernyng that matter wyche is al I wold do in this lytle tyme.

"Sir, for accompts of the Attornay ther ys none that I knowe, her was never any attornay, nor fynes, or amercyments assessyd or takyn by this Counsaill, bot about 2 yeres before the dethe of quene Mary, and then that matter was placyd in our Instructions at my suyte, for I thought yt wold be a means to bring the people to conformyte and make them ferefull bothe to do evyll and to disobey, and at that tyme my lord president that last was gote placyd therin as attornay Mr. Thomas Sutton, his servant, whoo occupyed that office 2 yeres, beyng nather bounden to accompte, nor yet dyd at any time accompte to my knowlege. At my beyng at London this tyme too yeres, the said Mr. Sutton dyd lett me se a note of his. Receyte for his tyme, and therby yt appered he hayd very lytle more then his awne fee, wyche ys appoyntyd 20l. by yere, to be takyn of theys fynes and forfetures, and at the makyng of our last Instructions your mastershyppe placyd in that Rowme Wylliam Woderoffe,* whoo at that time was sycke, and occupyed by a deputy 2 syttyngs and dyed, and aboute thys tyme twelve-month Rychard Whallay, somtymes of Grays Inne, was by the quenes Majesties letter apoyntyd, whoo hayth occupyed this yere, and ben so syckly that

---

* Thomas Woodrove, of Woolley, Esq., who married Elizabeth, daughter of Robert Waterton, of Walton, Esq., and died in 1549, had a son William, no doubt the person here indicated.

he could not come to accompt, and nowe he ys dede
also, so that as yet ther ys none accompte takyn for
that offiyce. I thynke ys fee were suffycyent to be
10*l.*, or 20 marks besydes his ganes.

" Sir,—The late L. president, whoys soule God
pardon, did lye for the most part (furth of syttyngs)
at his howse at Shefeld, wyche was the sowthyst parte
of his Commyssyon, and was therfor moche troble to
sutors, but for the most parte this 10 yeres I have
kepte the seale as Vice-president at myn awne howse
without any fee, allowance, or reward, the wyche in
dede was bot 14 myles more southe then Shefeld, bot
in myn openyon Yorke ys the metyste place for the
body of the Counsaill to remaine at for al sutors and
others that shuld repare to the Counsaill, and also for
the mayntenance of that pore cety wyche lakyng the
Counsaill's repare wyll in shorte tyme moche decay.

" Yt ys good to have yerly one syttyng in Northumberland, Westmoreland, or Cumberland as occasion
shall serve and there to continewe a moneth togethers
and to kepe in that syttyng one gaole delyvere, and
that was found to do moche good in King Henry the
8th's days.

"Nottynghamshyre ys not within the Commyssyon of
this Counsaill; Nottynghamshyre, Darbyshyre, Cheshyre,
and Lancashyre be all within the levetenancy of the
north, bot not wythin the Commyssyon of the president; ther ys only in that Commyssyon Yorkshyre, the
bishoppriche of Duryame, Northumberland, Cumber-

land, Westmoreland, the Cety of Yorke, Kyngston-upon-Hull, Newcastell, Carlyle and Barwyke. Thus ashamyd of my long and tedyous letter, I reffere myselfe to your goodnes and have herwith sent you certen notes, &c., &c.

At Kynslay, in hayst, the 10th of November, 1560.

"Your mastershyppes assuryd,

ever to command,

"THOMAS GARGRAVE."

"Our syttyngs and gaole delyvere her shuld begynne ather the 25th of this instant or the second day of December next, yf ordre be takyn for the dyetts, wyche I wold wyshe to be, bothe for that the cuntrye lokyth to have thayr matters hard, and ther ys also many persons in the gaole."*

SAME TO THE SAME.

"My deuty humble consyderyd to your good master-shyppe yt may please the same to be advertysyd that I with the Counsaill here have kepte our syttyng here at York and nowe endyd the same, we do repare every man to his awne howse, thanks be unto God, the people presently be in good quiett, savyng the troble thay fynd in the baser sorte of moneys, wyche be nowe refucyd to be takyn for any warres onles yt be by compulsion of some offycer, some do thynk that be-

* The above letter is contained amongst the Foreign State Papers of the reign of Elizabeth, No. 704 in the Calendar for the year 1560.

cause the cuntre ys so furre dystant from London, and
therfor a grett matter to convey thayr base moneys
theder, that a mynt placyd her at Yorke for a tyme
wold be grett ease and quiett to the people and
shortely bryng in bothe the sortes of the base moneys,
but for that the estableshement yerof and provysyon
of necessaryes yerfor wold aske some tyme. I do
suppose that yf one or 2 thowsand pounds of good
moneys myght be send hether for exchaunge of the
baser sorte of testons* of 2½d., or else that proclamations myght be mayd that the sayd testons shuld be
recevyd into the mynt as bullyon for 2 or 3 moneths
after the tyme thay be proclamyd to be currant, that
ather of theys ways wold fully quyett the people, and
especyally the grett nomber of the pore and ignorant,
as handycraftsmen, pore husbandmen, and laborers
(who may not spare thayr moneys, to send to London
for exchange).

"The southe parte of this shyre adionyng to the
shyres of Lyncolne, Darbey, and Nottingham haith ben
trobled wyth sundry rumors; in some parte yt was
said the quenes Majestie hayd sent men to take al
catall unmarked, wherupon the people mayd grett
haist to cutt the eares of thayr catall, and especyally
in Darbey shyre and Nottyngham shyre, and in other
places towerds Hull adionyng to Lincolnshyre. The
Reports were that the quenes Majestie shuld have,

---

* An English shilling was called a testone in Henry VIII.'s reign,
but in the time of Elizabeth the same name was given to a sixpence.

after a certen day, for every maryage 10s., for every buryall 6s. 8d., and for every crystenyng 3s. 4d., so that some prests therupon maryed upon a soden (sudden) some five coples, and some 2 or 3; we have hayd too of theys prests in ward, and dyvers others, and have apoyntyd severall sessyons for the Inquirye and punyshement thereof, we can nott by any means fynd furth the furst Inventors, for that yt came into this shyre furth of the shyres before namyd bot upon the furst brute* therof ordre was here takyn, so that the brutes and rumores entered not furre, bot stayd upon serche for thoffendors, and I tryst that by the opyn ponyshement of some offendors, the people for a good tyme wyll avoyde the lyke offences.

"As I perceive by Mr. Sayvell, your mastershippe supposyd I shuld have some occasion to repare to London, wherof I wold be ryght glad, trysting I shuld by your good meanes, fenyshe myn old suyte, bot as your Mastershyppe knoweth, I am apoyntyd vice-presydent of the Counsail here, and yf I shuld repare to London, I have not auctorite to apoynt one in my place duryng myn absens, wherfor I shall humble desyre your Mastershyppe ather to obtene me the Quenes Majesties letters, or the Counsaills letter declaryng her majesties pleasure to licence me to apoynt one to occupye the place of vice-presydent duryng myn absens, and therupon I shall take ordre ac-

---

* Bruit, noising, news.

cordyngly, and repare upe wyth that spede I can, or as your Mastershyppe shall apoynt me.

"Thus I am bold often to troble your mastershippe with my tedious letters, desyryng you to bere with thereyn with me, and to my power I shall remayn at your mastershyppes commandement, and beseche Almyghty God long to preserve you in helth with moche honor. At Yorke, in hayst, the 17th December, 1560.

"Your mastershippes ever assuryd
to command,

"Thomas Gargrave."*

Queen Elizabeth's second Parliament was not summoned until early in 1563. A different Speaker was chosen at the first meeting, and there is an entry on the Journals of the House, under date 4th March, that Sir Thomas Gargrave, one of the knights for the County of York, had leave of absence granted to him, for great affairs, with the rest of the Council of the North Parts. The "great affairs" would appear to be further difficulties with the Scots on the Borders; as we find that in August he was appointed one of the Commissioners to treat with our unpleasant neighbours for a due settlement of the disputes which had arisen.

In March, 1564, Gargrave was busy levying troops in Yorkshire to march for the relief of Berwick, and

* This letter is from the same source as the preceding one, and is numbered 809 in the Calendar.

shortly afterwards he appears to be acting as a Commissioner to survey and report upon Sandal Castle, called "the chief house within the Queen's Majesty's Lordship of Wakefield."* Again in the following year he was at work on the musters, and a letter of his to George, Earl of Shrewsbury, shows the difficulties he met with in this service.

SIR THOMAS GARGRAVE TO THE EARL OF SHREWSBURY.

" My bounden deuty humble consyderyd to your good L. yt may please the same to be advertysyd that I have ben at York, wher I taryed untyll Tuysday last to have receyvyd the bokes of musters, and to have brought them to your L. bot nather at my commyng away was al the bokes certefyed, nor divers of them mayd so certen as was mete, therfor I causyd these uncertefyd to be wryttyn for, and thoders sent agane to be reformyd, and to be sent hether so shortely as they may be had. Yesterday I receivyd 3 bokes of

---

* A return made to the Privy Council about this time of " The names of such as have rule of certain of your Majesty's Castles and Seignories within this County of York," has this entry : " Sir John Tempest, knight, is steward of the Lordship of Wakefield, and hath the order of the men, and keeping of Sandal Castle, and is a rule of men of service." Sir John's qualifications for the post are summed up in a marginal note thus—" not hable to rule himself nor the men ;" but it is added that Sir Thomas Gargrave dwells within three miles of the same, whose neighbourhood is a great " stay " to the people there. Sir John Tempest was of the Bracewell and Bowling family, and succeeded his father, Sir Richard, as Steward. He died about 1566, and Edward Carey, the Queen's cousin (as we shall see in this chapter), was his successor.

the partes, and not one of them certen, and therfor I
sent them agane to be made certen, and to have the
armor of all men certefyed, wyche in thayr certefycatts
was omyttyd, I never se any matter go so evyll for-
wards, bot ignorance ys an evyll executor of al
thyngs; some makyth excuse by shortenes of tyme,
others by letts* by reason of evyll wether and grett
waters, wyche was moche more northwards then here
in these partes.   The waters at Yorke and Tadcaster
wås very grett the last weke.   So shortly as I can
gett in the certefycatts I shall, God wyllyng, wayte
upon your L. with them, and shall in the mene
tyme make suche a brefe note as I can of the bokes
I have for your L.   I shall also bring al the bokes
at large, wyche wilbe grett, and many able men
certefyed, with lytle armor, thus ceasyng to troble
your good L.   I humble beseche Almighty God long
to preserve you in helth and honor.   At Kynslay,
in haist, the first of November, 1565.

"Your good L., ever humble
to command,

"THOMAS GARGRAVE."†

* Lets, hindrances or impediments. The verb, *to let*, had
formerly the same signification; thus says *Hamlet*—
"Unhand me, gentlemen—
By Heaven, I'll make a ghost of him that *lets* me."
† This letter is preserved amongst the Talbot MSS. in the
Heralds' College. The writer takes this opportunity of placing
upon record his deep obligations to the late Mr. T. W. King,
F.S.A., York Herald, for the kind help given him during his
visits to the College.

From this time up to the period when the Rebellion broke out, at the end of the year 1569, Sir Thomas Gargrave was actively occupied in Yorkshire with the duties arising from his position on the Council of the North. He seems to have been one of the very few statesmen of those days in whom the Queen and her eminent Secretary, Cecil, placed unlimited trust. The President of the North, the Earl of Sussex, writing to Cecil on the 10th of October, 1568, recommended the bearer of his letter, Cotton Gargrave, the only son of Sir Thomas, to the favourable notice of the Secretary, and took the opportunity of expressing the high opinion which he had of the father. "Sir Thomas Gargrave," he says, "has at all times, and especially since the death of the late Archbishop, used great diligence in the service here, and is a great stay for the good order of these parts. By his travail I find the country much more in order, and where there is any lack, I find him willing to assist me."

In January, 1568-9, the Queen wrote to him, commanding him to assist Sir Francis Knollys in conducting Mary, Queen of Scots, from Bolton to Tutbury. A stronger proof of confidence in her servant could hardly be given. A letter, addressed to the Lord President at York shortly afterwards, makes allusion to this service in the following terms :—

SIR THOMAS GARGRAVE TO THE EARL OF SUSSEX.

" My deuty humble remembred to your Honor, yt

may please the same to be advertysyd, that I do here
for serten that my L. of Shrewsbury hayth licens to
remove the Scotyshe Quene to his house at Wingfeld,
in Derbeshyre. His L. hayth so provydyd that the sayd
quene hayth herd wekely at this lent 13 sermons, every
Sonday, wednysday and friday one, wheryn she
hayth ben well perswadyd to the Redyngs of Scryp-
tures, and she ys as I am advertysyd very at-
tentyfe at the sermons, and dothe not lose one
sermon. . . . Frome Kinslay, in hayst, the 3rd
of Aprell, 1569.

" Yr. good L., ever humble

to command,

" THOMAS GARGRAVE."*

We have now reached the most interesting point in
Gargrave's career, and, indeed, a most important
episode in the annals of the county. The events
connected with the outbreak and suppression of the
Rebellion of the North have been very summarily
dealt with by historians of this period, from the difficulty that has existed in gaining trustworthy information. Some selections, therefore, from the State correspondence will throw great light on the subject. A
few words are first needful on the constitution of the
Council of the North.

Thomas Radcliffe, Earl of Sussex, was appointed
President of this Council in the year 1568, having

* Cotton MSS., Calig. B. IX., in the British Museum.

previously filled the office of Lord-Lieutenant of Ireland. He chose Sir Thomas Gargrave as his Vice-President, and other leading members were Sir Nicholas Fairfax,* Sir Henry Gate,† John Vaughan,‡ William Tankard,§ and Henry Savile.‖ Thomas Eynns was the Secretary. All these counsellors received fees for their attendance; the President was paid 1,000 marks, or £666 13s. 4d. per annum, but he was bound to entertain the members of the Council during the sittings at York, as well as their servants, the number of which latter was proportionate to the dignity of the master. The fee of the Vice-President was 100 marks per annum, with an allowance for "horse-meat," &c.

For some time before the insurrection actually broke out, there had been various rumours current of an intended rising in the North. The Justices of

---

* Head of the Fairfax, of Walton, family, the son of Sir Thomas Fairfax and Anne, daughter of Sir William Gascoigne, of Gawthorpe. In 1563 he sat in Parliament as member for the county, and held the office of steward of the lands lately belonging to St. Mary's Abbey, in York.

† Of Seamer. He was condemned, and narrowly escaped execution as an adherent of Lady Jane Grey. For his services in the suppression of the Rebellion, he had numerous grants of land in Yorkshire, including a lease of the parsonage of Hunmanby. He died at Seamer 7th April, 1589.

‡ Of Sutton upon Derwent.

§ Of Boroughbridge, which place he represented in the Parliament of 1553.

‖ Of Lupset, near Wakefield, commonly called the Surveyor. He was High Sheriff in the tenth year of Queen Elizabeth. He first appears on the list of counsellors in 1556.

the Peace for Yorkshire appeared before the Council
on the 1st of October, 1569, and were specially ad-
vised as to the execution of the trust committed to
them; they were directed to cause good watch to be
kept in all borough towns, market towns, and places
throughout the shire, and to apprehend any persons
uttering seditious speeches. It is said that they returned with "good-will and diligence" to execute
their charge. The Earl of Sussex wrote to Sir
William Cecil a few days later to the effect
that the reports were becoming so prevalent that
Sir William Ingleby and Francis Slingsby,* who
had the custody of Knaresborough Castle under the
Earl of Cumberland, had secretly repaired there
with some other gentlemen dwelling thereabouts,
and remained to keep the Castle, promising to be
ready with their lives and forces at one hour's warning. Sussex did not appear to have any fear of any
immediate rising, for, as he expressed it, "the time
of the year will shortly cool hot humours."

On the 27th of October the Privy Council wrote
letters to several of the Yorkshire gentry, intimating that they had heard in various ways of some

---

* Both these gentlemen were connected by marriage with
some of the principal rebels; a confirmation of the saying of
the Earl of Sussex, that "he is a rare bird that hath not some
of his with the two Earls." Isabel, daughter of Sir William
Ingleby, of Ripley, knight, was married to Thos. Markenfield,
of Markenfield, near Ripon, Esq. Francis Slingsby, of Scriven,
Esq., married Mary, daughter of Sir Thomas Percy, second
brother of the Earl of Northumberland.

late troubles, or some rumours of troubles, in the
North parts, and thought it needful that they should
understand where these rumours had had their beginning.   They, therefore, desired the person whom
they addressed, "being assured of his fidelity," to
furnish them, speedily and secretly, with such information as he could gain relating to these matters.
Sir Thomas Gargrave was one of the gentry thus
addressed.   He made the following reply :—

SIR THOMAS GARGRAVE TO THE PRIVY COUNCIL.

" My duetie humblie considered to your Honors. It
maye please the same to be advertised, that I receyved
your good L.L. lettre of the 26th of Octobre upon
Sonday last, and synce that time I have conferred with
suche as I thought mete, to learne what I coulde of the
occasions of the late rumors in thies partes, for at
myne owne house or in the parts where I dwell (beinge
in the Sowthe parte of this Shire), I coulde not learne
any thinge therof, by reason of the distannce frome
the places where the same beganne, which was in the
bishopriche of Durham, and in the north parts of
Yorkeshire, for untill I was sent for to L. President I
harde not at all therof, and being sent for to my Lorde
President upon the 8th of Octobre last, I came imydi-
atlie to his L., and founde with hym Sir Henrye Gate,
and Mr. John Vaghan, who also his L. had sent for,
and there his L. declared to us that he had herd frome
others that the rumor abrode was a commotion was

intended in thies yarts to be begonne, eyther the night
then last past, or the night then next to come, or the
night next after that, and that it was thought his L.
shulde be taken in his house, and that it was then
feared that the Erles of Northumbreland and Westmoreland shulde be privie therunto, and his L. said
he could not heare, nor knowe, of any speciall awthor
of the said Rumors nor of any facte or words of creditt
spoken to affirme the same. And hereupon his L. and
we consulted togither, what upon this sodan (sudden)
was best to be done to prevent and anoye them, and to
kepe frome them, Yorke, Hull, and Ponntfrett Castell,
and emongest other things, consideringe that both the
aforesaid Erles were nye unto Yorke, it was thought
good to send for them to mete my L. President and
Counsaile at Yorke the next day, and by that meanes
the truthe might bettre appeare, whereupon they were
sent for and came bothe the next daye, whereby the
greate feare was taken awaye, and upon conferrence at
the Counsaile borde here, they bothe agreed they had
herd suche rumors, but they affirmed they neyther
knewe the auctors, nor the causes therof, but they
wold both endeavor themselfes to enqueare thereof and
to se thoffendors punyshed, And the Erle of Westmoreland protested that if any commotion shulde arrise, he
wold be the firste that shulde adventure his life to represse it, and therle of Northumbreland said he wold do
the like, and (to my knoweledge) what by this dayes
worke, and the repaire to the Corte of the Duke of

Northfolke, all the brutes and rumors here were sodenlie ceassid, and not herd of in the contrye where I dwell over a weke after this tyme. And surelie I cannott certenlie lerne the causes or occasions of the said rumors, otherwise then by coniectures and uncerten reports. As some thinke when the brute was here that the Duke of Northfolke shulde marie the Scottishe quene, it was thought Religion wolde alter, and in the necke therof it folowed that the said Duke was gone into Norfolke, and sundrie in the northe parties of this Shire and in the bishopriche about that tyme beinge towards the said Erles toke upp their horses into the stables as was bruted, and many also at the same tyme prepared plate cootes and privie cootes,* and at the same tyme, the Justices of peace were called togethers and commaunded to represse rumors and to prepare themselves, and their lawfull powers in readynes, and for the more savetie of the contrye were commaunded to cause streyte watches to be kept for a tyme. All thies together or some of them, with the brute of alteringe of Religion weare (as it is thought) the causes of the brutes and rumors for other apparaunt causes is not knowen, but whether any horses were taken upp otherwise then in tymes past hath bene used I knowe not.

" And of any inconvenyent assemblies at unlawfull tymes, or preparinge of munition or armor (other then

---

* A privy-coat is a light coat or defence of mail, concealed under the ordinary habit.

before I have said) surelie I cannot certenlie undre-
stand, I have herd that the common people in their
greate feare bruted suche matters of armies of assemblies
in wodds, but. there is not knowen any certentie thereof
neyther of the place nor of the persons, some feare also
might be in the peoples heads of other matters, not appa-
annte, nor knowen to me. Surelie in myne oppinion if any
assemblies or confederacies were made it was done by
some fewe selecte persons, by whose examynations
nowe appointed to be had in thies parts, it is like that
some more mattre will appeare, if there be any.   Thus
I am tedious to your Honors in thies uncerten matters
besichinge yowe to accepte it in good parte, and to
my power, duringe life, I shall remayne readie to serve
the quenes Majestie accordinge to my most bounden
duetie, most humblie besichinge almightie God longe
to preserve your Honors in health and felicitie to
contynewe—from   Yorke in haste the Seaconde of
Novembre, 1569.

> " Your humble servant
> to command,
>
> " THOMAS GARGRAVE."*

Sir Henry Gate's reply to the Privy Council gives
us a few personal details.   On the evening of the 7th
he was at Mr. Vaughan's house at Sutton, with other
gentlemen, when a letter came from the Lord Presi-

---

* From the Addenda to the Domestic State Papers of Elizabeth, Vol. XV.

dent, desiring them to repair to him forthwith, at
Cawood, eight miles distant. They arrived there
between five and six in the morning, and his Lordship
came forth in his night-gown, bare-legged, to confer
with them. They debated the matter for an hour, and
Sussex then desired them to consider further, while he
slept for an hour, as he had not done so all the night
before, and by that time Sir Thomas Gargrave would
be come. Two hours afterwards Sir Thomas arrived.

Mary, Queen of Scots, was at this time imprisoned
in Tutbury Castle. The ambitious designs of the
Duke of Norfolk upon her hand had become known
to Elizabeth, and he had been thrown into the Tower.
Shortly after the Earls of Northumberland and Westmoreland had appeared before the Council at York, the
Queen summoned them to her presence. Instead of
obeying this command, Northumberland fled precipi-
tately from Topcliffe,* where he lived, and joined Westmoreland at Brancepeth. On the 13th of November,
Sir George Bowes reported to the Council of the

† Topcliffe is a parish-town on the river Swale, 24 miles
from York, formerly called the Jordan of England, because
Augustin and Paul are said, in the year 620, to have baptized
in this river between Topcliffe and Helperby 10,000 men in
one day, besides women and children. The population of the
neighbourhood of York may be accepted as somewhat scanty
and scattered at that period, so one hesitates to regard the
above statement as strictly accurate. Leland calls "Topeclif
an uplandish town, whos praty manor place stands on a hill
about half-a-mile from the town on the ripe of Swale." Charles
I. was a prisoner in this house of the Percies, which is now in
ruins.

North that the two Earls, old Richard Norton* and his sons, Thomas Markenfield,† and other gentlemen were assembled together in arms. Two days later they were reported to have entered Durham, and committed various outrages in the cathedral; so that there could be no doubt of their rebellious designs.

The Council of the North took prompt measures to meet this movement. Letters were addressed to the

* Of Norton Conyers, near Ripon. He was one of the Council of the North, and High Sheriff at this time. From his great age he was called the Patriarch of the Rebellion.

† Of Markenfield, near Ripon. There is preserved an interesting survey of the forfeited estates of Norton and Markenfield, of which the following is an abstract:—Richard Norton has a brick house, which looks fair, but is all out of order within. It is well placed, with apt grounds for gardens and orchards, wherein he had pleasure; within half a mile of his house he has a park of one and a-half miles, well stored with timber. It has been stored with deer and conies, which are now almost spoiled. Of his demesnes, part is good ground lying about the river Ure, but the grounds on the rivers are not so good as those by the rivers in the south. His demesnes are about 650 acres. As Norton's house lies two miles from Ripon, N.E., Mr. Markenfield's is one mile, S.W., an ancient house, built all of stone, to the outward show fair and stately; the hall and the lodging side embattled, more in length than breadth, and three sides environed with an evil moat, but the house is served with a conduit very plentifully. Against the entry of the court are built the hall and kitchen; on the right hand of the court the lodgings, and on the left the stables, brew-houses, and offices. The hall and lodgings are all vaults, and were at first built all about one high room. Besides the vaults, the walls are of a great height, without order, whereof part is divided at the mid-transom of the window, so that the rooms are all out of order. The house is placed in a park of the like quantity of Mr. Norton's, but better ground, and well planted with large timber. There is a demesne adjoining of 800 acres, with no quantity of water meadow, but much hay is made in seasonable years.—See Domestic State Papers, Addenda, Eliz., Vol. XVIII.

Justices and principal gentlemen of the county, requiring them to levy all the horsemen and footmen
they could, and bring them together at certain appointed places.

Henry Carey, Lord Hunsdon,* had been appointed
Governor of Berwick, and was soon on the march
northwards to defend Newcastle. From Doncaster he
made the following report to the Privy Council :—

Lord Hunsdon to the Privy Council.

" It may plese your LL. too be advertysyd that by
reson of long tarryynge for horsys by the way, and
the extreme fowle ways, yt ys thys Sunday nyght
byfor I cowld reche thys towne of Dankaster, wher I
fynde my L. Darcy,† who beynge as far as Pumfrett
onward towards Yorke was fayne too returne hythar
for feare of beynge taken, for yesternyght one Mr.
Tempest havynge the karyage of 150 men to Yorke
beynge yn Todcaster, was taken, and all hys sodyars,
by the rebels, beynge 200 horsmen. The erles and
theyr cumpany ar cume a thys syd Burrobryg and
what theyr determynacyon ys eythar too cume forward

---

* He was the Queen's own cousin, being the son of Sir
William Carey and Mary, the sister of Anne Boleyn. He is
described by contemporary chroniclers as a valiant man, very
choleric, but not malicious.

† George, Lord Darcy, was restored to the dignity in 1548.
His father, Thomas, took part in Aske's rebellion, called "The
Pilgrimage of Grace," and, being convicted of high treason on
a charge of delivering up Pontefract Castle to the rebels, was
beheaded on Tower-hill, 20th June, 1538, when the barony of
Darcy fell under attainder.

or too seke too gett Yorke ys nott knowne, theyre number ys nott knowne sertenly, but yt ys howlden heare for trothe that they ar 7 or 8000, and the most parte very well appoyntyd, ytt ys nott possybell for me too pase too Yorke for ytt ys sayde playnely that all the passagys ar stopte, and I wold be lothe too be theyr pray, and therfor I meane presently too ryde to Hull wher I wyll doo the best I can too pase too Newcastell, sum by way or els by sea, onles I may heare the contrary from your L.L., for seynge the Rebels ar cume so far hytharward and Newcastell safe I may the bettar remayne att Hull tyll I may know your pleasurs. I perceive by my L. Darcy that heare ys grete want of armor beynge men suffycyent, sewrly ytt ys necessary for her Majestie too put sum goode force in redynes thys way, for ytt appeares playnly that they meane too go thuro withall, I cannot see how my L. of Sussex can eythar heare from your LL. or sende too youe, the passagys are so stoptt, ytt appeares that Egremund Ratclyfe and Gynny, that was Mr. Norrys Secretary, ys also with them, for they ar bothe exemt owt of the procla-macyon whyche was proclaymyd heare agenst the Erles and serten theyr confederates yesterday, yt ys sayde that theyr proclamacyon is fyrst too refurme relygyon bycawse strangers shall nott, seconde too remove serten cownselars from her Majestie ; sum of my L. Darcys men affyrme that theyr meanynge ys too take the Skottyshe Q., and therfor for god sake lett her nott remayne where she ys, for theyr gretyst force ar horsmen. And I am credably advertysyd that Cudberd Collyngwoode, who ys Northumberlands man, and was shreve of Northumberland thys yere, ys cummynge after them with 600 horse of the owtlawse of Yngland and Skotland, whyche ys the more cawse too dowght the Skottyshe Q. I can wryght but by hersay as the common brewt of thys towne by the cummers hethar ys, and so leve ytt too your better consyderacyons, and so commyt your LL. too god— from Dankaster, thys 20 of November, att mydnyght.

"Your LL. too command,

"Hunsdon."

"If I can gett yntoo Northumberland I wold know your LL. plesurs what I shall doo with suche of theyr howsys as ar with the Rebels, as Swynburns and Cutberd Collyngwoods, for ytt ys sayde playnly that they spoyle all men as they pass that ys nott of theyr faccyon."*

The prospects of the rebels' success were very much increased by the great unwillingness of the Yorkshire-men to serve against them. There were many large Catholic land-owners in the county who were unfavourable to Elizabeth's government, though the majority had sufficient respect for its power to be restrained from joining the two Earls. They lent, however, as

* Dom., Addenda, Eliz., Vol. XV.

little assistance as possible in checking the movement.
The most effective, and least compromising, course they
adopted was to leave their homes for a time.   Sir
Thomas Gargrave reported that many of the gentlemen about him had gone out of the country.   He
feared, therefore, that the number of horsemen would
not be so great as was hoped for.   From other places,
too, news came that, with the exception of a few Protestants and well-affected ones, every man sought to bring
as small a force as he could of horsemen, and the footmen found fault with the weather, and otherwise spoke
their minds very freely.   The Earl of Sussex, in one
of his letters to Cecil, says : "He is a rare bird that
has not some of his with the two Earls, or in his heart
wishes not well to their cause."   He begs him also not
to be sparing of money, and to send some good force
that he may trust in these parts, for he fears this
country will hardly match the rebels with horsemen, and it will strike but faintly against them.   The
force of the two Earls, when they reached Wetherby
or Boroughbridge, was reckoned at 1,200 horsemen,
very well appointed, and at least 5,000 or 6,000 foot.
To oppose this array a much inferior force had as yet
been got together, as appears by the following
letter :—

The Earl of Sussex to the Queen.

"It maye please your moste excellente majestie, I
forbare these two dayes to write, partly for feare of in-

terceptinge by the Rebells who had sente certen horsemen alongest all the passages ou the farre side of the
river of Owse, and partly for that I wolde see whether
they bente ther cowrse from Wetherby, where they
have remayned two nights. And understandinge they
be now gone to Knaresborough, I thoughte fete to
write presently this moche, and do forbeare to write
at more leingth untill the waye be surer, which I hope
wilbe this nighte or to morowe.

" I have written to Westmorelande and Comberlande
for 500 horsemen, and into Northumberlande for other
500 horsemen, if they may be spared from the service
there, or els for so many as may be spared, and to
ioyne with Sir George Bowes at Barny (Barnard)
castell.

" I have written againe to levye all the force of horsemen in the este ridinge, and in other places where they
may with suertie come to me and did not come apon
the other Commission.

" I have allredy 2500 fotemen furnished as the
contrey will serve besides the force of the citie, and
have sent for 800 more owte of the Este ridinge.

" I have sent 200 men to Hull, and other 200 men
to the place your majestie commanded to be loked to
by your lettres of the 16th which my Lord of Hunsdon
sent by the post.

" Sir Thomas Gargrave is at Pomfrett, and hath fortified the passage at Feribrige.

"I have written to Newcastell for armor, munition, &c.

"From York the 24th of November, 1569.

"Your Majesty's most humble and
        faythfull subject and servant,

                "SUSSEX."*

On the 24th of November John Vaughan reported from York that the two Earls, with all their servants, tenants, and friends, had entered Yorkshire, levying soldiers in the Queen's name to maintain their actions, which they put forth to be for religion. They had mass daily, yet committed great spoil. They have passed, he adds, all this part of Yorkshire—viz., Richmond, Ripon, Knaresborough, Wetherby, Tadcaster, Cawood, Selby, and now are returned towards Topcliff.

We have seen, from a passage in the last letter quoted, that Sir Thomas Gargrave was now at Pontefract, and had fortified the passage at Ferrybridge. This announcement is verified by a letter from Gargrave to the Earl of Shrewsbury on the 25th of November, from which I give the following extract. It will serve to illustrate still further the present position of affairs :—

"Yestr nyght the twoo Erles returned to Burobrigg, and callyd backe al ther compenys; and required them to repair from thens toward the forest of Galtres, as though they wold go to York, on the farr syde of Owse. They perswade theyr solders to adventure to

* Dom., Addenda, Eliz., Vol. XV.

wyne York, wher they may have gaine, and have lyen
the winter; and say, yf they atteyne York all ys theirs,
and yf they mysse yt, yt were better for them to dye
lyke men, then to be hanged. I fere not York; it is
stronge enoghe to repulse them. They mynded to
have seized this house,* and to have wyntred here, and
at Wakefield, and at Doncaster, yf they could have
gotten them all. The only lack I fere here, ys money
and gonne powder, whereof I wold gladly have helpe,
for I cannot get any from York. Ther comyth to
serve the Queen's Majesty a thousand light horsemen, from the fronteyrs, towards Scotland, and
four hundred harquebusses; and ther comyth, also,
from the Southe, five hundred light harquebusses, and
other munytion, which I loke for to be here, and to be
conveyed to York, within four or five days; and, when
the provision comyth, I trust ther will be a short
ende of the rebellyon."†

On the 26th November Sussex wrote in a much
more hopeful tone to Cecil. He said: "At the beginning of those matters, the people were so affected
to these Earls for the cause they had in hand, that what
was had for the Queen's service was got out of the
flint, and those that came, save a number of gentlemen, liked better of the other side. Now I have gathered some good force, delivered them some money,
used some persuasions with all degrees to open their

* *i.e.,* Pontefract Castle.   † Talbot MSS. in the Heralds'
College.

D

rebellious intents, and published abroad their delusions
of the people and abuse of this realm." Sussex
further added that the discreet were now beginning to
distrust the Earls, and the soldiers to wax more trusty.
The wealthy were afraid of spoil, and the hangers-on
of the rebels, finding little money or plunder forthcoming, were getting dissatisfied.

On the same day it was announced to the Queen that
the rebels had retired from Wetherby to Boroughbridge, and from thence still farther northwards. They
found themselves checked in their efforts to levy an
additional force in the West Riding, owing to the
vigorous measures taken by the different members of
the Council of the North. Lord Hunsdon told Cecil
that, but for the great diligence of the Earl of Sussex,
Her Majesty had neither York nor Yorkshire at that
hour at her command. The intention of the rebels
had been to surprise York,* and so gain the control of

* The Corporation records of York abound with curious
notices of the proceedings at York, for placing the city in a
respectable state of defence. For instance, on the 18th Nov., it
is ordered for the "more surety" of the city, that the keels and
boats be kept within the city, and that the "fery-bot" be
"eyther sonken, or otherwise kept by discretion of Mr. Beane;"
and that the wardens shall raise "a common day work in
bearying of stones to the citie walles for defens." On the same
day the Lord-Lieutenant orders a levy of all the Queen's subjects within the Aynstie, "beyng hable men, as well horsemen
as fotemen," to come to York; and he also directs the Lord
Mayor, &c., to command all the Queen's subjects in the city of
York, "upon the first warnyng, to attend upon him." On
the 19th, the Mayor, &c., order the wardens to bring all the
"sties or ladders" from the suburbs into the city; and all the
inhabitants of the suburbs are ordered to make their abode in

the entire county. The city had not, at the time of the
first outbreak, one single piece of ordnance wherewith
to resist them, and the inhabitants were more addicted
to them than to the Queen. All the gentlemen, save a
few in the East Riding, had remained in their houses as
neutrals, but their sons were with the rebels. Nevertheless the Earl of Sussex had not only made York
past surprising, but had brought the soldiers who were
disposed to favour the rebels to think very ill of them.

In the meantime Lord Admiral Clinton and the
Earl of Warwick were engaged in making levies in
Lincolnshire, Warwickshire, and Leicestershire. Clinton remained for some days at Lincoln, where he
gathered together a considerable body of men. He
writes from there a letter to Sir Ralph Sadler, a
portion of which runs as follows: "I have sent a

the city, "this troublesome tyme," to be ready to serve; and
that "his honour" shall name the captain of the city soldiers—
namely, Mr. Robert Stapleton, Esquire. All pitch and tar is
ordered to be taken forth of the streets, &c. On the 21st
earth or stone is directed to be raised against the posterns; and
four shillings allowed for watching the "great gonnes" remaining the last night "upon Ouse." The wardens are directed
to "foresee, by their good policies," that no wheat, malt, nor
victual, want in their wards. Lights are directed to be placed
in the windows; and the Lord-Lieutenant orders that "whensoever any alarme shall happen within this citie, no manner of
men, women, or children, shall make any showtyng, crying,
or noyse, but to kepe sylens." The old "gonnes and ordenance" are ordered to be mended. On the 22nd November,
Mr. John Ingleby is appointed "capitayn of the citie levy of
100 men;" and a general muster is made of the men of the city
of York, on the 24th November. (See note in Sharp's *Memorials of the Rebellion.*)

letter herewith to 'master Carie,' being at Sandal Castle, near Wakefield, by commandment from my Lords of the Council. I pray you that the same may be sent him with all diligence, that I may get answer from him as soon as possible."

At this time, Edward Carey, son of Lord Hunsdon, was Constable of the Lordship of Wakefield, and lived at Sandal Castle, he having obtained a grant of that stronghold from the Queen. He appears to have responded to the sudden call which was made upon his resources with great vigour. Sir Ralph Sadler, who was appointed paymaster of the forces raised to meet the rebels, writes to Cecil that Carey is gone to Doncaster, to levy as many men as he can within "his rule of Wakefield;" his intention was then to join Lord Darcy, and keep the town of Doncaster, and annoy the rebels as much as he can, "whereunto," adds Sadler, "I see he lacketh neither goodwill nor good stomach, but I have given him my advice to be careful not to hazard too much without some advantage."

To Lord Clinton's letter, Carey replied as follows :—

EDWARD CAREY TO LORD CLINTON.

"My very good Lord: Havinge my firste direction to Yorke, there to receave my further chardge by the Lord Leifetenants appoyntemente, being then forestopped of my dyrect passage thyther, I made my repaier to my Office, where since my comynge, I have bene busied in musteringe of the Stewardeshippe of

Wakefelde, and preparinge my self in a reddynes to sett forwardes to Yorke, whoe beinge allmost at poynte to take my jorney thyther, have receaved the Councelles lettres countermandinge my firste direction, and appoyntinge me to thorder of your Lordship, to the which most willingelye I submytt myself with hartie good will, beinge now readye to awayte uppon your Lordship with my poore companie at one haulf daies warninge when and where yt shall please you to appoynte. My Lord, the contrey ys greately destitute of armor and munytion, whereof I have allredie certefyed the Councell, who, regarding our wants, have sente me their lettres appoyntinge me to receave supplye thereof at your Lordship's handes. It may therefore please your Lordship to stande thus farre our good Lord, as to help us with 300 corseletts furnished and one hundred bowes, and that yt may be sente to Pomefrett Castle, where Sir Thomas Gargrave is, the which passinge by Doncaster may be garded and safeconducted from thence to Pomefrett, by thassistance of my Lord Darcie, and soe from Pomfrett hyther to Sandall Castell eyther by suche as Sir Thomas Gargrave shall appoynte, or otherwise by suche ayde as I will provide my self for better conveyannce thereof hyther. Allso whereas by the Councells appointemente I am to receave 200*l.* of your Lordship for better defrayinge of our chardge in this service. I shall desier your Lordship to kepe yt in your custodie untill my comynge unto you, partelye for that I would

be lothe to hazarde the transporte thereof hyther, and
partelye for that I doubte not otherwise to serve my
torne here till then. Wherewith wisshinge unto your
Lordship felycitie, I leave further to troble you.

"From Sandall Castle,* the firste of December, 1569.

"Your Lo. at commandemente,

"EDWD. CARYE."†

The Earl of Warwick kept his head-quarters at
Leicester, and his levy of men proved numerous. It
was arranged that Clinton and he should join forces at
Doncaster. The gradual march of Clinton northwards
can be traced by the dates of his letters to the Secretary of State, Cecil. On the 1st of December he is

---

* The following report of a survey of Sandal Castle, made in
the year 1545, will be read with some interest :—

The Castle of Sandal is very fair and stately, a little mile
from the town of Wakefield, defended with a fair wall of seven
foot thick, hath the situation on a rocky hill, environed with a
deep and broad dry ditch. The towers, which are five, standing near together on the west part of the Castle, whereof three
are in a convenient state of repair, covered over with lead ; the
rest begin to decay in the timber work. The lead of one of
these being already taken down, and the other standing untiled.
Gate and entry strongly builded and with the wall in a good
state, save that a piece of the wall in the fore front is fallen
down, and will cost £10 to restore. The principal lodgings, as
Hall Chamber, Chapel, and Houses of Office are wholly prostrate,
except the kitchen, which is fair and large. The Steward's and
Constable's lodgings, divided from the rest, are of slight timber
work meet to be maintained, serving not only for the stewards
for the time being, but for the keeper of the park and gaoler
charged with the keeping of the prisoners committed to the
castle for arrears of the King's rent, trespassers, and such
like. The park adjoining is forty acres well paled, and there
are thirty fallow-deer or thereabouts.

† Dom. Eliz., Vol. LX.

still at Lincoln, from which place he reports that his
horsemen and harquebusiers are in want of training,
and there is a lack of arms and armour. On the 3rd
he writes from Newark. With his letter from the
same place on the 4th, he enclosed the following from
Sir Thomas Gargrave :—

SIR THOMAS GARGRAVE TO LORD CLINTON.

" My duetie humblie remembred to your Honor, It
maye please the same to be advertised, that my L.
Darcye and my self be appointed by my L. lieutenante
in thies partes to mete at Doncastre such munytion
and treasure as your L. doth send towards Yorke, and
bycause we wold be readie to do our dueties therin, and
for that also that my said L. lieutenante requireth to be
advertised when the same shalbe at Doncastre, to
thintent his L. maye send further supplye for the save
conduction thereof. Therefore I am so boulde humblie
to desire your L. to advertise eyther the L. Darcye or
me by the post when your L. thinketh the same
munycon and treasure shalbe at Doncastre, and we
shall not faile (god willing) to mete it there, but also
advertise my said L. lieutenante accordinge to his L.
direction. Thies parts of the contrye (thanks be to
god) be quiett, for the two Erles and their complices
be furre of in the bishopriche of Durisme where they
lye quyett for anythinge I here, but the brute is, they
mynde to attempte some enterprice against Newcastle,
or Barnaycastle, where Sir George Bowes lyeth, and
other saye they will take Hertilpole, beinge a stronge

scyte almoste enveronyd with the sea at every full
water, and there vittell, and fortefie themselfes, and
others saye they loke for money frome beyond the seas,
and if that come not they will flee by sea. Thus I am
boulde to advertise your L. of suche uncerten newes as
I have, &c.

"Frome Ponntefrett Castle, the thirde of Decembre,
1569.

"Your good L. ever humblie to commande,

"THOMAS GARGRAVE."*

On the 5th, Clinton reached "Tuxford in the Clay,"
from which place he reports that the greatest part of
the bands under his charge have marched to Bawtry.
On December the 7th, he dates a letter from Scroby;
in which he says that his men are much wearied by
marching with their armour in foul ways, and are unwilling to advance above five or six miles a-day. Lord

---

* Dom., Eliz., Vol. LX. The account rendered by Sir Ralph
Sadler of the expenses connected with the suppression of the
Rebellion has the following items :—

Sir Thomas Gargrave, Knight, by warrant of the Lord-Lieutenant, dated the last of November, 1569, for the charges of
himself and 100 soldiers appointed for the safe keeping of Pontefract Castle and the passages at bridges at Ferry-bridge,
Castleford-bridge, Swillington-bridge, and Leeds-bridge, extending over the River of Aire—£112 10s.

Cotton Gargrave, Esquire, captain, his wages 12s., lieutenant
6s., 5 officers at 12d. "the pece," and for 43 soldiers at 8d. per
diem "the pece," for 32 days, beginning the 21st of November,
and ending the 22nd of December, and for 245 soldiers at like
rate, for 12 days, beginning the 11th of December, and ending
the 22nd—£192 3s. 4d.

See Sadler's "State Papers, &c.," published in 1809.

Clinton arrived at Doncaster on the same day. Here the forces remained five days. On the 10th, the Earl of Warwick and the Lord Admiral rode over to Sherburn, to meet the Earl of Sussex, and others, from York. There they conferred together respecting the means to be pursued for the more speedy suppression of the rebels, and arranged that all their forces should be joined at Northallerton or Durham. Warwick and Clinton reached Wetherby on the 13th, and after two or three days' halt, marched to Ripon, at which place intelligence reached them that the Earls, without waiting for their attack, had dismissed their infantry, and fled with their cavalry to Hexham. From there they shortly afterwards escaped across the Borders into Scotland, and thus the rebellion ended.*

* It has not been thought necessary, in this chapter, to follow the rebels after they withdrew from Yorkshire. Most of the original documents relating to their proceedings in the more northern counties have already been printed in Sharp's "*Memorials of the Rebellion*," so it will hardly fall within the plan of this work to reproduce them here. In that volume will be found some interesting accounts of the siege laid by the rebels to Barnard Castle, then held by Sir George Bowes, before which place they appeared about the 1st of December. On the 12th, Lord Sussex, Lord Hunsdon, and Sir Ralph Sadler, writing from Cesawe by Topcliffe, report to the Council : "This day Sir George Bowes, Robert Bowes, his brother, and diverse of the gentlemen that were with him in Barnay Castell, came hether to us ; by whom we understand that the soldiers that were in the Castell, did daily, by great nombers, leape over the walls to go to the rebells. And on Friday last, ther leaped over the walls at one tyme, about the nomber of fourscore ; since which tyme they had growen to such mutinies, as upon Saturday, 7 or 8 score of them that were appointed to garde the gates, and had always been of the best disposed, did sudenly

As soon as the flight of the rebels was clearly ascertained, the President of the Council issued warrants to the Sheriffs of Northumberland, the Bishoprick of Durham and Yorkshire, to seize into the Queen's hands all the lands, goods, and cattle of the rebels and their supporters, and to apprehend their persons. It was ordained that in every special place where they gathered any strength, and in every market town or great parish, execution should at once take place, by martial law, of such as had " no freehold, nor copyhold, nor substance of lands." The members of the Council were engaged at different places in examining those suspected of participation in the rebellion. The meaner sort were quickly disposed of, and there were numerous executions at Ripon, Topcliffe, Wetherby, and Tadcaster, of the West Riding delinquents.

We have seen that one of the principal leaders in the Rebellion, always spoken of as old Richard Norton, was Sheriff of Yorkshire for this year, and, on his attainture, some other gentleman had to be found to fill his place. Sir Henry Gate was the first one thought of; but he excused himself on the ground of illness, and the choice then fell on Sir Thomas Gargrave. That Sir Thomas was by no means pleased with the

sett open the gates, and went to the rebells; wherupon Sir George Bowes, seeing the falshode of his men, was dreven to composition, and is with all his men, horses, and armor that remayned there, come away in saulftie. He hath had long lacke of drink, and was scanted of bread; and yet, if his men had been trewe, he might, and wold have kepte it untill he had been releved," &c.

honour thus thrust upon him is amply shown by his communication to Cecil, of the 19th of December, 1569, in which, after giving tidings of the rebels, he goes on—

"I have now ben twyse sheryffe of this shyre in 4 yeres, and so hayth not any other ben that can be remembred, the chargys therof ys presently so grett, both with the Justyces & thayr Retennors, & also in theschequer wher the charge ys treble to that yt was within 30 yeres, and ys rysyn by penall lawes & tenures, ... & otherways, also the Corts of Wards & first fruits & tenths dothe inchrese moche thayr charges, yt ys enogh to undoo a pore man, and althoghe ther be at the lest 4 knyghts or 5 that may dyspend three tymes the valewe of my levyng, yet I am callyd to more charges in all servyces than any of them, and to my power I have bene, am, & shall be, most redy & wyllyng to serve the quenes majestie, & my contry to the uttermost of my power and knowlege, yt hayth in servyce this yere past, cost me above 200 marks. I humble beseche you to have such consyderation towerds me, as I may remayne able in power to serve, & my delygence & good-wylle shall never fale, god wyllyng."* . . . .

But, however much Gargrave might feel the injustice of his position, he was not the man to shirk the duties of it. His principal work lay just now in gaining possession of the lands and goods of the higher

* Cotton MSS. Calig. B. IX. in the British Museum.

class of rebels; and his next letter fully illustrates the busy nature of his employment.

SIR THOMAS GARGRAVE TO SIR WILLIAM CECIL.

"My deuty humble remembred to your Honor yt may please the same to be advertysyd that one Crystofer Danbye,* one of the chefe Rebells for Religyon, hayd a lease at the hands of Mr. Gerard, brother to Mr. Attornay [General], a lease of a colemyn & certen lands at Beston [Beeston], in Yorkshyre, duryng the mynorite of young Beston, the quenes majesties warde, the wyche lease shall nowe I tryst come agayn to her majestie by his attayndor. I shall humble desyre your mastershyppe to be good mr. to this berrer, Martyn Byrkheade,† of Grays Inne, and to help hym to a newe lease therof, or els to her majesties tytle theryn, and this beror beyng a very honest man shalbe bounden to pray for your honor, and shalbe able I tryst to do ther moche good amydyst a sorte of papysts, the wyche ys one cause whye I do wyshe an honest man ther. Sir Thomas Danby, brother to the sayd Crystofer, beyng not well affectyd in Religyon,

* The son of Sir Christopher Danby, of Farnley, near Leeds, Knt. Dorothy, one of his sisters, was married to Sir John Nevile, of Liversedge, another leader of the rebels.

† A native of Wakefield. He lived in a house which still stands in Southgate, where may be seen an excellent ceiling bearing his initials and arms. See Banks' *Walks about Wakefield*. He was M.P. for Ripon in the Parliaments of the 13th and 14th of Queen Elizabeth, and was appointed Attorney of the Council of the North in May, 1574. He died 6th July, 1590, and was buried in the parish church of Wakefield.

clamyth now althe beasts and goods of the sayd Crystofer by a dede mayd 2 yeres ago, and not knowen untyll now, and therfor I do suspecte the same, the sayd Crystofer (the same dede notwythstandyng) hayth by hymselfe and his servants occupyed & inioed the hole untyll nowe.

" Here hayth ben so many grett spoles and dystruction in the contrey of late of the goods and catills of the Rebells, and also of many trewe subiects, that the store in thes partes wyll not be hayd agayn a good tyme, and I thynke the scarsetye willbe feld this 2 or 3 yeres bothe here and else where, and the same shall lose the quenes majestie the most part of al the forfetures wyche I thynke (yf they myght have come to her majesties hands) wold have borne a good pece of the charges.

" As I do here ther ys some that takyth upon them to promes pardons of lyffe lands and goods of the Rebells, and of some chefe Rebells, wheryn I tryst her majestie wyll have good consyderation, for therby she shall lose her majesties escheats and forfetures, and besyds that norysh styll amongst us the opyn ennemyes to God, her majestie, and realme, and suche as herafter wyll not fale when tyme and ayde may serve to attempte the lyke enterprises.

" I do wyshe a parlyament for 10 or 15 days for 2 causes, the one for attayndors of the prinsepall Rebells lest thayr tenants and frends shold lyve styll in hope of ther pardon or feare of thayr dysplesure.

" The other cause for a stricter law for Religyon &
agaynst papysts and suche as practyse yerin here, or
elswhere, and yf any refuce the servyce or communyon, I wold wyshe them convyncyd by opyn disputation
in every shyre before Commyssyoners and yf they wyll
not relent to the treuth, I wold wyshe them attayntyd
in *premunire* for one yere, and yf they stycke at the
yeres ende, then to be dethe for herysey or treson.
Thus I am bold to wryte my fantesye to your Honor,
humble besechyng God long to preserve you in helth
and honor.—From Yorke, in haist, the 6 of January,
1569-70.

> " Your mastershypps, ever humble
> to command,
>
> " THOMAS GARGRAVE."*

Gargrave met with considerable difficulties in the
carrying out of some of his instructions. The whole-
sale seizure of the cattle and sheep, for instance, had
led to complications for which he was wholly unprepared. He plaintively asks Cecil what he is to do
with the flocks and herds which were driven up from
all parts of the country. " I have," he says, " no meat
for them. If I buy it, they will soon eat up their value.
Some have died by driving and lack of meat.   The
Queen orders me to keep the goods without diminish-
ing, but it would be better husbandry to sell some
than keep all."

* Addenda, Dom., Eliz., Vol. XVII.

SIR THOMAS GARGRAVE TO SIR WILLIAM CECIL.

" My deuty humble remembred to your Honor yt
may please the same to be advertysyd, that amongst
others the rebells at thayr beyng together in the
busshopryke of Durysme, dyd spoyle this berror Sir
Thomas Calverlay beyng a yong man, and hayd newly
sett up howse and furnyshed the same to his power,
thay lefte hym nothyng nather to relyffe hymselfe his
wyff and famely nor to pay his Rent wyth all.   Ther
was non that was known to favor Relygyon that they
left unspolyd.   This berror proclamyd them traytors he
levyed men from the busshopricke and went hymselfe
with them to Barnar Castell to Sir George Bowes and
left the men ther and returnyd to Newcastell, wher he
servyd and kepte watche and warde and was delygent
to sett furth the servyce ther for the defence of that
towne to his power.   He was of Lyncolnes Inn, and
ys lernyd in the lawes and ys honest in Religyon and yf
yt be thought convenyent to releyffe any, I humble
beseche your Honor to stand his good mr. and helpe
hym.   Thus I am ever bold to troble your mastershyppe
and not able to serve you other ways then with my prayers,
good wyll and affection, the wyche I am bounden to
owe you and do humble beseche God long to preserve
you to his pleasure and your good contentation.

" Frome Yorke in hayst the 30th of January, 1569-70.

" Your Mrshipps ever bonden to command,

" THOMAS GARGRAVE."*

* Domestic—Addenda, Eliz., Vol. XVII.

On the 10th of January, 1569-70, the rebellion being virtually at an end, Elizabeth wrote to Gargrave to the effect that she had been informed in sundry ways of his diligent and faithful service in that late troublesome time in the North, done both in his own person, and with all the power he could make; she could not, therefore, omit to give unto him by those her letters her hearty thanks for the same, assuring him that as occasion should serve she would not fail to remember him.

Possibly the vague promise held out in the above tempted him to add the concluding paragraph of this following letter to Cecil :—

THE SAME TO THE SAME.

" My deuty humble remembred to your Honor yt may please the same to be advertysyd that I have herwith send to the Ryght Honorable and my synguler good L. and others of the quenes majesties privey Counsall, the examynations of the Lady Nevyle wyffe to Sir John Nevyle, wherof parte were taken by me and by Hughe Savyle,* and parte by the sayd Mr. Savyle and Mr. Ric. Hammond, who were bothe jonyd with me in the sayd counsalls letters for that purpose. Surely her husband in myn openyon ys of a good nature, and fully of late confermyd in popery and false doctryne, which at the begynnyng he was misselyd in by doctor Robynson in Quene Maryes days, and al

* Of Wrenthorpe, near Wakefield, descended from the Saviles, of Newhall, in Elland.

kyng Edwards days was a protestant. His wyffe hayth
10 chyldren, ys lefte in a very pore estate, and she
verely thynkyth yf her husband myght have his lyffe
he wold come in and submytt hymselfe to imprisonment
or otherwyse as shuld please the Quenes majestie, as
in my letter to the Right Honorable privey Counsalle
more at large apperyth.

" Aboute Saterday come senyght I tryst to be able
to make a good certeficett of the lands & the goods of
the Rebells or of so moche therof as ys in this shyre and
can be herd of, and so shortly as I can I shall send yt to
your Honor with all the notes I can lerne of the goods
takyn away by others ather with warrant or withoute.

" Ther be nowe so many sutors that I am ashamyd
to be one, and yet my charge at Pontfrett Castell in
the styrre of the Rebells and nowe aboute the serche of
Rebells goods and the stay of them, and that to come
for the shriffaltye (shrievalty) wilbe more charge unto
me than I shalbe able to bere and I shall be forcyd to
seke some releffe. If her majestie wold lett me have
to me and my heyrs 100*l.* or 100 marks yerly in lands
and to pay for theme halfe in 6 yeres equall paments,
and the valewe of thoder halfe to be payd of the hole
as a fee ferme, I shuld spend the same in her majesties
servyce as I do the rest I have and be the more able
to serve her hyghnes, and I wold seke to have no lands
ather replenyshed with woods or grett commons or
other commodyties for I wold only seke the land adionyng ny wher I inhaite (*sic*) beyng non of any stately

E

seignory, nor replenysed with other commodyte bot
the large rents—thus I am ever bold to troble you as
my synguler good master and friend, humbly besechyng
God long to preserve you in helth and honor—frome
Yorke in haist, the 13 of February, 1569(-70).

> "Your good mastershipps ever
>   humble to command,
>
>   "THOMAS GARGRAVE."*

SIR THOMAS GARGRAVE TO SIR WILLIAM CECIL.

"My deuty humble remembred to your Honor, yt
may please the same, I have herwith sent to my Lords
& others of the privey Counsaill with the artycle
subscrybyd by the Justyces of peace whoys herts &
hands for a good nombr of thame I tryst do agre,
and althoughe I muchdo wyshe, blody lawes, nor dethe
in matters of consyence, yet by experyence I se in
Kyng Henry the viij^{th's} days, sharpe lawes kept the
evyll quiett and in dew obedyence, wher nowe they be
bothe ferce and stowte, wherof evyll Insuyth, & more
not unlyke to folowe. I wyshe yt myght be expery-
mentyd by some lawe, whether they wold abyde Imprisonment with losse of thayr lyvyngs duryng theyr
lyffes, that do refuce to use and receive the servyce
and sacrements acordyng to the lawe. Long suffer-
ance of evylls bredyth herdnes yerin wherof Insuyth
trobles and dayngers; yt ys tyme in myn openyon to

* Domestic—Addenda, Eliz., Vol. XVII.

stycke ernysly to the Churche and stoutly to resyst
the malyce of thenmye (the enemy). Cancred or sotell
enmyes wyll herdly by gentylnes or other meanes become assuryd frends, bot at the most wyll flatter, dys-
semble & snache when the tyme servyth. I humble
beseche almyghty God to represse thayr malyce and
to turne thayr harts to godlynes. And long to preserve the Quenes Majestie and this realme frome thayr
malyce & dysseyts, & to kepe your Mastershippe in
health and honor—frome Yorke in haist the 21 of
June 1570.

<blockquote>
"Your Honors ever humble to

command to his power,

"THOMAS GARGRAVE."
</blockquote>

"I am so bold to send herwith a pakett of letters
from my lady of Sussex, at her request, to Sir Henry
Ratlyffe."*

SIR THOMAS GARGRAVE TO SIR WILLIAM CECIL.

*   *   *

"The next syttyng of the Counsaill here, bothe for
causes off sutes, and for the oyer determyner aud
gaole delivere, ys apoyntyd the first of Decembre next,
and yf ther be any matter to be ther preferryd for the
Quenes Majestie, wyche ys not here knowne, yf yt be
advertysyd yt shalbe preferryd to the best of our
knowleges.

* Domestic—Addenda, Eliz., Vol. XVIII

"I have herwith sent your Honor the names certefyed by Mr. Inglebye of theys that be thought able,
and refucyd to pay the lone money requestyd, with
suche notes theron as I thinke trewe and mete to in-
forme you withall.

"I have also sent you the examynation of Thomas
Leyghe for suche words as he shold speke in Cheshyre.
Surely Sir, he ys a yonge man moche gyffyn to
huntyng, and of myn awne knowlege I do knowe that
in the heate of the troble, when Christopher Danbey
and others of the rebells wyth 200 horsemen came to
Ledes within lesse then ij myles of his howse, he kepte
hym frome them and came to me to Pontfrett castell,
to serve the Quene's Majestie, and because he dyd
dwell ny Ledes, and on the southe syde of the water
of ayer (Aire) that comyth by Ledes I ioinyd hym in
commyssyon with divers others to fortefye and defende
that bryge lest the rebells shold ther passe over the
water southeward, where he servyd well and also he
dyd send and sett furth to the Lord leuetennant here
bothe horsemen and fotemen to serve the Quene's
majestie. So that in all that tyme of Rebellyon so
farre as I could here he servyd the Quene's Majestie
accordyng to his deuty. He hayd a yonger brother
that servyd therle of Northumberland, whoo hayth sub-
myttyd hym selfe and payd his fyne, the sayd Thomas
Legh hayth ben syckle moche of this somer. I
beseche your Honor yf this case may bere yt to
be his good master for this tyme.

"This berrer Mr. Calverly myndyth to be a sutor for some releyffe for the spoyles by hym and his father-in-lawe sustenyed in the tyme of the late Rebellyon, this berrer to his power servyd in Newcastell and also musteryd and caryed men to Barnard castell to Sir George Bowes. Mr. Allan Bellyngham hayth a sute with a college in Cambryge, and hayth requiryd me to move your Honor to be so moche his good master as to be a meane that the matter may have some frendly ende without extremyte, and yf he be in the wronge he will make recompence or compounde as shalbe thought resonable, thus I cease to troble your Honor humble besechyng you to bere with my boldness and to my power I shall remayne at your comandement duryng my lyffe besechyng Almyghty God long to preserve you in helth and honor—from Nostell in haist the last of October, 1570.

"Your Honors ever humble
to command,
"THOMAS GARGRAVE."

Attached to the above letter is a document headed—
"Thexamynation of Thomas Leighe* of Middleton esquier takyn at Nostell, the   daye of Auguste 1570, before Sir Thomas Gargrave knight, upon the Interrogatories hereunto annexed." The following are extracts from it.

* * * * * * * *

* The Leghs, or Leighs, of Middleton, in the parish of Roth-well, held the manor of Middleton at least as early as the 14th

" To the third Interrogatorye he saith that he herd
not of any Musters in Yorkeshire untill the daye or ij
before his comyng awaye homewards, and then one
came to hym frome his owne house in Yorkeshire, and
said he muste on the Mundaye folowinge be at a
Muster at Rothwell Haigh in Yorkeshire before Sir
Thomas Gargrave, [and have a horseman furnished
there.

" To the fourth he saithe that upon a Sondaye he
was with his cosyn Mr. Leighe aforesaid at . . . at
a bearebaytinge at after none, where the dogge that
did best wonne a bell for a price, and in ridinge home
towards Mr. Leighes house in a towne he se hym that
kept the dogge that wonne the bell goo into a house
with the dogg, who called this examynate and prayed
hym to drynke, and so he came to the dore, and was
desired to light, and so he did and went within the
house dore into the entrie, and thider came to hym

century. Hopkinson says (see Harleian MS. 4630 in the British
Museum) that Gilbert d' le Leghe gave this manor to his second
son John and Clarice his wife, and to their heirs for ever, by a
deed dated at Middleton, Friday in Easter week, 1332, and wit-
nessed by Sir Roger of Leedes, knt., Sir John Fleming, knt.,
Bryan of Thornhill, Henry of Olton, and others. William
Legh, of Middleton, was attainted of High Treason with Edmond
Tattersall, a clothier, and Ambler, a priest, and executed in the
year 1541. He was seized of lands in Cheshire, and in Wakefield, Lofthouse, Carleton, Rothwell, West Ardsley, Westerton,
Wombwell, Blacktop and Long Liversedge, in the County of
York. His son Gilbert married Dorothy, daughter of Thomas
Woodrove, of Woolley, and Thomas, the eldest surviving son of
this marriage, is most likely to be the subject of the examination
above recorded.

the aforesaid man who he thinketh was called Coppell,
and with hym dyvers others whome he · knew not and
they brought this examynent a selybube to drynk and
this examynate dronke therof, and in communycation
he said he was sent for home to be the next daye at a
muster, & he wolde ride home to it, and he further
saith some in that companye asked hym where the Erle
of Northumbreland was, and what was become of hym,
and he said he thought the said Erle was in Loughle-
byn in Scotland, and that the said Erle before his last
offence was verie well beloved of all gentlemen, and he
this Examynate, if the said offence had not bene
shulde have bene his servante.   Then some of ye
company asked hym what newes in the northe, and
he said he knewe none, but said forasmuche as there
is a muster appoynted, it maye chaunce that some of
our men may be put awaye, or that thother parte is
comynge towards us, whereof I wolde be sorye for it
wolde greve me to drawe my sworde againste the
⸺ said Erle that had so muche bene his frend.   And
yet he saith he then said he wold adventure hymself
as furr in the service of the Quenes ma^tie as any
man will do ; examyned why he said he wolde not drawe
his sworde against the said Erle, and he saith he never
said nor mentt so, but that he wolde be sorie to do it
for the good will before he ought hym.   And he said it
is well knowne that when the said Erle and his com-
plises were upp, and a good sorte of their horsemen
come within two myles of this examynates, he kept

hymself frome them and served the quenes ma^{tie} to his charges, bothe with sendeinge horses and footemen to Yorke to my L. lieutenants, and also hymself was one that had charge to kepe the bridge at Ledes. that the Rebells shulde not passe over sowthward. And he said he was in Ponntfrett Castell with me the said Sir Thomas for advice howe to kepe the said bridge.   And althonghe he wolde be sorie to drawe his sworde againste the Erles person, yet if he came agaynste the quene and Realme, he saithe he wolde be as readie to resiste hym as any man wolde, and this above confessed is all (he saith) that he can saye or remember towchinge the premisses.   And he saithe he never ment evill, but the next daye, he saith, he repaired home, and went to the place appoynted of musters in Yorkeshire, and caried a light horseman with hym as he was appoynted and there he founde before Sir Thomas Gargrave a good nomber of horsemen, both launces and light horse, and there he undrestode it was no common muster, althonghe it was by the people so termyd, but was a viewe appoynted to se that men had their furnyture of horse and armor accordinge to the Statute.

" Exd. *per me,*

" THOMAS GARGRAVE."*

* Domestic—Addenda, Eliz., Vol. XIX.

SIR THOMAS GARGRAVE TO THE EARL OF SUSSEX.

" My boundon deuty humble remembred to your
Honor yt may please the same this contrey I tryst
dothe remayne in quyett ordre, in the last privey
watche ther was not found any suspecte persons other
then certen knowne beggers and wacabonds wyche
were punyshed acordyng to the lawe.

" I have travelyd this iij wekes and more daly excepte
Sondays for thassessement of the subsedy, I was forcyd
to sytt in vij severall places for lacke of Commyssyoners, I have hayd more to do to bryng yt to any
convenyent some than ever I hayd before, nor I have
not herd the complaynt so generall of povertye as yt
nowe ys.   They have ben moche touchyd with the late
trobles, also the pament for armor, the assessement for
repare of bryges overthrowne the last wynter, above a
dosan, pament of grett fynes and Inhancement of
rents, lacke of traffycke with Flanders, & otherways, &
besydes thes moche trobled with commyssyoners for
concelyd lands & goods, for sale of wynes, owtlaryes
& suche lyke surely the people ar moche trobled yer-
with at the present when they be callyd on for the
xvth & tenthe, and subsedy, for of every paryshe ther ys
a nomber of persons callyd before some of the sayd
Commyssyoners, I would they hayd stayd untill the
subsedy haid ben ratyd, and then to have procedyd
for thay have ben some lett with troble to ye people.

" At the last gaole deliverye ther was one Cuthbert
Athye attayndyd at Yorke for stelyng of a mare, and

because he ys a talle man and hayth servyd long in
Yrland (Ireland) as he sayth and heryng of your
Honors beyng in Scotland gott lycens of his capten to
come to have servyd ther under your L. & beyng on
the sea was be force of wether dryvyn into Scotland,
wher he was spolyd and his money and al he hayd
takyn frome hym, and for nede and by persuasyon of
an evyll man as he sayth toke the sayd mare at the
other mans hands and was persewed and takyn at
Ferybryge. He ys repreved untyll yt shalbe knowne
whether your Honor wyll procure his pardon or not, &
yf your L. wyll not, then he to be executed before
alhalowtyde (Allhallowtide). I have herwith sent your
Honor the byll he sent me.

" Ther was a pore mans house aboute a yere sins
robȳd (robbed) in servyce tyme, and before Chrys-
tymes last a riche preste robyd, beyng as ys sayd a
grett usuror, the brute of yᵉ roberyes were grete &
yet non offenders could be founde. I awardyd iij
severall commyssyons for the fyndyng and trying·
furth therof and at the last yt was founde owte by Mr.
Thomas Farefaxe and others to whome I hayd dyrectyd
one of the commyssyons. The Roberyes were com-
myttyd by vij pore men inhabitants ny the places and
ther was a gentylman one Gabryell Grene* a man

---

* One of the Greens, of Horsforth, near Leeds. Hopkinson
writes that " Thomas Green, of Horsforth, son and heir of John,
married Jane, daughter of Mr. Robert Hunt, of Carleton, near
Rothwell, and had a son Gabriell. This son was one of the pur-

about xxx*l.* or x*l.* land, beyng pore and nedy that was
accessary to the same. He was acceptyd very honest,
and hayd the love and credytt of his nebors and gentylmen wher he dwelt, & yet by bying of a pece of
land so moche overchargyd hym selfe that he was pore
& nedy and as well by the persuasion of the evyll persons as by his nede became an assentor to the same
roberyes. At the last assyses al the offendors were
indytyd, and v of them executyd, one that confessyd
the matter and broght yt to lyght repreved, and the
sayd Grene and one other of the offendors be fled.
Divers of the sayd Gabryell Grenes frends, in consyderation that he hayd a wyffe and dyvers chyldren,
wold make amongst them as they say cc*l.* to have his
pardon, & as they allege the most of his lands ys in-
tallyd, and cannot be forfett bot duryng his lyffe, so
that the Quenes Majestie can have no grett commodyte yerby, the wyffe of the sayd Grene was Thomas
Lyster daughter, of Cravyn a ny kinsman to Lyster
your L. servant, yf yt wold please your Honor ather by
your selfe or others to cause the pardon be procuryd
the money wylbe deuly payd. I am bold to wryte thys
moche to your Honor because I here so moche good
report of the sayd Grene, and that he ys moche la-

chasers of the manor of Horsforth, from Lord Clinton, Earl of
Lincoln, and Leonard Irby, Esq ; he married Alice, daughter
of Mr. Thomas Lister, and had issue, John, William, Thomas,
Anne, and Rosamund." Gargrave's account is an interesting
confirmation of part of the above.

mentyd wher he dwelt, and therfor have hope he wold
herafter be an honest man.

"Yf yt please your Honor to procure a pardon for
Athye, upon knowlege frome your L. I shall cause yt
to be drawne and send to your Honor.

"Ther ys certen felons in the gaole at Hull, for the
delyvere whereof I have apoynted a gaole delyvere at
Hull the xiijth of this moneth wher I tryst Mr. Seriannt
Wray wyll also be. Thus I cease to troble your Honor
humble besechyng the same that I may knowe your
Honor pleasure in the premisses and I shall beseche
the Almyghty God to assiste your L. in the weghty
affares of the realme and long to preserve you in helth
and honor to your L. good contentation, frome Nostell
in haist the vjth day of September 1571.

"Your good L. ever most humble to commande,
"THOMAS GARGRAVE."*

SIR THOMAS GARGRAVE TO LORD BURLEIGH.

"My boundon deuty humble remembred to your
Honor yt may please the same to be advertysyd, that
so farre as may appere by any talke or doyngs of the
late erle of Northumberland at or before his dethe he
contynewed obstynate in Relygyon, and declaryd he
wold dye a Catholyke of the popes churche, he ac-
comptyd his offence nothyng and especyally after he
knewe he shuld dye, but before he semyd to confesse
he hayd offendyd, and wold qualyfye yt sayng he dyd
that he dyd by compulsyon and for feare of his lyffe.

* Domestic—Addenda, Eliz., Vol. XX.

He confessyd he was reconsylyd to the pope, he affermyd this Realme was in a scysme, and that al were sysmatyks, he sayd here was nather petie nor mercy, in his talke with divers he namyd hymselfe symple Thome, and sayd symple Tom must dye to sett up crewell Henry; at his dethe he wyshyd his brother to be of his Relygyon, and then yf he hayd his lyvyng he trystyd he wold pay his detts, and helpe his chydren and servants.

" He dyd not here ather pray for the quenes ma^{tie} nor ever wyshed her well, nor yet wold confesse he hayd offendyd her ma^{tie} wherat many was offendyd and thought he hayd no deutiful consyderation of her ma^{tie}, and on the othersyde the scysmekyd papysts recevyd moche of his stedfastnes in that trade of popyshe Relygyon. I beseche the almyghty to preserve the quenes ma^{tie} and all good subiects frome thayr decetfull and crewell practyses the wyche in myn openyon they intend, yf tyme wold serve. They have to moche lybertye and stepe and waxe herd hertyd wylfull and stoborne. The L. resyste thayr malyce and defende his electe and al the good and crystyan people, and thus besechyng your Honor to beare with my boldnes I cease to troble you humble besechyng the Almyghty long to preserve your good L. in helth and honor— from Yorke in haist the 23 of August 1572.

" Your Honors ever humble to command,

" THOMAS GARGRAVE.*

* Cotton MSS., Calig. C. III., in the British Museum.

The Same to the Same.

"My deuty humble remembred to your Honor, with
my lyke thanks for al your Honor's goodnes towerds
me, and for your late advertysement of the L. Presydent apoyntyd,* of whome I have herde so moche good
reporte and espescyally in matters of crystyan relygyon,
wyche here I tryst his L. shall further with his good
countenance and ayed; and also by thadmynystration
of justyce indeferently well execute his offyce, to the
glory of God, the Quene's Majesties contentation, his
awne honor and to the good and quiett of thes partes
that I have grett hope of goodnes to growe therby,
and my L. Archbusshope beyng placyd in the Commyssyon of this Counsall, lying ny Yorke may be ever
a good assistant to his L. My L. Archbusshope as
yet ys not placyd a Counsalor in thes partes. I am
and shalbe this vj days occupyed here in the contree

* Henry Hastings, Earl of Huntingdon. A letter of his,
dated 26th April, 1573, shortly after his establishment in
office, reports as follows on the state of Yorkshire—(see
Harl. MS., 6991)—"Wee have here begunn ye musters, And in
sum mo placys I have gone my selfe for my better knowledge
of ye cuntrye, and settyng forward of ye servys, then els I
wolde have seene ; where surleye I founde greate numbers of
talle men, and a people most wyllynge and readye to serve byr
Ma^{ty} even in *Craven*, wheare they are most ignorant of God and
relygion ; so as yf they may have good guydes, in my opinion
no parte of thys realme doth breede better subiects, then they
wyll be heare . . . but one greate one of ye contrarie disposition may doo heare muche more hurte then in any parte of
ye realme."

for the assessement of the subsedy wheryn I was
hynderyd almost a fortenyght by my severall iorneys to
Yorke about thexecution of the late Erle of Northumberland, whoo dyed the xxij of August at iij of the
clocke at afternone. And because I cannot untyll
tuysday next conferre with the L. Archebushoppe, I
have wryttyn unto hym to consydre of the choys of
persons mete to be connselors in these partes and after
that day I shall advertyse your Honor therof.

"Yf Sir Henry Gate and Sir George Bowes with Mr.
Vaghan wold make thayr abode in thes partes they wold
be good assistants for men of wurshippe and for knowledge in the lawe, here ys non mete besydes theys
alredy placyd, and Mr. Tankerd ys agyd and so trobled
with the stone and strangurs that he may not well
travell; and yf we lacke hym here ys non bot Mr. Meres,
that knoweth the lawe, for that lytle I hayd ys for-
gottyn because yt ys xxviij yeres sins I left the study
of the lawe and so long have I remanyd here of this
Counsall. And yf yt were no hynderance to Mr. Raufe
Rokebey I do wyshe he were placyd here as
an attendant, and for others I shall when I have
conferryd with my L. Archebusshope advertyse your
Honor, and send unto you suche remembrances of the
Instructions as ar to be referryd in myn openyon, thus
I am bold with your Honor humble besechyng you to
contynewe my good L. and to helpe me furth of my
present cares, and to my power I shall ever duryng

lyffe remayne at your Honors commandement &c.—
frome Nostell in haist the 2 of September 1572.

"Your Honors ever humble to command,
"THOMAS GARGRAVE."*

THE SAME TO THE SAME.

"My deuty humble remembred to your Honor, accordyng to your L. late letter I have conferryd with
my L. Archbushoppe towchynge mete persons to be
counsaillors in thes partes, ather for thayr credytt and
power, or for thayr knowlege in ye lawe bot we have
not takyn upon us to preferre any, bot I have herwith
send your Honor a byll of the names of the men of
most wurshyppe and of the grettyst lyvyngs in thes
partes, and also of suche as be lernyd in the lawes.

"The people be here I thynke as in other places of
the Realme, on sorte ys pleasyd with the late facte in
Frannce,† a seconde sorte moche lament yt, and become fearfull and moche appaulyd at yt, a thyrde wold
seme indeferent as newtralls and thoys are the grettyst
nomber and may be termyd dyssemblers and yet many
of them obedyent subiects and ar to be ledde by the
auctoryte, and by thayr landislords and offycers.

"The Quene's Majestie hayth many grett seignoryes
in this shyre, and yf the offycers were resyant (resident?) and wold well intrete the people, the Quenes
Majestie without grett charges myght with some

* Domestic—Addenda, Eliz., Vol. XXI.
† The Massacre of St. Bartholomew, August 24th.

delygence of thoffycers, accordyng to ordre to be takyn, have in redynes upon any sodan ny *mm.* (2,000) tranyd soldyors, and the offycers and captens beyng well chosyn, the parcell and charges shuld not be grett, and I do thynke the wyckydnes of the tyme suche, that with fayth and feare in good, delygence ys to be usyd with care, to prevent the malycyous and wykyd practyses of the evyll, and the L. God I tryst wyll worke with us and for us, yf we call upon hym, and endevor ourselfes to do our devor* to resyst his ennemyes. King Henry the viij abandonyd the pope and stode stoutly to yt and hayd good lawes to brydle his enmyes, I have herd them termyd blody lawes bot yt ys to be fearyd our to gentyll lawes, wyll not resyst crewell blodeshedyng, yt ys a common saying the weapon betokenyth peace.

"Yf my Lord of Huntington do not come downe at mychelmes his Lordship ys to take ordre for the stay here, as well for thappoyntyng of a vice-pr. as for the dyett of hym and the counsaill.

"His Lordship is to have one commyssyon for the counsaill for heryng of causes, one other Commyssyon of oyre and determyner; the instructions for the Counsaill; a warrant to the recevor for the fees allowed, and a warrant for venyson towerds the dyett to be takyn in all the Quenes Majesties forests chasses and parks be north Trent, one stag and one hind in every place of rede dere, and ij buckes and ij does in every place of falowe dere.

Endeavour, duty; as in French, *devoir*.

F

"I humble beseche your Honor to be my good Lord in my suyte to the Quenes Majestie my symple servyce within this vij last yeres hayth cost me ny a thousand pounds besydes all allowances, yf yt be my chance to wayte of your Honor at this parlyament I shall then be an humble sutor unto your Lordship, as well in my sayd suyt as for my impost for wyne; my late Lord Tresurer every yere untyll the ij last years allowed me for iiij tonnes yerly and the to (two) last yeres I hayd only for ij tonnes, I beseche your Lordship yf I may not have myn old allowance of iiij tonnes that then I may have for iij tonnes and yet the hole iiij tonnes hayth not servyd my house, bot yf the Quenes Majestie be not good to me I shall abate that and more besydes; thus I humble beseche your Honor to bere with my boldnes and to my power I shall remayne at your Lordships commandement, &c.—from Nostell in haist the xviij of September 1572.

"Your Honors ever humble to command,

"THOMAS GARGRAVE."*

Names of the Princepall gentlemen in Yorkshyre.

ESTE RYDYNGE.

d† Sir John Constable.[1]

mp Sir Marmaduke Constable.[2]

wp Sir Wylliam Babthorpe.[3]

---

* Domestic—Addenda, Eliz., Vol. XXI. The list of Gentry which follows is enclosed with the letter.

† The marks before each name are explained at the end of the list.

[1] Of Burton Constable. [2] Of Everingham. [3] Of Babthorpe Hall.

. John Vaghan.[1]

. Xpor Hyllyerd.[2]

Thomas Boynton.[3]

mp Robert Aske.[4]

. Edward Ellerker.[5]

: John Hussey.[6]

. John Hothome.[7]

wp Peter Vavasor.[8]

. Rauf Boucher.[9]

NORTH RYDYNGE.

Lord Latimer.[10]

. Lord Eure.[11]

. Sir Henry Gate.[12]

wp Sir Thomas Danbey.[13]

mp Sir Ric. Chulmeley.[14]

mp Sir William Farefaxe.[15]

. Sir William Bellases.[16]

mp John Sayre.[17]

d Xpor Francis Wasfurth yonger.[18]

d Xpor Rokebye.[19]

. Roger Ratlyffe.[20]

wp Roger Tocketts.[21]

---

[1] Of Sutton upon Derwent. [2] Of Winestead in Holderness. [3] Of Barmston. [4] Of Aughton. [5] Of Risby. [6] Of North Duffield and Hemingborough. [7] Of Scarborough. [8] Of Bellasize. [9] Of Benningborough. [10] Of Snape. [11] Of Malton. [12] Of Seamer. [13] Of Scruton. [14] Of Roxby. [15] Of Gilling. [16] Of Newborough. [17] Of Worksall. [18] Of Kirklington. [19] Of Moreton. [0] Of Mulgrave. [21] Of Langburgh.

wp William Wyclyff.[1]

wp Francis Wyclyff.

wp   Pudsay.

d Ric. Aldburgh.

. Thomas Layton.[2]

wp Xpor Wyvell.[3]

. John Constable of Dromanby.

. Roger Ratlyffe.

.· Thomas Gowre.[4]

. Thomas Savile.[5]

WEST RIDING.

. Comes Salop.

d Lord Darcy.

d Sir Ingrame Clyfforde.

: Sir Thomas Gargrave.

. Sir Symon Musegrave.

mp Sir Ric. Stapleton.[7]

mp Sir Willm. Mallery.[8]

d Sir Willm. Inglebye.[9]

. Ryc. Tempest.[10]

. Thomas Farefaxe.[11]

mp John Vavasor.[12]

d Francis Wortley.[13]

---

[1] Of Whitby. [2] Of Saxham. [3] Of Osgodby. [4] Of Stittenham. [5] Of Welburn. [6] Second son of Henry, Earl of Cumberland. [7] Of Carleton, near Snaith. [8] Of Studley, near Ripon. [9] Of Ripley. [10] Of Bowling. [11] Of Walton and Gilling. [12] Of Weston. [13] Of Wortley, near Barnsley.

mp Thomas Wentworth.[1]

d Willm. Tankerd.[2]

d George Savyle.[3]

mp Willm. Plumton.[4]

. Ryc. Malleverer.[5]

d Edmond Eltoftes.[6]

. Franncis Slyngesbey.[7]

wp Bryan Stapleton.[8]

wp Walter Calverley.[9]

d Wyllm. Hungate.[10]

d Willm. Hawmond.[11]

wp Ric. Gascoigne and his brethern.[12]

. Thomas Waterton.[13]

d Thomas Reresbey.[14]

. Francis Woderoffe.[15]

d Willm. Lyster.[16]

. John Lambert.[17]

. Ryc. Beamond.[18]

d John Beverley.[19]

[1] Of Wentworth Woodhouse. [2] Of Boroughbridge. [3] Of Northgate-head, *alias* Haselden Hall, in Wakefield. [4] Of Plumpton, near Knaresborough. [5] Of Allerton Malleverer, near Wetherby. [6] Of Farnhill, near Skipton—described as of Knottingley, in 1584. [7] Of Scriven, near Knaresborough. [8] Of Wighill, near York.(?) [9] Of Calverley. [10] Of Saxton, near Swillington. [11] Of Scarthingwell, near Sherburne. [12] Of Lasingcroft. [13] Of Walton, near Wakefield. [14] Of Thribergh, near Rotherham. [15] Of Woolley, near Wakefield. [16] Of Midhope and Thornton, in Craven. [17] Of Calton, in Craven. [18] Of Whitley. [19] Of Selby.

Gentylmen of mener degre.

ESTRYDYNG.

d   Robert Wryght.[1]

d   Robert Hawdenbye.[2]

mp Marmaduke Cunstable.[3]

.   Arthur Dakyns.[4]

.   William Strycland.[5]

d   Bryan Lacy.[6]

     Marmaduke Lacy.

d   Gabryel Sayntquyntyn.[7]

d   Constable of Corethorpe.

mp Thomas Dolman.[8]

d   Robert Sothebey.[9]

.   George Dakins.[10]

.   Xpor Legierd.[11]

d   Antony Smethley.

NORTH RIDING.

mp Antony Cateryck.[12]

wp Robert Rokebye.[13]

.   Xpor Lepton.[14]

d   Roger Burghe.[15]

mp Henry Scrope.[16]

mp Micheell Wansfurth.[17]

     Avary Uvedale.

---

[1] Of Plowland, in Holderness. [2] Of Haldenby. [3] Of Cliffe. [4] Of
Linton. [5] Of Boynton. [6] Of Folkton. [7] Of Harswell, or
Harpham. [8] Of Pocklington. [9] Of Pocklington. [10] Of Brands-
burton. [11] Of Anlaby. [12] Of Carlton, near Stokesley. [13] Of
Manfield, in Richmondshire. [14] Of Kepwith. [15] Of East
Haukswell. [16] Of Danby. [17] Of Kirklington.

d Symon Dodisworth.[1]

William Davell.[2]

. Roger Dalton.

. John Place.

THE COUNTY OF Y⁰ CITY OF YORKE.

. Sir Robert Stapleton.[3]

d Sir Oswolde Wylsthorpe.

d Gabryell Farefaxe.[4]

d Vavasor.[5]

d John Ynglebey.[6]

WEST RYDYNG.

d Laurance Kythley.[7]

wp Willm. Hawkesworth.[8]

d Mathewe Redman.[9]

. Ric. Bunny.[10]

. Hugh Savile.[11]

. Robert Bradfurth.[12]

d John Lacy of Lenthorpe (Leventhorpe).

. John Lacy of Brerelay.

d Henry Tempest.[13]

mp John Hamerton of Cravyn.[14]

wp John Hamerton of Monkroyde.[15]

d Robert Rocklay.[16]

mp Thomas Drapere.

[1] Of Thornton Watlas. [2] Of Coxwold. [3] Of Wighill. [4] Of Steeton. [5] Of Hazelwood. [6] Second son of Wm. Ingleby, of Ripley. [7] Of Newall, near Otley. [8] Of Hawksworth, near Otley [9] Of Harewood. [10] Of Newland near Wakefield. [11] Of Wrenthorpe, near Wakefield. [12] Of Stanley, near Wakefield. [13] Of Broughton, in Craven. [14] Of Hellifield. [15] Near Pontefract. [16] Of Rockley, near Barnsley.

.   Willm. Wombwell.

d   Jerves Boswyle.[2]

d   Willm. Frobysher.[3]

mp Robert Ley.[4]

mp Pers Stanley.[5]

d   John Holmes.[6]

d   James Washyngton.[7]

wp Martyn Anne.[8]

d   Bartylmew Tregott.[9]

mp Herry Gryce.[10]

.   John Kay of Woodsome.[11]

.   John Kay of Okynshay.[12]

mp Xpor Nelson.

wp Henry Oglesthorpe.[13]

mp Xpor Hopton.[14]

.   Willm. Vavasor of Weston.

wp Wilm. Gascoigne of Caley.

wp Wyllm. Arthyngton.[15]

.   Bryan Bales.

Many mo evyll and dowtfull.

y⁵ markes {
.   protestant.
wp, the worste sorte.
mp, meane or lesse evyll.
d, doutfull or newtor.
}

[1] Of Wombwell, near Barnsley. [2] Of Ardsley and Newhall, near Barnsley. [3] Of Finningley, near Doncaster. [4] Of Hatfield. [5] Of Womersley, near Pontefract. [6] Of Hampole, near Doncaster. [7] Of Adwick le Street. [8] Of Frickley. [9] Of South Kirby. [10] Of Sandal, near Wakefield. [11] Near Almondbury. [12] Oakenshaw, near Wakefield. [13] Of Beaghall. [14] Of Armley, near Leeds. [15] Of Arthington.

The following papers in Gargrave's hand-writing, and endorsed with his name by Lord Burghley, are the last traces of him that can be found in the State Papers. They are undated; but from various considerations have been assigned to the year 1574 :—

SURVEY OF WAKEFIELD OLD PARK.

"A brefe note of the Survey of th'olde parke of Wakefelde beyng surveyed and mesuryd by me and presentyd by sundry gentylmen and others of good honesty beyng sworne for that purpose.

"The same parke ys a busshye and barran ground in the most parts therof and contenyth 340 acres with 16 acres wythout the pale usyd as parcel of the parke wherof 4 acres at 2s. ye acre, 200 acres at 16d. the acre, the residew at 4d. the acre.

"Ther ys no tymber wods yerin for repare of pale or loges bot the wods yerin be old rotyn dotyd* trees valued in all to 13l. 6s. 8d.

"Ther ys no copyses mynes or other proffett theryn.

"Ther ys fewe dere theryn and presently nather bucke nor sowre,† for the pale ys so in decaye that yt wyll not kepe in the dere.

* Dotard or doated, applied to trees, means beginning to decay, or stumpy—thus in *Friar Bacon's Brazen Head's Prophesie*, 1604—

> Then beetles could not live
> Upon the hony bees,
> But they the drones would drive
> Unto the *doted* trees.

† A *sower* is a buck in his fourth year.

" Ther ys yerin on loge and 2 lytle howses at the park gates, the wyche with also the parke pale be so farre in decay, that 40 tymber trees and 33*l*. 6s. 8d. ys convenyent to be bestowed for the present repare yerof.

" The Ryver of Calder hayth wastyd away 12 acres of the best ground yerof and for the defence therof the thornes and busshes in the parke, with 40*l*. in money is convenyent to be furthwith imploied.

" The yerly rent of the parke ys only by yere 10*l*. wherof goeth furth for fees to the keeper and palester yerly 5*l*. 15d., and remanyth there towerds the charges of the repare yerly 4*l*. 18s. 9d., so that al the premysses consyderyd, the same parke for lacke of woods, and for the grett charges therof ys not to be contyneud as a parke, for the contyneuance yerof wilbe more charges than ather pleasure or profett.

" Ther ys 3 other parkes wythin a myle therof, and 4 mo parkes within 6 myles yerof and al be the Quenes Majesties grounds.

" My suyte ys to gyffe the Quenes Majestie 200 marks wyche amountyth to 30 yeres purchace of her Majesties clere rent and yet *communibus annis* her Majestie hayth not 40s. by yere, and I to have the grant of the sayd parke in recompence yerof and of my suyte and to discharge her hyghnes of the aforesayd fees, to me and to my heyres for ever and to pay yerly to the Quenes Majestie and her heyrs 10*l*. rent as a fee ferme.

" This my suyte ys in manor of a purchace and yet the

Quenes majestie shall have her full revenew, and be also dyschargyd of 5*l*. fee yerly, and of all repare.

" 2 suyte.—Yf the Quenes Majestie wyll not departe with the fee symple, I have bot . . . same and I shall humble require to have the same to me and to my heyrs males in fe ferme and I shall gyffe the Quenes Majestie 40*l*. in money and yerly duryng ten of the furst yeres ten pounds by yere and ever after 16*l*. by yere, and I shall also dyscharge her Majestie of the rents fees and repare.

" My suyte ys for to have my herytance yerin because the fencyng stubbyng and dressyng of the ground wylbe very chargeable, and ar not to be borne by any fermor, and I wold also buyld me a dwellyng howse yerin for that yt ad-ioynyth to the place wher I was borne, & wher my land lyeth.

" Yf I may attayne ather of thes too suytes, I shall thynke my selfe well satysfyed and be redy to spend the rest of my lyffe with my lyvyng in suche the Quenes Majestie servyce and affares as I shalbe apoyntyd unto.

" 3 suyte.—Yf the Quenes Majestie wyll not departe with the inherytance then I tryst her Majestie wyll grant yt to me upon the surrender of th'old patent for terme of my lyffe and 21 or 30 yeres after wyth lyberty to take and stubbe the trees and bushes, and I shall gyffe her majestie duryng my lyffe 10*l*. rent, and dyscharge her majestie of the aforsayd fees and charges, and after my dethe duryngo the said terme I shall gyffe her majestie 16*l*. rent by yere.

" Or yf her majestie wyll graunt yt unto me upon the

surrendr of the former patent for 40 yeres, I shall gyffe the Quenes Majestie 20*l.* and 10*l.* rent yerely for ten of the furst yeres, and yerly after 16*l.* by yere, and I shall also dyscharge her majestie of the aforsayd fees and charges of repare.

"Provydyd always that the same parke be not kepte as a parke for dere nor I chargyd with any kepers.

"In this last suyte I tryst the Quenes Majestie wyll not stycke, bot I wold moche rather obtene ather of the 2 former suytes, because I wold buyld me an howse yerin, and end my lyffe ther."*

SIR THOMAS GARGRAVE'S WILL.

"In the name of God, Amen. I, Thomas Gargrave of Nostell in the Countie of Yorke, knight, being in health and good memorie (praised be unto God) consyderinge the uncertaintie of man's lyfe, and the troubles that often arise for the lands and goods of the dead, and also the cares and troubles of the sicke, yf order bee not therein taken before. Therefore I mynde to prevent the same by God's grace so much as in me is, by the makeing of this my will and testament written with my owne hand and sealed with my seale as hereafter herein is declared ; and before I enter further therein I doe hereby declare my selfe to beleve that all thinges written in the olde and new Testament (that is to say) in the Canonicall Scriptures bee written for our learnynge, and that the same is profitable to

* Domestic—Addenda, Vol. XXIII.

teache and instructe in all rituousness, and therein wee
bee taughte that we be all synners, and that yf wee
say that wee have no synne we deceyve ourselves and
the trueth is not in us."

* * * * *

After a very long elaboration of his religious views,
wholly expressed in the words of Scripture, Sir Thomas
proceeds :—

"And I will my bodie shalbe buried in the upper-
most Queer on the South Syde of Wragbie Churche,
and yf I make not a tombe before my death, then I will
that my heires or executors shall make one within six
yeres next after my death, and I will that mention be
thereon made of me and both my wyfes and of my
children, and I will that the day of my funeralls there
shalbe a Sermon made by some learned man, and xii
moe sermons to bee made at Wragbie Churche on
xii of the next Sondayes after my said funeralls, and I
will that other xii sermons shalbe made at Hemesworth Churche on xii Sondayes next after the said
xii Sondayes, that is to witt upon everie of the xxiii
Sondayes one sermon, in all which sermons I woulde
have the people taughte there dueties in prayer, and
in the comaundements of God, and in charity towards
their neighbours, and their justification by faith in
Jesus Christ. Then I will that my mortuaries shalbe
paid according to the lawes of this realme ; and I will
that the day of my funeralls shall be gyven and
bestowed to thinhabitants of everie cottaige in the

parishes of Hemesworth and Wragbie, and in the
towns of Havercrofte and Upton XIId., and to everie
poore scholler of the Scholes att Hemesworth and
Wragbie IId. and to everie one of the Hospitall in
Hemsworth IIIId.; and I will that there shall be dis-
tributed the day of my funeralls to the poore of
Wragbie parishe one quarter of wheate and one of rye
in breate att their houses; and I will to bee paid within
one moneth next after my death to the Churchwardens
of everie parishe hereafter named to bee putt into the
poore man's boxes in the said severall parishes for the
releife of their poore, to Wakefield XXs., to
Pontefract Xs., to Wragbie Xs., to Hemesworth
Xs., to Felkirke VIs. VIIId., to Crofton VIs. VIIId.,
to Baddesworth VIs. VIIId. I will my wyfe shall
have all her mornynge apparell with all other
her apparell with her cheyne and her broderie
for her French hoode, and all her rings and jewells;
I will that my wyfe's two maides have everie of them
one blacke gowne, and her man one blacke coate; I
give to Bridgett Haighe *alias* Tempest XLs.; and to
Frances the wife of Mr. Thomas Wombwell XLs. in recompense of all things they or eyther of them may
clayme of their father's gyfte or bequest, and I consyderinge my wife's aige and impotencie, and by
reason of her aige, the decay of her seighte and
hearinge, I do will and desyer her my said wife to
remaine in house with my sonne or other my heire
duringe her lyfe, and that she shall have convenient

chambers and lodgeings with bedds fyers and other
necessaries, for her selfe, her two maids, and one
man. And for her chamber, if she like, the chamber
wherein she now lyethe, that then she shall have
and keepe the same with the two chambers next
within the same with the bedd clothes and therein and
convenient meate and drinke for her, and her said
servaunts; and I will that my heires shall pay her fiftie
pounds rents yerely att Pentecost and Martynmas by
even portions furthe of all my lands, tenements, and
hereditaments; and for defaulte of payment thereof
or of anie parte thereof, att anie of the said dayes of
payment, and by twentie dayes after that then my
heires to forfeyte to my said wife in the name of a
paine therefore, for everie tyme fyve pounds of lawfull
moneys, and that ytt shalbe lawfull for my said wyfe
and her assignes and everie of them to enter and dis-
trayne in all my lands and tenements for the said rent
and arreragies thereof, and for the said somme *sub
nomine poenæ,* and the same distresse and distresses to
impounde and reteyne untill the same with th'arreragies
thereof, yf anie bee, shalbe fully satisfied and paid, the
which bequest of this my will and therein specified
with meate drinke lodginge and the said rent of fyftie
pounds by yere I will shalbe in full recompense and
satisfaction of her dower of all my lands tenements and
hereditaments, And I will that to be parcel of that
recompense she shall have paid within one moneth next
after my death the somme of twentie pounds of law-

full money ; and I will she shall farther have VI sylver
spoones gylte, and VI with appostills on the ende, the
sylver aile cupp and cover gylte, the which spoones and
cupp were Sir John Wentworthe's;* And I will she
shall ymediatly after my death have the mannor of
Holey with all that was her joynter of the Myrfeilds
lands.   And I will and bequeath by this my will and
testament to my said wife, that yf she agree and accepte
the legacies and bequests of this my will according to
the intent thereof, that then she shall have the bedd
whereon she lyeth and the ymplements thereof with
two paire of sheets and three . . . to bestowe upon
her children att the time of her death, so they live
quietly without troublinge or vexinge my heires or executors or any of them for anie thing that was their
fathers.   And where Hector Wentworth my wifes
sonne hath heretofore had and receyved of my wyfe
one aile cupp of sylver, and the cover all gylte, to the
value of foure pounds or thereabouts, and also one
tablett of Golde with two stones therein to the value
of VIII*l.* att the least, the which I will he shall have
and reteyne to his owne use with also VII*l.* XIIIs. IVd.
in money to be paid within one yere after my death, so
within the said time he do release to myne heires executors or administrators all actions and demaunds, or yf
he shall not so do, then all my bequests unto him to

* Gargrave's second wife was the widow of Sir John Wentworth, of North Elmsall, and daughter of Roger Appleton, co.
Kent.

bee voide : and yf my said wife be not content with
these my bequests in this my will, and to accepte them
in full recompense of all her dower of my lands tenements and hereditaments, and for and in full recompense of all such portions of my goods and cattells
and of the goods and cattells of her former husbands
as she may have and clayme by anie meanes, then I
leave her to have that the lawe will, and all my former
bequests to be voide to her for ever, but I verelye trust
and deayer my said wife well to consyder of her aige
and quietnes, and I chardge my sonne even as the
father may chardge the sonne before God, that hee bee
gentle and good unto her as unto his father's good wife
as hee hath good cause, yf he call to remembrance her
rare diligence and goodnes towards him in his youthe,
and her kyndnes nowe to his children. I bequieth to
Susane Wentworth yf she remaine with my wyfe att
my death X*l*. of money towards her marriage ; and to
˙Thomas Wentworth father of the said Susane VI*l*.
XIIIs. IVd. bothe the saide two last devised to bee
voide, if the said Thomas ˙Wentworthe, his Executors
or Administrators or anie of them shall att anie time
after my death vexe sue or impede myne heires or executors or anie of them for anie the bequests or goods
or cattells that was his father's. I will that Christopher Penson have during his life the house wherein he
now dwelleth in Wakefeilde with all houses gardens
crofts and grounds in Burmantofte, and now in his
occupation, hee yerely payinge the out rents thereof and

G

the makeinge and doeinge all necessarie reparacions of
the said house and grounds. And I give to Jane Pear-
son his daughter V*l.* towards her marriage to bee paid
at the time of her marrage. And further I will and
bequieth to Thomas Gargrave my servant XL*s.* yerely
furthe of my lands at Nostell untill he shalbe preferred
by marriage or otherwaies to a lyvinge of IIII*l.* yerely. I
give and devise to everie one of the children of James
Byrkeby and Thomas Sands that shalbe unmarried at
the time of my death X*s.*; and I will that everie of my
waiting household servants att the time of my death
shall have one blacke coate and X*s.* in money over and
besydes his wages then due. And I give will and
bequieth to Frauncis Roids, Serjeant at lawe,* and to
Robert Bradforth of Stanley, Esquire,† the third part
of all my manor lands and tenements for VI yeres
next after my death to the intent that they with the
rents and profitts thereof shall pay my debts and legacies; provided alwaies that when they have receyved
so muche as will satisfie the same, that then this
bequeste to bee voide; and one other full thirde parte
of my lands tenements and hereditaments I do lease to
the Quene or Prince during the infancie and nonaige
of myne heire, and yf Cotton Gargrave my sonne shall
fortune to dye before me, then I will unto my daughter

---

* Rodes, of Great Houghton; afterwards Justice of the
Common Pleas.

† The son of Brian Bradford, of the same place, an attorney.
Robert Bradford was a Justice of the Peace, and treasurer for
lame soldiers, 36-40 Eliz. He died about 1598.

in lawe his wife my mannor of Darton with th'appurtenances and XL*l*. yerely rent chardge owt of my mannor
of Wrenthorpp to bee paid at Pentecost and Martynmas
yerely duringe her lyfe by even portions; and I give
and bequieth to the said Frauncis Roids and Roberte
Bradfurthe and to their heires all my mannors lands
tenements and hereditaments with th'appurtenances in
the severall parishes of Wragbie, Crofton, Fetherston,
Ackeworth, Baddesworth, Hemesworth, Felchurche,
and in everie of them to the onely use of Cotton Gargrave my sonne, and to the heires mailes of the bodie
of Bridgett his first wife lawfully begotten, and for
default of such issue then to the use of the heires
mailes of the body of the said Cotton Gargrave of his
seconde wyfe the doughter of Thomas Watterton lawfully begotten, and for defaulte of such issue to the use
of my right heires for ever. And I will and bequieth
to the said Frauncis Roids fyve pounds for his paines,
and to Robert Bradforthe for his pains III*l*. VI*s*. VIII*d*.
And I do make Cotton Gargrave my sole executor of
this my last will and testament. In witnes whereof &c.
the 27th day of Marche, 20 Eliz.: (   ) there beinge
witnesses James Byrkeby, Matthew Usher, Thomas
Clerke, Thomas Gargrave, Richard Tempest, and
Thomas Tayler."*

Sir Thomas Gargrave died on the 28th March 1579.

* From a copy in Additional MS. 24,475 (one of Hunter's
Collections) in the British Museum, taken, we believe, from the
original in the possession of Viscount Galway.

There was an inquisition taken of his estates on the 1st May following,* at Wragby, when it was certified that he held the manors of Winterset, Crofton, West Hardwick, Wrenthorpe, Hemsworth, Upton, Kinsley, Darton, Ryhill, Askern, and Havercroft; a tenement called Santingley Grange; a windmill in Crofton; the advowson of Hemsworth Church; messuages and lands in Ackworth, &c. He also held a "park called the Old Park of Wakefield," granted by the Queen to himself and his heirs.

A few words on the unfortunate descendants of Sir Thomas Gargrave will bring this chapter to a close. Sir Cotton Gargrave was the only surviving son of Sir Thomas. He was 39 years old at the death of his father, and only enjoyed the estate ten years. He seems to have taken but little part in county affairs, beyond serving the office of High Sheriff in 1584. One letter of his has come under our observation, written to Thomas Randolph, who, it seems, had just returned from an embassy to Scotland. It is short, and so may as well find place here:—

SIR COTTON GARGRAVE TO THOMAS RANDOLPH.

"My L. Ambassadoure and my good cousen, I am most glad to hear of your helthe, as God be thankid

---

* The commissioners were Ralph Rokeby, George Woodruff, and Brian Hammond, Esquires. The jury was composed of Robert Lee, Jervase Nevile, James Washington, John Holmes, Thomas Barmby, Christopher Nelson, Thomas Savile, Esquires, and Thomas Storthes, Thomas Tempest, Thomas Crosby, George Watterton, Hugh Wentworth, Richard Tempest, Robert Usher, gentlemen.

1 leaft your wieff and chydren whan I came from London, and I am glad to hear of your returne owt of Scotland in helthe. I praye you lett your frend see you at his poore howse in your passayge, it is not owt of your waye you shalbe as welcome to my howse as unto any frend his howse in Ingland y^t you have. Newse I can writt you none because they ar ye thynges I aske not often. God send you well unto my howse at Nostill & from thence as it shall plese God & you to London whear ther is many y^t wold be most glad to see you, & I to receyve some few lynes from you of your returne as you passe & at whatt tyme & . . . I committ you to ye Lord. Nostill this fyrst day of May 1586.

" Your kinsman & assurid frend,

" COTTON GARGRAVE."*

Sir Cotton's son Thomas succeeded to the family estates in 1588. He was tried and executed at York for the murder of his servant, some seven years afterwards, leaving a daughter, Prudence, who married Dr. Richard Berrie, of Hodroyd. Richard, the half-brother of Thomas, then inherited the property. In 1605 he served the office of High Sheriff; and it is told of him that as he rode through the streets of Wakefield he "bestowed great largesses upon the common people, in congratulation for so wise, peaceful, and religious a

---

* Harl. MS. 6994, in the British Museum. Gargrave is erroneously printed "Mowgrave" in the Calendar.

king as England then enjoyed." Sir Richard was a
gambler and a spendthrift, and by little and little the
great estates upon which he entered were parted with
to support his extravagance. Nostel was disposed of in
1613. Dodsworth wrote of him in 1634 that " he now
liveth in the Temple for sanctuary, having consumed
his whole estate, to the value of 3,500*l.* per annum at
the least, and hath not a penny to maintain himself but
what the purchasers of some part of his lands in reversion after his mother's death allow him, in hope he
will survive his mother, who hath not consented to the
sale." Hunter, writing in 1830, says, "The memory
of his extravagance and his vices yet lingers about
Kinsley; and Kinsley, not Nostel, is supposed to
have been the scene of the murder. The rustic moralist
still points his counsel with the story of Sir Richard
Gargrave, who could once ride on his own land from
Wakefield to Doncaster, and had horses innumerable
at his command, but was at last reduced to travel with
the pack-horses to London, and was found dead in an
old hostelry, with his head on a pack-saddle."

The little that is known of Mary Gargrave, one of
Richard's sisters, is hardly less sad. She was maid of
honour to Anne of Denmark, the Queen of James I.
Between the years 1631 and 1639 she presented several
petitions to Charles, praying for protection against her
creditors. In the first of these she stated that her
pension had been already made over to them, and "she
still in much peril, having nothing to live upon." A

year later, she prayed for the renewal of her protection, being then 1,000*l.* in arrear, " to prevent an old servant of the king's late mother from dying miserably in prison."*

Richard had only female issue. His younger brother, Francis, had many children, one of whom, Cotton, was chaplain to the first Lord Irwin. The family, however,. gradually declined, and some years ago there was a Gargrave, believed to be of this family, who filled the humble office of parish clerk at Kippax.

---

* She was baptized 17th Jan., 1575-6 (see Banks' *Walks about Wakefield*, p. 283), and so would be about 56 years old at this time. The petitions quoted from are preserved among the State Papers of the period.

CHAPTER II.

SIR MARTIN FROBISHER.

Both the birth-place and the parentage of Sir Martin Frobisher have been the subjects of much discussion a; various times, without any satisfactoay result. The compilers of biographical dictionaries, copying one from another, content themselves with the assertion that he was born in the neighbourhood of Doncaster. If this off-hand assumption be traced to its source, it will be found to be based on the fact that there lived a Francis Frobisher in Doncaster about this time. He was a member of the Council of the North, and served the office of Mayor in the town where he lived. No traces of any other person of the same name can be found in the neighbourhood. Now, Francis Frobisher died in 1562, and shortly afterwards, as was usual in those days, a jury was impanelled to certify as to the estates which he held, their mode of tenure, his heir, &c. The report of this jury is still preserved, and is strictly legal evidence. It states that William is the son and heir of Francis, and that he is 24 years old. No other son is mentioned in this inquisition, nor is any other attributed to Francis in the pedigree compiled by the Heralds on their visitations.

There seems little reason to deprive Altofts, in the

parish of Normanton, of the honour of having produced him. John Frobisher, of Altofts,* farmer of the king's domain there, had a son John, who married a Freston, of the same place. There were several sons issuing from that marriage. One of them was Francis, of Doncaster, above-mentioned. Anthony, another son, was vicar of Normanton. A third, Barnard, it appears by the Heralds' Visitation of Yorkshire in 1584, married Ada, daughter of John Yorke, of Gowthwaite, in Netherdale, near Ripon,† and Martin was one of the offspring of this union.‡ This statement is further confirmed by the fact of an entry in the Normanton Parish Registers of the baptism of Margaret, daughter of Barnard, whilst the inquisition taken after Sir Martin's death, as will presently be seen, shows him to have had a sister of the same name.

* " John Frobisher, of Newland," occurs on the subsidy roll for 15 Hen. 8, under Altofts and Normanton. The roll for 1546 contains the names of Edmund "Frobishore," who is taxed 10s. in lands and fees, and of Johanna "Frobishore," under Altofts, and of Richard "Frobishore," under Normanton. In 1572 Gregory "Frobyser" is the only contributor; he pays 2s. 8d. on lands.

† The fifth son of Sir Richard Yorke, knt., of the city of York, who died in 1498.

‡ See the pedigree of the Yorkes in Harleian MS., 1571, in the British Museum. The expression there is "Sir Martin and others"; it will be seen by the *inquisition post mortem* that Martin had two brothers, John and David, and one sister, Margaret, who attained full growth. Sir John Yorke, presently alluded to as Martin's kinsman, was a son of John Yorke, of Gowthwaite; he was Lord Mayor of London. It is worthy of observation that Sir John's son, Peter, succeeded to the Gowthwaite property, and that John Frobisher's son, also named Peter, was made Martin's heir.

When Martin was under examination in May, 1566, his age was stated to be 27 or thereabouts, so we may regard his birth to have taken place in the year 1539. Michael Lok, who seems to have been one of his early friends, and whom we shall meet afterwards in connection with Frobisher's three voyages, wrote in one of his letters that Martin "was born of honest parentage, ' gentlemen ' of a good house and antiquity, who sent him to London to school; his kinsman, Sir John Yorke, perceiving him to be of great spirit, bold courage, and natural hardness of body," thought a seafaring life best suited for him, and sent him on a voyage to Guinea. Lok's narrative, unfortunately, breaks off at this point. However, the fact that Frobisher took a voyage to Guinea is curiously enough confirmed by the first mention of him that occurs in the State Papers. A document is preserved amongst them, called a "Declaration of Martin Frobisher, who was in the first and second voyages in the parts of Guinea, and there remained by the space of three quarters of a year in the Castle of Mine." The date of this is 27th May, 1562. Just three years after this— that is, on the 26th May, 1565—Frobisher was reported to be in command of a ship forming one of a fleet alleged to have been engaged in spoiling sixty-one Spanish ships. That Frobisher was at this time engaged in the active pursuit which now-a-days we should plainly designate as piracy, we would hardly venture to assert; but that he laboured under a reputa-

tion of that kind is plainly shown in the next particulars that can be ascertained about him. The following letter tells its own story :—

THE MAYOR AND BURGESSES OF SALTASH TO THE PRIVY COUNCIL.

" Pleasith your Honors to be advertised that the
fiveth day of this present moneth June we receved
your Commyssion by this bearer Thomas Naryse the
Queens Majesties Servant for the apprehension of a
shippe of the burden of six score or therabouts,
wherof is owner Martyn Furbusher, and capiten or
cheiff Ruler, John Furbusher his brother, and before
this present tyme wee have not herde of any souche
shippe or companye to be within the precincte of the
liberties of this Town of Saltaysh, but from hensfurth
accordyng to our bounden dutie wee wyll from tyme
to tyme diligently watche and serche if anye souche
shippe or companye doe come or arryve within our
liberties, to apprehende and surely kepe aswell the
sippe as also the persons therin beyng hopyng your
Honors conceyve noe lesse opynyon in us but that we
have bene and are alwayes redye to showe ourselves as
trustye and obedyent subiectes, &c.; from Saltayshe in
Cornwall the fiveth day of June, 1566."*

However, the expedition which Frobisher had set out
upon, whatever might be its object, was already at an
end. Queen Elizabeth, writing about this time to one
of her ministers, Lord Montague, mentions the many

* Dom., Eliz., Vol. XL.

complaints of piracy, in the Thames and elsewhere, that have been made, and adds that one " Furbisher " and his partners have been committed to prison, and his ship arrested upon suspicion. That this person was none other than our hero, the following report is suffi-·cient evidence :—

EXAMINATION OF MARTIN FROBISHER.

"The 30th of May, 1566, before Mr. David Lewes, Doctor of Laws, judge, &c. ; in the presence of me, John Lewes, public notary.

"Martyne Furbisher of Normanton,* in the county of York, gentleman, of the age of 27 or there abowtes.

" Beinge examined what shippinge he hathe, saythe he hathe one shipp called the Mary Flower which he bought of John Baxter, gent., abowte 12 monethes past then called the Mathewe of the burthen of an hun-drethe Tonnes or there abowts, beinge a black shipp.

" Beinge demanded what voyadges he hathe made with the same shippe & what voyadges he intended to make saythe, that he haythe made none yet, but in August last intendinge a voyadge for Gynney he rigged and trimmed the said shipp at Newcastell uppon Tyne. And in December last he sett furthe from thence to the sea with the same shipp havinge then aborde abowte ·36 men, whereof he had not as he saythe above 4 gen-tlemen, viz.: John Baxter, George Norton, William

* This description of Frobisher is additional proof of his early ·connection with Altofts, that place being in the parish of Normanton, as has been already pointed out.

Kinge, nowe deceased and Thomas Yonger and the rest mariners.

" Beinge demanded for howe longe tyme he had victualls Seithe for a monethe and no more for that he minded to be victualled in the west contrey for the said voyadge or els to gyve over the same.

" And as for merchandizes he had none as he saythe. But intended to have had sum Linnen clothe Wex Karseys and other thinges necessary for that voyadge in the west contry.

" He seythe he had in mony with him of his owne abowte fifty pounds and one Mr. George Claxton of the Bishopprick of Dyrham, gent., had promised for that voyadge the adventure of two hundrethe poundes, whereof this examinant receyvid at Newecastell one hundrethe in mony after his departure and the other he promised shuld be delivered unto him in the west contry.

" Beinge examined howe many other gentilmen were appoyntid to goe with him in that voyadge saythe that the said Claxton one Robert Laxton and Raffe Hasylby and noe more of his knowledge.

" And these three personnes he commanded by his Letters to one Richard Erisye of Cornewall and willed them to tary abowte Plimowthe (Plymouth) for his arryval.

" Beinge asked what munition or ordinannce he had abord his shipp at his settinge furthe sayethe that he had one Saker 2 quarter slings six bases, and 2 faw-

kens, 20 corseletts, tenne Jackes, tenne bowes; tenne
Curryers and 2 or 3 dosen of pykes.*

" And further seithe that after they entrid the seas
they saylid noe further then Hull, by reason of greate
tempest and contrary wynde whyche happenid the
Sunday after Christenmas day last past by occasion
whereof he spent all his mastes and sayles and thereby
was dryven to arryve at Scarborowghe where he abode
by the space of 3 monethes for the furnishinge of the
said shipp agayne for the said voyadge.

" And becawse he sawe his evill luck and lacked money
to furnishe his said voyadge in such sorte as was
requisit he left of the same, and minded either to sell
the said shipp or els to make sume shorter voyadge
therewith.

" And at Scardborowghe one Mr. Edward Rye, a
servant of the Lord Darcy of the North came to this
examinant and lent him fifty pounds but the said Rye
ment not to goe on the said voyadge toward Gynnye,
but wold have gon into Fraunce in the said shipp
if she had gon thether to see the country, And
saythe that one Ogdon a servinge man came in company withe the said Rye.

" And from Scarborowghe this examinant was sent
for, by the Lorde Archebishopp of Yorke, under whose

---

* Saker and falcon were species of artillery. Dampier, in his
Voyages, 1688, writes, " Of guns the long *saker* is most esteemed."
The falcon carried a ball of a pound and a-half, and measured
two inches in the bore. Corslets and jacks were leathern coats ;
we still speak of " jack-boots."

chardge he continewed untill he presented·him self to
the Lords of the privey consayle.

"Beinge asked what suertyes he put in for his good
behaviour and his cumpany in the said shipp before the
same passed to the seas, saythe that he, John Baxter,
and the said Claxton were bounde in the summe of
twelve hundrethe pounds to the effect aforesaid before
Mr. Thwinge and Mr. Standeven, Viceadmiralls at
Yorcke.

"Beinge examined whether he knowethe or hard say
that his said shipp was arrested at Scarborowghe
at the sute of one Kinge, saythe that sithence his
cumminge therehens he herd say that the said shipp
was arrested by vertue of proces that came owte of
thadmiralty at the said parte, but howe or when she
went therehens he knowethe not, for that he herd
nothinge from his brother John Furbisher whome he
left there his deputy. Howe be yt he herd say that
she departed from thence abowte the 6th or 7th of this
present monethe. And as for letters or other messengers
he received none from his brother or from the said
shipp sithence he came hether to London.

"And seythe he was not privey of her departinge from
Scarborowe to the West parties for he had geven order
that she shold have gon to Newecastell for coles and
from thence to Rochell for salt.

"And he saithe he never herd of eny spoyle or other
thinge don by the said shipp after her departure from
Scarborowe nor eny tidings of her untill Walter Darby

came to London uppon Sonday last from the said shipp and told him that she was gon westward, wheruppon he made motion to my Lords grace of Yorck, declaringe that the sayd Darby was cumme from the said shipp and that she was gon westward withowte her ladinge of coles that he might have commission to goe or send westward for the stay of the same for that he knewe not in what order she was gon.

"MARTYN FROBISHER."

"ON THE 11TH DAY OF JUNE, 1566.

"The foresaid Martyn Frobisher farder examined this day before the said Mr. Lewes what ordennance and munition his seid shipp had or was appointed to have at eny place—

"Seithe,

"That at his departure and cumminge from her at Scardboroughe she had one saker of iron, 2 fawkenetts of iron, one fowler, 2 small slings, and 6 single brases and more she had not.

"He seithe, that he had the 2 fawkenetts and 2 small slings of John Bennett of Newe castle, Master of the Quenes Majesties ordenance, for the which he payed to him as he nowe remembrethe 8*l.*

"The residewe of thordenance he bought with the said ship.

"He seithe that he should have had 2 peeces of Brasse of the said Bennett, so as he could have putt him in band for the sure delivery of them agayne, which at that presente he was not able to doe.

" And other ordenance or munition he had not of the said Bennett nor made eny covenants or bargayne withe him for eny more..

" Beinge examined whether he herd enythinge of his foresaid shipp since his last examination he seithe that he hathe not understoode enythinge of her.

"MARTIN FROBISHER."

A few days previous to this, Dr. Lewes had been engaged in examining Walter Darby, another of the crew. He is described as of Barnard's Inn, gentleman. Darby said he had been acquainted with Martin "Furbiger" ever since his brother and he were in trouble at the suit of Mr. Appleyard, about two years before. Martin had proposed to him, about Easter, 1565, that he should go on a voyage to Guinea, the ship called "Mary Flower" having been just purchased. Early in September, he rode down into the North with Sir Henry Percy,* knight, John "Furbeger," who was then Sir Henry's man, and a son of Sir Anthony Cooks. He found the Mary Flower not yet properly fitted out, so he spent the remainder of the year about the towns of Tynemouth and Newcastle. About eight days after Christmas he embarked, having for his companions "Marten Furboger," John Baxter, one Longer, Waisher, Sprent, Kinge, Norton, Sydenham, Rogers, and one Todder, *alias*

---

* The brother of the Earl of Northumberland, a leader, as we saw in the last chapter, of the Northern Rebellion. Henry stood loyal to his Queen, and in 1576 was summoned to Parliament, in succession to his brother, as Earl.

Trowblefield, and so went to the seas, purposing to
have gone to the West Countries.   From Darby's narrative we get additional particulars of the first voyage
of this ill-fated ship.   When they left Scarborough
they were victualled for a month, having with them
three tons of biscuit and a hogshead of beef, besides
butter, cheese, and fish.   From Scarborough they went
to Burlington Road, "a kenne or a half" from Scarborough, and stayed there a day and a half.   At Burlington they landed John "Furbiger" to go to a friend
named "Mr. Boynton,"* from whom he obtained fresh
victuals.   John returned the following afternoon with
a sheep, capons, and bread.   Yarmouth was their next
port, which contrary winds hindered them from reaching in less than a week.   Here they stopped four
days.   The "Mr." went on land, and was immediately
apprehended by the bailiffs of Yarmouth, and threatened
with imprisonment for having "spoyled twoo island
shipps of theire victualls."   This charge having been
with some difficulty rebutted, the Captain regained his
liberty.   They reached the North Foreland on the 14th
of May.   Darby denied having boarded any ship

---

* William Frobisher, son of Francis, of Doncaster, and
therefore John's cousin, married Margaret, daughter of Matthew
Boynton, of Barmston, Esq.   Barmston is some 6 or 7 miles
from Burlington, and was no doubt the place of John's visit.
The connection between the two families was still further
strengthened by the marriage of Sir Thomas Boynton, knt.,
with Frances, daughter of Francis Frobisher.   Francis Boynton,
of Barmston, one of the issue of this last marriage, was named
an executor of Martin's will.

during their cruise, and taken from it any anchors, cables, kerseys, or other cloths, of which act he was accused, but said he had heard that a "trill blacke shippe muche like to theirs being a Scottisheman" did board a Flemish boat at the mouth of the Thames before Margate, and did take various wares from her.

But little is known of Frobisher's doings for some time after the risk he ran of being convicted as a pirate. There is small reason to doubt that he obtained public employment in a sea-faring capacity. On the 22nd of May, 1569, he signed a bond for the payment of £13 8s. 7d. to Richard Bramley, citizen and butcher, of London, and the following letter, bearing no date, which is addressed to this same Bramley, very likely belongs to the same period :—

"Mr. Bramle,—My harte comendasyons I pra you hellpe me with 40s. till I retorne apon Satarda and then you salle have it agane upon my word. I have stade all thes mornynge for money of Mr. . . man, and I cannot spe till Saturda. I pray you doe not thenke muche of my boldenes for I wolle aquyte all youre frendsepe.—Youre asured frend,

"MARTIN FROBYSHER."

Attached to this paper are two others, on the first of which is written :—

"Summe of Mr. Furbesher's reckonninge is sence the bill of his hande was made is £15 8s. 1½d."

And on the second :—

"I wolle se thes pade.   MARTIN FROBYSHER."

In 1571 we have positive evidence that Frobisher is
engaged in the Queen's service. On August 28th in
that year, one Captain Edward Horsey wrote from the
Isle of Wight to Lord Burghley, and stated, among
other things, that he had expedited the fitting out of
the hulk for Martin Frobisher, and a few days later
another correspondent of Burghley's alluded to a
number of mariners at Portsmouth, in Frobisher's
service. The particular object of this expedition does
not appear.

Frobisher was back again in England in the following year, and on the 4th of December he was summoned to appear before certain Commissioners to explain his connection with some proceedings of the Earl
of Desmond, an Anglo-Irish nobleman, who had just
been imprisoned in the Tower. Frobisher's explana-
tion, signed by himself, is still preserved. He told the
Commissioners that Ralph Whaley, servant to the said
Earl, went to him, "Martyn Furbusher," at his
lodgings in Lambeth, about "Bartilmewetide" last
past, and told him that he had a great secret matter
that he would utter unto him, if Frobisher would not
disclose it. This assurance being given, Whaley went
on to say that the Earl of Desmond had recommended
him to come to Frobisher to see if he would lend his
help in conveying the Earl privately out of England.
An ample recompense was promised for the risk. For
about a fortnight Whaley passed to and fro between
the Earl and Frobisher, and divers plans were sug--

gested. When Frobisher asked what amount of money
would be forthcoming for the purchase of a ship, it
was replied to him that the Earl would never be at a
loss for a thousand pounds. At last came a suggestion
from Desmond that an oyster-boat should be taken to
convey him down the Thames; in that way he hoped
to pass the Queen's ship at Gravesend without being
challenged. The Earl would rather have taken the
high road into Kent, had he not been a bad horseman, and unable to mount without assistance; besides,
he feared that some of Sir Warham St. Leger's men
might meet and recognize him. Frobisher fell in with
this plan, and was straightway commissioned to provide
a bark for the purpose. He undertook this, but, according to his own account, had no intention of assist-
ing them in any way—to use his own words, " for that
they should think I would procure the same I went
into Kent, and so returned back again to London, an-
swering Whaley that I had provided a bark." The
negotiations went on, and the reward offered to Frobisher and Whaley, in case of the Earl's getting away
in safety, was a ship worth five hundred pounds, and
the Earl's Island of Valencia. Some five or six weeks
passed, and matters being no further advanced, Frobisher told Whaley that he could wait no longer, as he
was sadly in want of funds. Whaley assured him that
there would be no lack of money soon, but in the
meantime the ship must be got ready. The delay was
still continued, and Frobisher then declared his belief

that the Earl was playing fast and loose with him, and
intended to go away by some other means, which
Whaley stoutly denied : " And thus," adds our hero,
"·they have continued all this time with divers talks
and devices." An end was put to all by the apprehension of the Earl of Desmond and Whaley.

Nothing appears in this declaration to show that
Frobisher was in communication with the Government
during the progress of these negotiations, but it would
be difficult to believe that his promise of secrecy to
Whaley had not been at once broken. He could hardly
otherwise have come out of the transaction with such
perfect impunity.

Our hero is next heard of in the year 1574, lodging in
the house of one Brown in Fleet Street. He was then
anxious to start upon a voyage for the discovery of
Cathay, but lacked means for the undertaking. However, the services he had already performed for the
State seem to have been of some account, as he had
secured the good offices of Lord Treasurer Burghley,
and others of the Council. Armed with letters from
these high dignitaries, he presented himself to the
Muscovy Company, and besought their aid in the
matter. This was at first refused. Just after this
Michael Lok, a mercer in London (as he himself tells
the story), renewed his old acquaintance with Martin
Frobisher, and, " finding him expert, fit, and ready to
execute so great. attempts, he joined with him." He
treated him as his fellow and friend, opened all his.

own private studies, and the fruits of twenty years' labour to him, and showed him all his books, charts, maps, and instruments. Lok adds, "My house was his house, and my purse his purse at his need; and my credit was his credit to my power when he was utterly destitute, both of money, credit, and friends." Frobisher left Fleet Street, and took up his abode at "Widow Hancock's house in Mark Lane," so as to be nearer Lok. This last-named person, it appears, had some influence with the Muscovy Company, and the second application of Frobisher met with better success. In February, 1575, the Company granted a licence to Lok, Frobisher, and such others as would be adventurers. It was upwards of a year, however, before sufficient confidence in the scheme was generated to induce speculators to aid with their money. Indeed, in the end Lok had to provide more than half the cost of the outfit, which amounted to 1,600*l.* In later years, when Lok and Frobisher were not only estranged, but when the ruin of one and the disappointment of both had made them enemies, Lok asserted that this want of confidence was owing to the little credit Frobisher had at home, and that it was entirely by Lok's efforts and recommendations that his associate got the command of the expedition.

For the first enterprise two barks and a pinnace were furnished; the two barks, of 25 tons each, being the Gabriel, Christopher Hall, master; and the Michael, Owen Griffin, master. Martin Frobisher was described

as captain and pilot of the expedition. There were
in all 34 persons, and they sailed from Gravesend on
the 12th June, 1576. A great storm arose soon after
they got to sea, in which they lost sight of their
pinnace with three men, "which they could never
since hear of." After about a month the Michael
was separated from its companion, and came to Labra-
dor, "but found it so encompassed with monstrous
high islands of ice that they durst not approach;" so
they sailed homeward, and reached London on the
1st September. The Gabriel continued its course, and
various dangers to it were averted by the valiant
courage of the captain, as the chronicle tells us. The
straits which now bear Frobisher's name were discovered; also an island upon which the captain and
six of his men landed and found seven strange boats.
The people who inhabited this island, one of whom
came on board the ship, and "made great wondering
at all things," showed such inclination to fierceness
and rapine, that the captain, unprepared for defence,
made haste to depart to a neighbouring island.
Five of the mariners, anxious to have traffic with the
natives, rowed out of sight of the ship, and were not
again heard of. The ship remained a day and a night
at anchor in the hope that they would re-appear, and
at the end of that time a number of boats and men of
the country came towards it. Signs of friendship
were exchanged, and small presents were given from
the ship's side to one of the strangers, whose boat and

himself the crew tried to detain by a boat-hook. The capture of this native was at last effected by Frobisher himself, who suddenly seized him as he was receiving the present of a bell, and dragged him on board by main force. At this his companions departed in great haste, howling like wolves. Their prisoner is described as having a broad face, and being very fat and full in the body; legs short and small, and out of proportion; long, hanging, coal-black hair, tied above his fore-head; little eyes and a little black beard; skin of a dark sallow, much like the tawny Moors; countenance sullen or churlish, but sharp. Frobisher, previous to this adventure, was oppressed with sorrow lest he should have to return home without an evidence or token of any place where he had been; but, being now possessed of an undoubted curiosity, he had regard to the weak state of his crew, now reduced to thirteen men and boys, and so set sail for England. They arrived at London on the 9th October, and we read that " they were joyfully received with the great admiration of the people, bringing with them their strange man and his boat, which was such a wonder unto the whole city and to the rest of the realm that heard of it, as seemed never to have happened the like great matter to any man's knowledge."

Immediately after Frobisher's return, Commissioners were appointed to examine him concerning the passage to Cathay, before whom he vouched, according to one account, absolutely, with vehement words, speeches and oaths, that he had discovered the straits to Cathay, and found good harbours for all the Queen's navy. By one of his party a black stone had been found "as great as a half-penny loaf." This stone was given to Lok on their return, tested by "divers men of art," and declared to be a mineral ore of a gold mine. There was great marvel at this, and Commissioners were appointed for setting out a second voyage. Frobisher affirmed "with great speeches and oaths" that there was enough ore to be had where he had been to lade all the Queen's ships, and he promised to fill all the ships of the second voyage with it.

About this time Frobisher petitioned the Queen that in respect of his late discoveries in the North-west, and his great charges, letters patent might be granted to him, and his heirs for ever, appointing him High Admiral of those seas already or hereafter to be discovered by him, with government by land of all people in those discovered parts; also five per cent. upon the clear gain of everything brought from such lands, and one per cent. to his heirs for ever; also, to make free of this voyage six persons yearly, and to receive one ton freight of every hundred tons brought from thence. The answer to this was a grant from her Majesty to the "Company of Cathay." In this grant, Michael Lok, of London, mercer, is named Governor for life, in consideration "of his industry, good direction, and great travail" in Frobisher's first voyage; and Martin is appointed Admiral of all new discoveries for life for

" his industry, good order, and great travail " in his
late voyage ; and for his good service he is to have one
per cent. for ever upon all goods exported.

At a council held at Westminster in March, 1577, a
letter was written to the Lord President in the North,
stating that " last year a voyage was taken in hand by
Master Furbussher for the discovery of some parts of
the world unknown, where there is great likelihood
that the continuance thereof will be beneficial to the
whole realm, and particularly to such as are venturous
in the same ; and for that some encouragement might
be given for the following thereof, her Majesty is
pleased to contribute largely towards such charges as
are now to be employed ; their Lordships think good
to desire that seeing, by the success of the last year,
such hope hath been conceived of the profits of that
voyage, as both her Majesty and their Lordships have
entered into some charges, and could wish that others
would do the like, &c. : the Lord President would
signify to the inhabitants thereabouts, to the merchants
of York, Newcastle, Hull, and other places under his
jurisdiction, who shall be willing to contribute."

There was no lack of adventurers for the second
voyage. The Commissioners had reported to the
Queen that the matter was one well worthy of
encouragement. Subscriptions rapidly flowed in. The
Queen herself advanced 1,000*l.* ; the Lord Treasurer,
the Lord Admiral and other prominent men also
lent their aid. The hope of finding gold was doubt-

less of considerable effect in swelling the list of
speculators.

Frobisher set sail a second time on the 26th of May,
1577. On the same day Lok memorialised the Queen
for recompense and help in the great matter in which
he was engaged. He stated he had been at great expense during the two years Frobisher had been in
London, who " eat the most of his meat at my table
freely and gladly."

Ten convicts, out of various prisons, were taken by
Frobisher on this second voyage, probably with the
intention of making them work the mines of gold ore
which were expected to be found. Lok afterwards
declared that not one of them actually went to voyage,
but that they were set at liberty by Frobisher " for
friendship and money."

And now comes the most mysterious part of this
story. Just after the departure of our hero, one Isabel
Frobisher, "the most miserable poor woman in the
world," presents a petition to Secretary Walsingham.
She asserts that she was formerly the wife of Thomas
Riggat, of Snaith, co. York, a very wealthy man, who
left her in very good state, and with good portions to
all her children ; but she afterwards took to husband
Mr. Captain Frobisher (" whom God forgive "), who
has spent all, and put them to the wide world to shift ;
and she adds that the children of her first husband are
with her in a poor room at Hampstead ready to starve.
She prays that one Kemp may be ordered to pay 4*l.*

due to her husband, and for other relief until Frobisher's return, to keep them from famishing.

We are unable to state the result of this appeal. There can be no doubt that Martin Frobisher was the man here presented in so unfavourable a light; though no other record of this woman seems to be in existence. That Frobisher had a wife at a later period of his existence is well known, but her name was Dorothy, and many particulars can be given concerning her, which, apart from the difference in name, point to another person than is indicated in this petition. We must be content for the present to leave the matter as it stands.

The instructions given to Frobisher on his second voyage directed, among other things, that he should enter, as Captain-General, into the charge and government of three vessels—namely, the Aid, the Gabriel, and the Michael—with all that appertained to them, and that he should appoint, for the fitting out of these vessels, one hundred and twenty persons, of whom ninety should be mariners, gunners, carpenters, and other necessary men to serve for the use of the ships, and the other thirty to be miners, refiners, and merchants; this number he was in no way to exceed. The Aid was a ship of some 180 tons, and was lent by the Queen herself; the Gabriel and the Michael were about 30 tons each, commanded respectively by Masters Fenton and Gabriel Yorke. On taking leave Frobisher had the honour of kissing her Majesty's hand, "who dismissed him with gracious countenance and comfort-able words."

They sailed, as has been already stated, at the end of May, 1577. Approaching Friesland, they were hampered with drift ice and large ice-bergs, some of which are declared to have been seventy or eighty fathoms under water, and more than half a mile in circuit. They entered the strait of the previous year's discovery round Hall's Island. Frobisher took the gold-finders with him near the spot where the black-stone had been found, but the whole island did not furnish "a piece as big as a walnut." Two savages made their appearance, whom some of the Englishmen tried to seize, but they got away from them, and making use of their bows and arrows, "fiercely, desperately, and with such fury, assaulted our General and his men, that they chased them to the boats, and hurt the General behind with an arrow."

Proceeding up the strait, they landed on a small island on the southern shore, and "here all the sands and cliffs did so glister, that it seemed all to be gold, but upon trial made, it proved no better than black-lead, and verified the proverb, 'All is not gold that glistereth.'"

On another small island they found a mine of silver, and four sorts of ore, "to hold gold in good quantity." They also found and brought home the horn of an unicorn fish, which was afterwards sent to Windsor, and preserved as a jewel in the Queen's wardrobe. In

York Sound they had a skirmish with the natives, and
slew five or six of them. Two women they took
prisoners, "whereof the one being ugly, our men
thought she had been a devil or some witch, and
therefore let her go." The season being now far
advanced, they set to work to fill their ships with the
ore, and in about twenty days got on board their ships
about 200 tons. They set sail for England on the
22nd of August.

Another account of the second voyage is preserved,
evidently been drawn up by no friend to Frobisher,
which records many instances of Frobisher's violent
temper. This account speaks first of the great hazard,
uncertainty, and charge of this voyage "attempted by
this bold captain." The chief conduct was committed
to him by the Queen's patent, and Commissioners were
assigned to see him furnished and dispatched. He
would needs have had three tall ships and two barks;
he vented "no small raging and outrageous speaking"
before his departure; he would have all authority in
his hands alone. Because he could not be furnished to
his will, "he flung out of the doors, and swore by
God's wounds that he would hip my masters the ven-
turers for it, at which words Captain Fenton plucked
him secretly, and willed him to be modest."

He returned to Milford Haven on the 20th Sept.,
1577, laden with rich ore, worth 60*l.* or 80*l.* a ton, as
he affirmed with great oaths (which, as Michael Lok
temperately remarks, " is not yet so found "), "and

such plenty of precious stones, diamonds, and rubies
as he had discovered. No small joy was had of his
arrival, and no small increase of his reputation, so as
now 12 or 20 men were too few to follow his horse
upon this return."

'In October, 1577, the Privy Council directed the
officers of the Mint to receive into the Tower certain
ore brought out of the North-west parts by Martin
Frobisher, by weight, which from time to time was to
be melted down, as directed by the Commissioners
appointed to overlook the operation. A month later
Lok reported that the ore was not yet brought to per-
fection, the three workmasters being jealous of each
other, and loath to show their coining; but, he adds,
the ore is very rich, and will yield better than 40*l.* a
ton, clear of charges. These three workmasters afterwards gave totally different opinions of the value of the
ore; one engaged that two tons would yield 20 ounces
of fine gold, another certified that "he has proved it
to the uttermost, and finds not such great riches as is
here spoken and reported of." The third declared
that he found neither gold nor silver, or next to none.

But whatever reports were spread of the bad success
of this second venture, they must have been quickly
suppressed, or little trusted. Officers of State, Lords
as well as Commoners, sought to be sharers in another
venture, and before the truth could be fully ascertained
of the value or worthlessness of the ore, the necessary
expenses for a third and more costly expedition than

the two preceding were quickly promised. The Queen, " understanding that the richness of that earth is like to fall out to a good reckoning, is well pleased that a third voyage be taken in hand," gave instructions to " our loving friend Martin Frobisher for the order to be observed in the voyage." It was proposed to send ships for 5,000 tons weight of ore, and the charges thereof were calculated, besides the maintenance of 100 men in the country eighteen months. When directions were given by the Privy Council in March, 1578, to proceed with a third voyage, Lok declares that Frobisher " grew into such a monstrous mind that a whole kingdom could not contain it, but already, by discovery of a new world, he was become another Columbus." Eleven vessels were fitted for this expedition; they sailed for Harwich on the 31st of May, 1578, the Queen, herself a large adventurer, watching their departure, and, it is said, wishing them success.

Articles and orders to be observed by the fleet were set down by " Captain Frobisher, general," and delivered in writing to every captain. Some were to banish swearing, dice, cards, and playing, and to serve God twice a day. If the accounts of Frobisher's enemies are to be believed—and, unfortunately, no others are preserved—he did not set a very good example in his own person of the rules he thus laid down. Many complaints were afterwards made of his disorderly dealings, his forcible language, his arrogant and obstinate government at sea; and he is described as

I

full of lying talk and impudent of tongue. It does not
appear that he was at the pains at any time to defend
himself from these attacks; indeed, it is easy to imagine
that a man of his hardy and impetuous nature would
ignore them altogether. There can be little doubt that
his temper became soured from disappointment on this
last voyage; and it must be admitted that the command
of a ship is a difficult position in which to cultivate
the Christian virtues of fortitude and forbearance.

The fleet reached Friesland on the 20th of June,
without anything happening worthy of note, except
that the Salamander (one of the squadron) struck on
a great whale with her full stem with such a blow that
the ship stood still. " The whale thereat made a great
and hideous noise, and casting up his body and tail,
presently sank under water."

On attempting to enter Frobisher's Strait, they
found it barred up with mountains of ice, and the bark
Dennis received such a blow that she went down.
The loss was doubly unfortunate, in that this particular
vessel had on board the houses and furniture for the
settlers; and thus one plan of the expedition was
frustrated. Other disasters quickly followed. A storm
dispersed the whole fleet; some vessels were swept
into the straits, some out to sea; and when they got
together again, they were so bewildered by the snow
and mist, and so driven about by tides and currents,
that the pilots hardly knew where they were. The
greater part of the fleet followed Frobisher to the

north-west coast of Greenland. Captain Best, of the
Ann Francis, one of the missing ships, discovered a
great black island, in which such plenty of ore was
found, "as would reasonably suffice all the gold
gluttons of the world." To this black island, for good
luck's sake, the captain gave the name of Best's
Blessing.

The end of the summer was now approaching, and
a council of the captains being held, it was decided,
for a variety of good reasons, that each captain and
owner should look to the lading of his own ship, and
that by a certain day they should set sail for England.
After a stormy passage, in which the fleet suffered
much distress, they arrived at different parts of England about the middle of October, with the loss by
death of forty persons.*

---

* Thomas Churchyarde, gent., celebrated this third voyage
in some verses which he styled "A welcome-home to Master
Martin Frobusher, and all those Gentlemen and Soldiers that
have been with him this last journey in the country called
Meta Incognita." They will be found entire in Nicholls' *Pro-
gresses of Queen Elizabeth*, Vol. II., pp. 233-4. A few extracts
will suffice us here—

"Five hundred times most welcome home, my friends that far have been,
When thousands thought that all was lost, your fleet came safely in ;
To glad their hearts that long bewailed your toil and hazard great :
O give me leave, in English verse, a while on this to treat ;
That doth deserve such world's renown, and come to such good end,
As forceth friends to favour much, and foes may well commend.
You slothful snails, that creep not far, and love your shells so well,
And you cold crusts, that have small crumbs, in cottage poor that dwell,
Now will you blush, or bend the brow, to see how travellers thrive ;
Nay, now you ought go help yourselves, and rather seek to strive
Against ill-hap, that holds you here, when others work for wealth,
And trudge abroad, to lengthen life and nourish wished health.

Frobisher seems to have had a quarrel with his old
partner shortly after his return, for we hear of his
openly abusing Lok, calling him "a false accountant to
the Company, a cozener of my Lord of Oxford, no
venturer at all in the voyages, a bankrupt knave," and,
as Lok himself says, he raged like a mad beast. On
one occasion Frobisher entered Lok's house with a
retinue of some forty men, and made like charges
against him. This seems very hard and ungrateful
treatment of poor Lok, who had risked about 6,000*l.*
in these adventures without the least return. The real
value of the ore brought home by Frobisher never
seems to have been correctly ascertained for some years,
though the Queen, and those interested in the result

But addle-heads, and idle brains, and babbling tongues, I trow,
Had rather sit in smoky house (or on the dunghill crow
Like craven cocks), than go abroad where fortune may be found,
And search where gold and treasure lies in bowels of the ground.

If each man were alike in wealth, as rogues and beggars are,
And none had skill, nor great foresight, for country's cause to care,
Adieu, good rule and riches too, and farewell virtue's praise ;
But God be thanked, that we are born to live in happier days,
When wits will work for wealth's avail, and sundry ride and run ;
Yea, hoist up sail, and go themselves as far as shines the sun,
Through thick and thin, and fear no foil, as though to their good minds
The gods had made the land and seas, the skies, the air, and winds,
To follow that they have devised that take these toils in hand.

O Frobisher ! thy bruit and name shall be enrolled in books,
That whosoever after comes, and on thy labour looks,
Shall muse and marvel at thine acts, and greatness of thy mind.
I say no more, lest some affirm I fan thy face with wind,
I flatter for affection's sake ; well, God shall witness be,
In this thy praise (and other books) I speak but right of thee.
A book I made at thy Farewell, in prose (where'er it is),
Another for thy welcome-home thou shalt have after this,
If this mislike thee any whit. So here, mine own good friend,
I bid thee welcome once again, and therewith make an end.

of the "proofs," must have been fully convinced that
to expect a large amount of gold from the ore would
be a delusion. All doubts were finally set at rest by
two assays made in July, 1583. The two minute par-
ticles of silver found in 2 cwt. of "Frobisher's ore"
were not nearly so big as a pin's head, and they remain
to this day fastened by sealing wax to the report—an
evidence of the worthlessness of the ore.

As a last effort to regain some portion of his losses,
Lok petitioned the Council, and besought their consideration, having, as he said, for three years past taken
charge of all the businesses of Frobisher's voyages,
and paid 6,250*l.*, "whereby himself, his wife, and
15 children are left to beg their bread henceforth, *unless God turn the stones at Dartford* (whither
the ore had been taken) *into his bread again.*"
The total amount allowed by Lord Burghley for
Lok's three years' service and expenses was 430*l.*;
he demanded 1,200*l.* We are sorry to add that the last
we hear of this early patron of Frobisher is as a petitioner from the Fleet Prison. He was condemned at
the suit of one William Borough to pay 200*l.* for a
ship bought of him for Frobisher's last voyage, but, he
adds, it is not his debt. He complains that he has
sustained great troubles, many imprisonments, and
extreme losses to his utter undoing; and he prays for
his release, for the cancelling of his bond for 4,000*l.*
for the Queen's adventure, and for a warrant of protection from further trouble for debts owing by the Com-

pany of Cathay. There is evidence of his having been
six months in prison for the debts of the adventurers.

Numerous documents are still preserved, which show
that a fourth voyage was contemplated by Frobisher.
A large sum of money was subscribed, and instructions
were drawn out in February, 1582, for Frobisher to be
captain-general of the expedition. For some unassigned
cause, one Edward Fenton was suddenly appointed in
the place of Frobisher. These instructions stated that
this voyage should be undertaken rather for the purpose of trade than the discovery of the North-west
Passage. This latter was Frobisher's darling project,
and there is every reason to believe that, when he found
himself so fettered by these instructions, he threw up
the command. At any rate, it is certain that he did
not go on the voyage. *

For two or three years we hear little or nothing of
our hero; we may assume, however, that the Queen,
with whom Frobisher appears to have been a great
favourite, in spite of the ill-luck which attended her
money investments with him, gave him employment in
her navy. We should not otherwise find him appointed,
in the year 1585, as Vice-Admiral of a fleet fitted out
to annoy the King of Spain in the West Indies. This

* Most of the materials for the preceding account of events
connected with Frobisher's three voyages have been gathered
from the second volume of Mr. W. Noel Sainsbury's calendar
of Colonial State Papers. Mr. Sainsbury has given the writer
kind aid in other matters relating to the subject. Barrow's
" Naval Worthies of Elizabeth " has also proved of service.

mighty monarch had taken the first step towards a declaration of war with England, by laying an embargo upon all the English ships, goods, and seamen found in his ports. The fleet consisted of twenty-one ships and pinnaces. But little account is preserved of their doings. They captured a few cities and towns, and restored them to Spain on payment of a certain ransom, and were thus enabled to bring home substantial testimony of their service. The booty they secured consisted of some 60,000*l.* in money, and 240 pieces of brass and iron cannon.

In the year 1588, the formidable fleet of the King of Spain, known to us all as bearing the proud title of the Invincible Armada, appeared in the English Channel. To Frobisher was committed the important post of Vice-Admiral, in command of a squadron of the fleet fitted out to grapple the enemy. The Lord High Admiral, writing to the Queen, speaks of him as " one of those whom the world doth judge to be men of the greatest experience that this realm hath." An attack was made upon the rear division of the Spaniards on the first day they appeared off Plymouth, in which Drake, Hawkins, and Frobisher played so stout a part, that many of the ships opposed to them were completely shattered.

The final overthrow, and almost utter annihilation, of the Armada, are such well-known events in history, that no space need be taken up here in detailing them. For his great services in the matter, Frobisher re-

ceived the honour of knighthood at the hands of the
Lord High Admiral. Shortly afterwards mention is
made of an occurrence which shows the new-made
knight to be still liable to occasional outbursts; for
in August, 1588, a complaint is lodged against him
for certain unbecoming words spoken against Sir
Francis Drake, whom he called a cowardly knave and
traitor, and accused of merely remaining by one
Spanish vessel in order to plunder her; he vowed, too,
that he would make Drake eat his own words, or he
would have his best blood.

While the other commanders went in pursuit of the
remnants of the Spanish fleet, Sir Martin remained on
board the Triumph to watch the narrow seas. Several
letters of his, showing the vigilance with which he
carried out his instructions, are still in existence. Two
of them are selected for insertion here, as curiosities
for their style and orthography, rather than as having
much importance :—

SIR MARTIN FROBISHER TO THE LORD ADMIRAL.

" My Honorabelle good Lord,

" In sendenge the monne (money) tou ostedynde
(Ostend) she hathe taken a Lonnedragare (L'homme
de guerre ?) & a spanyare in her, bound for Don-
kerke, and the spanyarde caste onare borde tou paketes
of Letares, & as he saythe, beye ordare from thos
that delevrede them tou hem: as sonne as I can ex-
samene theme I wolle send youre honare all ther

-exsamenasiones, for thate thes Letares of my Lord Tresarares requirede grete haste I coullde have no time, beynge neyghte. Dounes (The Downs) thes 6 of maye, at 8 acloke at nyghte, 1589.

"Youre honares moste hombleye,

"MARTIN FROBISER.

"To the reyghte honorabelle the Lord
Admeralle of Ingland : gev this.

"Shee is ladenede with ches, & nate elles (nothing else), & your honar shalle knoue as sone as I can undarestande it."*

THE SAME TO THE SAME.

"My Honnorable good Lord,

"I have sent your honnor the pase of this hoye hearein closed, and with all a letare wher in your honnor may se all her Ladinge, that she was dericktly bound for Dunkert, with this don John Detoledo.

"The marchant that is onnor of these goods ys called Hanse Vandeveck, dwellinge in Hamserdam.

"I have also examined this Spaniord: he confeses, as I advertised your honnor, that he was taken with don Deage de Pemnentelo, and that his name ys don John Detoledo, and that this marchant Hanse Vandeveck did get him Relesed for a mariner of Roterdam that was Presoner in Donkert. I have allso sent your

* Dom. Eliz., Vol. CCXXIV.

honnor his pasport, wherein you may se his name, and
the forme of his deliverie.

"Ther ys in her three pore men, their wifes and
childern, bound for honscot (?). I have sent the hoy
into Dover peare, and I have commanded the pore
men the wemen and childeren a land in Dover to
goe where they will. The hoy, the Skiper, and the
Spaniard, I kep in safe coustodie tell I know your
honnors pleasur hearin.

"When the Skipper did se he wase to be taken, he
willed them all to cast overbord ther leters, but they
swere all thay wher but one pore kinsmans to an other
of comendations and of ther parince.

"I pray your honnors deriction for these causes, and
what I shall doe foe the mendinge of my mast, and
shifting of my balis, which must be donne before I
take in any vitels. I have but 7 dayes vitels left, and
it plese your honnor the vitels myght goe to Harwige
that comes doune, and the ship may met ther vitels
ther and dispach all thinges in thre or fower days.
Thus comiting your honnor to the almitie. Downes
this 7th of may, 1589.

"Your honnors most humbely bound,

"MARTIN FROBISER." *

The remaining incidents of Sir Martin's career
though of signal account in the history of the nation,
require but a brief summary in this chapter. In 1590

---

* Dom., Eliz., Vol. CCXXIV.

he was Admiral of an expedition fitted out for the coast of Spain. The expedition was fruitless in one respect, as not a single Spanish ship was fallen in with worthy of being captured. It answered another intention, by wholly crippling the commerce of King Philip, inasmuch as he was compelled to keep in port the whole of the outward-bound ships, and also to send out instructions to the Indies, to detain the sailing of the homeward-bound ships till the following year.

From this time until his death Frobisher was continually engaged in operations against the Spaniards. The following letter will serve to illustrate part of this service :—

SIR MARTIN FROBISHER TO LORD BURGHLEY.

"My humble dutie my honorable good Lord. I sent the Gallion Rawley for England the fiftene of Julie wth a prisse of Brassill Sugar, wch I hope is well arived.

"I meette wth Captaine Crosse in the Forsight the one and thirtie daie of August, in fortie seven degrees, and he gave me to understand that the Forsight, the Row bucke, and my lord of Cumberland's shippes, wth the Daintie, and some other have taken one Carrecke, and another is burnte. And the third, it was my hard hape to misse at the Burlinges in a darke night, havinge sight of her light, the seventh of Julie. But I am of the opinion, that my staie upon the coast of Spaine made the Kinges fleette staie so longe from the Ilands as this Carrecke was the better come by, for I have kept everie daie upon the coast as by this letter herein inclosed your honours may partlie understand.

"I understand by Captaine Crosse that the Carrecke will want Ankers, Cabelles, and sailles, and for that I am able out of this shippe to furnishe her in all thinges, I will for the better safetie of her keepe betwixt the Lizard and Hushinge (*sic*) and so if God send wether bringe her aboute for the ylle of Wight for she draweth thirtie footte watter, and ther we will staie to know your honours further pleasure, excepte the wind force us to some other harbour. As touchinge the circumstances in takinge of her, I referred it to this bearer, who was as his companie reporteth it to me the cheefe autour in bourdinge and takinge of her. I will have as greate care as lyeth in my power to save all thinges for I understand all the men of war that hath bin at the takinge of this and the other Carrecke that burnt her selfe have made verie greate spoille and hath it abourd there shippes. I will staie all the men of warr and suffar nothinge to land as neare as I may till I heare from your honours.

"I have had since the first of August a great sickenes amongest my companie wch forceth me to put into Plimouth to land my sicke men but I meane not to staie there one howre yf the wynd serve. I have staide the Forsight wth me for that I heare some mutinie in the Carrecke wth the other shipps in her companie but I do not doubte yf I meet wth them but to pacifie all thinges till your honours further order—thus wth my

prayer to the Almightie for your honourable estates
and all happines this forth of Septembre, 1592. .

" Your honours most humblie,

"MARTIN FROBISER.*

" Lizard, aboord the Garland."

Endorsed by Burghley : " Brought by Tho. Tippyng
yᵗ served wᵗ Cap. Furbyser.."

THE QUEEN TO SIR MARTIN FROBISHER.
" ELIZABETH R.

" Trustie and welbeloved, wee greet you well : wee
have seen your [letter] to our Threasuror and our
Admyrall, and thereby perceive your [love] of our
service, and also, by others, your owne good carriage,
whereby [you] have wonne yourself reputation ;
whereof, for that wee imagine it wil be comfort unto
you to understand, wee have thought good to vouchsafe to take knowledge of it by our owne hand
writinge. We know you are sufficientlie instructed
from our Admyrall, besides your owne circumspection,
howe to prevent any soddaine mischiefe, by fire or
otherwise, upon our fleete under your charge ; and yet
doe wee thinke it will worke in you the more impres-
sion, to be by ourself againe remembred, who have observed by former experience that the Spaniards, for all

---

* Lansdowne MS. 70. The signature alone is in Martin's
hand—a fact which may perhaps account for the slightly
improved spelling. There is another letter of his in the same
volume, dated the 13th of September, from Dartmouth, and
addressed to the same, which there is no need to quote.

their boaste, will trust more to their devices than that they dare in deede with force look upon you.

"For the rest of my directions, we leave them to such letters as you shall receive from our counsaile.

"Given under our privie signet, at our mansion of Richmond, the 14th of November, in the 36th yeare of our reign, 1594. (L. S.)

"To our trustie and welbeloved Sir Martine
        Furbussher, Knight."

It was in an attack on the fort of Crozon, near Brest, that Frobisher got his death-wound. The enemy had strongly fortified this place, and they defended it with the utmost obstinacy. Our Admiral landed his troops, with a party of seamen; a joint attack was begun, and carried on with great vigour. The fort was captured at last, but the success was dearly bought, as many gallant English officers and men lost their lives. The sequel is best told in Frobisher's own words. This last letter of his is a remarkable evidence of the character of our hero; his hardy nature, the stern sense of duty which overrode all his personal injuries, is strikingly evident in it:—

SIR MARTIN FROBISHER TO THE LORD HIGH ADMIRAL.

"My humble dutie my honorable good Lord, the 7th (of this) monnth, by a battrie, ûndermininge, and a very dan(gerous)* assault, wee have taken this fort,

---

* The volume of the Cotton MSS. (Calig. E. IX.) in which this letter is contained was damaged by the fire which broke out in Ashburnham House, Westminster, in the year 1731, where the collection was at that time preserved; many words, and portions of words, are on that account wanting.

with the losse . . . . of our people, but non of any
accompt. They . . . . it verie resolutelie, And never
asked mercie; S(ome) were put all to the swoord,
savinge five or six that (hid) themselves in the rocks,
many of them were slaine . . . . our canonn and
greatt ordennance in defendinge of . . . . breatch with
there Captaine one Perithos. It was tyme for us to
goa through with it. Don . . . . is advanst within
six leaggs of our armie with an intente to have suc-
coured them. Sir John Norris doth rise this daie and
doth martch towards th(em) to a place called old
Croydon.

"Wee are about to gett in our ordenannce as fast as
(we) can, and so to make our repaire homewards, Sir
John Norris would willinglie have some five hundred
of . . . . sayllers for his bettar streinght again the
da(ie) of meetinge with Don John, which I would verie
willinglie have don yf we had vittles to continewe
our fleett heare for the tyme.

"I was shoott in with a bullett at the battrie alongst
. . . . huckell bone, So as I was driven to have an
ins . . . . made to take out the bullett. So as I am
neither to goa nor ride, And the mariners are verie
unwi(lling) to goa, except I goa with them myselfe;
yet (if) I find it to come to an extremitie we will . . . .
what we are able; yf we had vittles it were (very)
easilie done, but heare is non to be had. I have accordinge to your Honours derections tow shipps Plymouth and Dartmouth, we most presentlie . . . . away

yf they come not to us with vittles. This bearer is
able to certiffie your Honours all things at large. So
with my humble p(rayer) to the almyghtie for your
increase in hon(or).

"Croydon, this 8th of Novembre, 1594.

"Your Honours most h(umble) to Comande,

"MARTIN FROBISER."

The wound of which Frobisher here speaks was at
first regarded as a very slight injury, but the ignorance
or carelessness of the surgeon made it a mortal one.
It festered, and brought on a fever, of which Frobisher
died, on the 30th November, 1594, shortly after the
return of the squadron to Plymouth. "Thus fell,"
writes Fuller, "a man of undaunted courage, and
inferior to none of that age in courage and conduct, or
the reputation of a brave commander. He was very
valiant, but withal harsh and violent (faults which may
be dispensed with in one of his profession)."

Some interesting information about the estates of
Frobisher is furnished us by the report of the inquisition taken some months after his death, before the
escheator of Yorkshire; allusion is also made therein
to various members of the family. The following is a
very full abstract of it :—

"Inquisition taken at Wakefield the 4th day of October, 1595, after the death of Sir Martin Frobusher,
knight, late of Altofts, before Christopher Ashe,
Esquire, Deputy of the Escheator of Yorkshire, Timothy

Whittingham, Esquire, and the following jury:—
viz., Richard Sproxton, gent., Richard Clayton, gent.,
Thomas Harryson, Peter Grante, John Fairbourne,
William Tayler, Robert Hoyle, William Bromheade,
Thomas Aycroide, Aver Lyndley, Edward Claie, William Saxton, Richard Denton, Richard Copley, and
Edward Secker, who say upon their oaths that the said
Martin Frobusher was seised in his demesne as of fee
in & of the manor, capital messuage or tenement in
Brockhoales, in the parish of Cantley, and of one
hundred acres of land, arable, meadow, and pasture,
with the appurtenances in Brockhoales aforesaid. Also
of a messuage or tenement in Heath, with twenty acres
of land, arable, meadow, and pasture there. Also of
one capital messuage or tenement in Altofts, in the
parish of Normanton, called Frobusher Hall, and six
acres of land there, attached to the said capital messuage. And being so seised, he made his last will and
testament, in which he gave and bequeathed to Lady
Dorothy, his wife, in full satisfaction and recompense
of all titles, claims, and demands of her marriage portion, under certain conditions and provisions, the tenement called Frobusher Hall, and the lands in Altofts,
to be held by her and her assigns for forty years, should
she live so long. And further, he gave and bequeathed
to one Peter Frobusher, son of John Frobusher, his
brother, for the term of his life, the aforesaid manor
or capital messuage in Brockhoales, and the lands,
tenements, rents, &c., belonging to the same, and

K

situate in the parish or town of Cantley; and the
aforesaid tenement and lands in Heath; and the capital
messuage called Frobusher Hall, and all other lands,
&c., in Altofts; and his heir. Remainder to Darby
Frobusher, son of David Frobusher, brother of the
aforesaid Martin, deceased. Remainder to Richard
Jackson, son of Margaret Jackson, sister of Martin,
and to his heirs in perpetuity," &c., &c,

The jurors further certify that Peter Frobusher is
the nearest heir of Sir Martin, being son and heir of
John Frobusher, his brother, deceased, and was aged
twenty-three years at the time of the death of his
uncle.

The estates mentioned in the above inquisition are,
of course, all of which Sir Martin Frobisher was in
full legal possession. An entry in the Docquet Book
of the reign of Elizabeth, under the date of the 18th
November, 1591, certifies the payment of 948l. 17s. 3¼d.
by him for the Manor of Whitwood, in Yorkshire, and
Finningley Grange, Co. Notts, sold to him by the Queen.
The non-mention of these estates in the inquisition is
explained by another entry in the same book, dated
the 25th of January, 1596-7, of a re-grant to Peter
Frobisher, described as the cousin and heir of the late
Sir Martin Frobisher, on payment of 500l., of Whitwood and Finningley, forfeited by Sir Martin for non-
payment of 500l.

Frobisher's will was proved on the 25th of April,
1595. By it he commends his soul unto God his

maker, and his body to the earth, his mother, to be
interred where God call him, and as it shall be thought
fit by his executors. His funeral shall be solemnised
at the Parish Church of Normanton, and at his house
called Frobisher Hall, in Altofts. To his well-beloved
wife, Dame Dorothy, he] gives all the jewels, chains,
bracelets, pearls of gold, pearl "agglets," and rings
now in her possession, her wearing apparel, and so much
of his plate then at Frobisher Hall as should amount
unto the value of 200*l.*; the one half in silver plate at the
value of 5s. an ounce, the other half parcel gilt at 6s.
the ounce; and one-third of his linen and "napery,"
his two coaches, and furniture, and horses. He nomi-
nates and appoints Peter, son of John Frobisher, his
eldest brother, his executor; and for overseers nomi-
nates Mr. Francis Boynton, of Barmston, and Mr.
Francis Vaughan. The real estates are disposed of in
the manner indicated in the inquisition.

Peter Frobisher, it would seem, from a tradition that
Hopkinson has handed down to us, was also a sailor;
for Sir Martin Frobisher, it is reported, whilst he was
at sea, made his will, and devised all his estate to his
kinsman, Captain Peter Frobisher, who was then with
him; and upon his publishing the said will, an old
officer under him desired him to consider well thereof,
for his kinsman was a weak man, and not able to manage the estate; he had, too, other kinsmen as near as
Peter was, and more able to manage it. To which
Martin replied, "My will shall stand; it was gotten at

sea; it will never thrive long at land;" which proved too true.

Peter Frobisher was a justice of the peace for the West Riding in the early years of James the First's reign; but he soon lost both position and estates by his prodigality, and ended his days in London in most abject poverty.*

---

* He presented a petition on the 21st of June, 1609, to Robert Cecil, Earl of Salisbury. He describes himself as "Peter Frobisher, Esq., farmer of His Majesty's Manor of Altofts, on lease, by which he is allowed "howsboote, fyerboote, hayeboote, plougheboote, hedgeboote, and fenceboote, and chardged with many necessary repairations, and competent wood for colemyne there. In which mannor (continues the petition) his majestie hathe a Parke, unto which there is adioyning a little wood called Birkwood within the said manor, wherein are no great store of woodes fitt for tymber but standeth much upon Birch, Alders, Hollyes, and such other small trees, which will rayse very small profitt unto his majestie and yet the cutting downe thereof wilbe a very great defacingof his majesties said howse and parke, and out of which your petitioner should have his wood and tymber for his necessary uses aforesaid, and a speciall mayntenance for his majesties deere there. Nevertheless, Mr. Johnson, surveyor there, hath lately entered into the sayd wood, and hath made sale of 140 tymber trees at small values (there not being above 200 or thereabouts in all), and hath also made sale of 1,200 byrches at 7d. or therabouts a tree, and others at lower rates, to strangers, and none of his majesties, though your petitioner (being farmer of the sayd manor) desyred of the sayd Johnson that he and other the tenants might have the refusing thereof, and offered to pay as others would give for the same. Also the sayd Johnson hath sold a woode, called Gilkers, within the sayd mannor of Altofts, conteyning therein a parcel of woods than can in noe wise be spared without very great damage both to his majestie and his farmer which is not yet cutt or felled."

Peter concludes by praying that Johnson may be restrained, and the woods stayed from further damage.

CHAPTER III.

WHEN Dr. Edwin Sandys was appointed Archbishop of York in 1576, the memory of the Rebellion of 1569 was still fresh in the minds of the inhabitants of the northern counties. The prompt suppression of that outbreak had for the time being discouraged the favourers of the old religion from another trial of strength with the ruling powers, but their discontent was great, and they still hoped to gain the mastery. The Protestants, on the other hand, were quite as unsettled by their knowledge of the passions which were silently working in their midst, and which they were almost powerless to counteract. Many of them, too, had suffered heavy losses at the hands of the rebels, and of the marauders who followed in their trail; they hoped to indemnify themselves with the lands and goods of the Catholics. This forfeiture of possessions, on conviction of the holder's recusancy, became very common, and the facility with which it was done led to many acts of extortion and oppression.

The original documents, which will be found in this chapter, have been selected with a view to illustrate as much as possible the religious state of the inhabitants of Yorkshire in the time of Elizabeth. But first,

a short account of the rather notable man who was
called upon, as mentioned above, to preside over the
spiritual welfare of the northern counties, will not be
out of place.

Edwin Sandys was born at Hawkshead, in Lancashire, in the year 1519.   In 1532 or 1533 he entered
as a student at St. John's College, Cambridge.   There
he had for his contemporaries Redmayn and Lever,
both great lights of the Reformation, besides others of
inferior name, who continued in the hour of trial so
true to their principles, that, according to Baker, the
learned historian of that house, "probably more fellows
were, in Queen Mary's reign, ejected from St. John's
than from any other society in either university."   It
does not appear that Sandys ever became a scholar or
fellow of his college, but he served the office of proctor
for the University, and in 1547 was elected master of
Catherine Hall.   About this time, too, he obtained
several valuable ecclesiastical preferments; but a few
years later, on the accession of Queen Mary, he was
deprived of these, and he suffered some months' imprisonment for his religious opinions.   He escaped
the stake by fleeing abroad, where he remained until
the death of Mary again placed him on the road for
advancement.   He was successively Bishop of Wor-
cester, and of London; and finally, on the transfer of
Grindal to Canterbury, became Archbishop of York.
Little has been handed down to us of his private character; but as a public man he made, wherever he

went, few friends and many enemies. His affectionate
solicitude for his own numerous family had a good deal
to do with his unpopularity. To make suitable provision for his children, he preferred to live at some
obscure manor-house on his estate, and thus avoid the
semi-regal display which would be necessary at the
palace at York. One letter of Dr. Sandy's, written in
defence of himself, has been selected for publication
here; it certainly does not give a pleasing picture of
the church dignitaries of those days. The *Dean* so
frequently spoken of is Matthew Hutton, who, after a
while, became Bishop of Durham, and then Archbishop
of York.

THE ARCHBISHOP OF YORK TO LORD BURGHLEY.

"My honorable good Lord. The *Dean* spitteth out
his venome still, and hathe used means to infect the
verie Court; there is no end of his malice. He hathe
by his Patron, made her Matie to be enformed, that
before the LL. appointed to heare our cause, there was
no more matter but my *yea* and his *nay*, neither had
he said any thinge in the Consistorie, wch was not
convenient and alloweable, neither coulde any thinge be
proved against him. How true this is, your L. and
others appointed for that cause can well tell, to whose
reporte in that behalf I referr me; further her Matie
is informed, that I have geven diverse leases unto my
chyldren in revertion, and no fyne reserved thereof
unto the use of the Church. This is as impudent, for I
hould no lands of the Church, neither ever had the

Church any thinge of the Archb. of Yorke for the use
thereof. In truthe they have the Church lands and
should keepe a stock in the common chest for the defence thereof. But the overplus of the Revenue they
put not in the Treasurie Chist of the Church, but like
good fellowes divide it among them selves, and that is
the cause of their protestation, that I may not see into
their reckoninges in my visitations. There was not
many yeres since, Two Hundred pounds in their Chest
for the use of their Church. But my L. President's
men brake in and robbed St. Peter of everie penny,
and yet they escaped punishment, although it was
Burglary. But to avoide the like, they put it in their
private purses, and buy land wth it for them selves,
wch can hardly be robbed from them. I graunt that I
gave (as I lawfully might) to my six sonnes, every one
two leases in Reversion, for the confirmation whereof,
the Dean and Chapter had of me for every lease 4*l.*, in
the whole 48*l.* I am bound in conscience to take care
over my familye. I have no lands to leave them, as the
Dean hath a great deale, and as fitt for me to bestow
these upon my children (who I trust shall not be found
unworthie of such help) as upon my Servants or
Straingers. The Bushopricke loseth nothinge by it,
neither is it any whit in worse case. This complaint
smelleth of mere malice towards me and myne. The
Dean will not remember how that my Predecessor,
wthin two months that he was translated unto Canterbury, gave unto his kinesmen, his servaunts, and for

round somes of mony to him self, six soore leases and
patents, and even then, when they were thought not to-
be good in Lawe, and the Dean and Chapter confirmed
foure score of them, and that w^{th}out stoppe or mislike
and (as I suppose) *gratis*. He might doe any thinge,.
and you see my case, I may doe nothinge, but it shalbe-
complained of even unto her Matie. A Third thing
I was chardged w^{th}all, that I woulde needs geve a
Patent of the Chancellarship to a Boy of nyne yeres of
age. *O os impudens.* My Lord, I have a sonne at
Oxford, a M^r of Art of thre or four yeres standinge, and
the *Dean* him self will confesse that he is well learned,
and hathe ben a student in the Lawe (as I take it) now
two yeres, and will in one yere followinge be fitt to-
procead Doctor. I must confesse that havinge nothing
ellse to leave him, I was content to bestow this upon
him, and drawne thereunto by my learned and wise
frends. It is he who made report unto your L. of S^r
Robert Stapleton's frivolous submission. Your L. then
liked well of him, and since he hathe profited in
learninge wth the best; he is allmost 25 yeres of age,
and a great deale elder in discreation, sobrietie, and
learninge, yet I was content that a D^r of Lawes should
execute the office two yeres next to come, even such a
man as the Dean liketh right well of. My late Secretary, Symon Hill, had an office of the Registership of
the Officiall, and myne eldest sonne was ioyned wth him
in it, who hathe supervived him. He would surrender
his interest to two of his brethren wch have-

nothing to live on. The one being at Cambridge, of 19 yeres of aige, a good Student. The other a Scholar in the Gramar Schole at Yorke of 14 yeres of age. Bothe in Lawe capable of such a pettie office, and noe other cause why the *Dean* denieth to confirme them, but that they are my children.

" Seing he denieth to confirm them, neither doe I urge him unto it, what cause hathe he to complaine of me ? The L. President toulde the Queene, that he would iustify him self, and so doubtles he will, if he may be heard and beleeved. He is a man that hath no great regard what he saith, or what he sweareth, for nothinge is so manifest true wch he will not deny. Wth these moste untrue tales some had so wrought wth her ma^{tie} that hardly I could have accesse. The way by many means was stopped, belike by some Ladie. All this cunninge dealinge notwthstandinge, her ma^{tie} well accepted of me, gave me good leave to answere these Reportes, still remayninge most gratious towards me, sayinge, that if she heard anything of me, she would make my best frend my L. Treasorer acquainted wth it, and so wth good favor gave me leave to retourne to my chardge, and praied God to send me a good journey. He that durst doe thus when I was present, what dare he not doe when I am absent ? Now my cheefe refuge must be unto your L. as you ever have stood wth me in my iust causes, so do I knowe that you will not leave me in this. I shall humbly and moste hartely pray you to declare unto her ma^{tie} how the matter fell out, and in

what sorte I proved the speach uttered by the Dean in
the Consistorie; as allso let her ma^tie understand how
untrue these his accusations be. The speach testified I
sent unto you by Dr. Aubrey. I trust your L. will not
send him home to triumph over me, for you know what
wronge he hathe done me, ever an enemy since the
first tyme I knew him. . . . .
Huntington this Whit Sunday in the morning 1586.

> "Yor L. most bounden
>
> "E. EBOR."*

Sir Robert Stapleton, to whom allusion is made in
the above, had been convicted in 1582, with some
others, of a base attempt to damage the Archbishop's
character, and sentenced by the Court of Starchamber
to pay a heavy fine and undergo imprisonment.
Sandys died at Southwell in July, 1588.

(Signature torn off) TO SIR WILLIAM CECIL.

"Assuredlye the state of these partes is miserable, and
Daunger greatt, the people are after a sorte in a madde
desperation, manie secrett mutynies are amongest them,
wherof nether author nor witnes can be lerned owt.
But that (to our terror and grefe) dailie talke is in
manie places of the Rebells retorne, whiche is rather
wished after, than detested, for ought that I can
perceave. The comons are verie wanton still, and
thoughe manie have suffred, and manie shorne to the
bare pelche,† yet for so moche as verie fewe or none of

* Lansdowne, MS. 50.
† This word is occasionally used in the north as an adjective,

the gentlemen hathe tasted of judgement which only
were, yea, and are the Incentors to all this evell, the
danger is rather doubled then in anie respecte fordone.*
And in verie dede except that owte of hand the Quenes
highnes, whom God long preserve, and you of her right
honorable councell, prevent the daungers imminent;
undowtedlye *Novissima erunt longe periculosiora et
peiora prioribus.*

"I knowe they shoote chefelie at the life of the Quenes
ma^{tie}, at her crowne, the subversion of the estate, and
destruction of us all, that trewlie obey, and obediently
embrace Christes syncere relygion and her highnes
moste godlye lawes. I feare, her highnes goethe dailie
in great daunger. O Lord preserve her (from privie
conspiracie, poison, shotte, and all papisticall trecheries).
I knowe you are maligned, envied, and dysdained at,
of the papists and rebells faction, more then anie of
of the privie councell. And surelye they have soughte
all meanes to supplante you, and still will so practize;
for of all men they take you for theire dedlieste
enimie and greatest hynderer. O good Mr. Secretarie
have an eye to your selfe, beware whom you truste,

meaning *faint* or *exhausted*; but of the above employment of it
(in the sense of *skin* or *pelt*), we have met with no other
instance.

* *i.e.*, exhausted, overcome.

> Now the hungry lion roars,
> And the wolf behowls the moon,
> Whilst the heavy ploughman snores,
> All with weary task *foredone.*
>
> *Shakespere, Song of the Fairies.*

you knowe the world, all are not faithfull frends that shewe fairest faces; helpe to overthrowe the wicked conspiracie; if the heddes may still remaine, and be shuldred owte shortlye shall the whoole realme repente. *Misterium Impietatis.* The papists practize daye and nighte. *Judas non dormit. Sinon Incendia mistet.* Remember the councell of Sext. Tarquinius, Titus Livius, li. I. to. a.; so longe as they remayne as they doe, loke for no quietnes; and if they get libertie, loke not longe to lyve. Wel warned well armed.

"Thus am I, as may seeme, somewhat sawcie, and overbold to deale withe your Honor. Yt may be sayd *sus Minervam*, and I acknowledge yt. But if your Honor beare with my good meaninge, and consydre as trewthe is, that a faythfull harte and the feare of God, and verie dewtie enforcethe me thus to doe. When I consydre the daunger I tremble. I see, and yet I dare saye no more.

"If I might be bold some tymes to write, I could at tymes advertise you of things, not to be neglected. But if it shuld be knowen to some of our governors that I shold write, I were sure to be in daunger of displesure; for having writen no thing at all to your Honor hetherunto since these hurly burlies beganne here, yet am I maligned and suspected so to have done. And sithence I have begonne to write I beseche your Honor beare with me a lytle.

"Amongest other Rebells of the northe partes send uppe as prisoners, there is one, Oswald Wilkinson,

Jayler or keper of the castle of Yorke; óf whom I of
conscience am enforced to advertise you as followethe
which is undoubted trewthe. This man assuredlye is
the most pernicious, railinge, and obstinate papiste in
all this countrie, so reputed and taken of all men, and
therein he gloriethe. A lytle before this late rebellion
burste owte, he openly ware the ensigne and badge of
thordre of those rebelles, which Markenfeld and the
rest dyd weare, yt was a great crucifyx of gold about
his necke. And journeing towards the sowthe about
the erles busynes as is suspected, at Newarke uppòn
Trente, did openly and stowtely pronounce and utter,
in the heringe of Mr. Henrison, Alderman of that
towne, that within four dayes the masse shold be as
openly said in Yorkeshire, and as frely for all men to
repaire unto, as ever the Communion was; which he
colde not knowe excepte he had bene of the conspiracie or privie therunto. Of this I have witnesses,.
Gregorie Paicocke Alderman of Yorke, Raufe Micklethwaite, William Broke, merchants and others.

"Peter Wilkinson, brother to this said Oswolde
Wilkynson, and nowe attendante on him at London,
said openlye in the house of one Mr. Woodde, a
capper* of Yorke, a lyttle before the rebellion burste
owte, in the heringe of diverse persons, that within a
shorte space, he knewe the masse shold be openly
said, and receaved in Yorke and Yorkeshire; And that

* A cap-maker.

the Quene and her Councell wold further yt. If yt
lyke your Honor that he be convented and examined,
if he denie it, Mrs. Harte the wife of John Harte of
London, grocer, and her neighbour Mrs. Blakelaye
who were presente when he uttered the said words,
will witnesse the same.

" We have heare one Sir Thomas Metham, a knighte,
a moste wilfull and obstinate Papiste, he utterly refusethe to come to the divine service or here yt said;
to receave the Communion, to come to anie sermons, or
to rede anie bokes excepte they be approved (as he
saiethe) by the churche of Rome, or to be conferred
with all. He refusethe to answere and stand and be
tried before the Quenes Matie Commissioners for causes
ecclesiasticall. He usethe the corrupte Lovaine bokes.
And at Lovayne mainteinethe amongst those Rebells
2 of his sonnes, to whom he bothe writethe often, and
from them receaveth letters agayne. Yt is foure yere
sythence he and Dame Edythe Metham his wyfe
were fyrst commytted to warde, since which tyme he
hathe daylye growen more welthie, and more wilfull,
and assuredlye nowe semethe to be utterly incorrigible
and past hope of all reformation. He doethe moche
hurte here, and of the papists is reverenced as a pillar
of theire faythe. I caused him to be committed to the
Castle where he remaynethe, and dothe harm, yet more
wold he have done if he mighte lyve at large. If
therfore your Honor wold be a meane, that by autho-
ritie he might be removed hence to London, or else-

where as to the councell shall seme good, bothe shold
you ridde us and this countrie of a verie evill man, and
take away a greatte occasion of evill, which is manie
waies verie daungerously ministred by him to this
tyckyll* people in these partes.

"We are also sore encombred with 2 Archepapists and
Doctors, whom we can not call owt of theire circuites
limited to them by the Quenes commissioners ecclesiasticall above; to deale with them according to theire
desertes. Theire names be, Doctor Carter and Doctor
Siggeswike. Doctor Siggeswike was lymited to lye
and abyde at Richemonde or within 16 myles therof.
And Doctor Cartar was limited to lye at Thirske or
within 16 miles therof; where they have lurked since
the beginninge of the Quenes raigne, never conforming
themselves, but obstinatly refusing to obey the
godlye lawes and have so practized that those 2 townes
and the townes adioyninge have most rebelliously in
this late tyme of insurrections resen, and armed themselves for recoverie of theire popishe masse, above all
the residewe of this shire. When we wold deale with
them they will not obey, nor dare (say they) for feare
of forfeyture of theire Recognizances departe their
lymites. Thus are they lymited to practize and lyve
disordredly withowt controlment. If yt might, by your
Honor, be brought aboute, that either the Privie coun-

---

* *i.e.* unsteady, inconstant.
Courtiers are but *tickle* things to deal withal.
                                  Beaumont and Fletcher.

cell, or those that lymitted them wold call them and reforme them, or releysing theire bounds, remitted them to the Commissioners for causes ecclesiasticall here, I doute not but they shold be reformed or at leste so delte withall that they shold not hereafter so practyse as they have done in corners heretofore, amongest the sillye people.

"We have here also 2 Doctors of Phisicke, worse papists I think ther is none in Rome, D. Vavasour and D. Lee. We have hunted for D. Vavasor these 2 yeres but he is so frended that no officer will see him. He hathe had a numbre of masses said in his house of late, as some of his chappleines whom we have mette withall have confessed. He was not seene here since before the late Insurrection. D. Lee was with the erles at theire beinge at Richemond in the Rebellion tyme, thether he rode with the countesse of Northum. and was with her and assisted her when she toke the letters from the poste, which were sayd to have bene sende from the Quene to the regente. He goethe uppe and downe from papiste to papiste, and nothing is said to him. But undowtedlye excepte there be sharpe execution done on the hedds and Incentors (as they are altogether spared hetherto) we shall shortely feale a greatter smarte. For now beginne whisperings, and muttrings againe. '

" Thus beseching your Honor to pardonne me, bothe óf this grette temeritie, and that I have so longe troubled your Honor with my foule scribblings, and

L

that you wold take in good parte my poore goodwill
and faithefull harte, which is and ever shalbe, with all
that I have or shall have, ever most redie to doe anie
service that in me may lye at your commandmente.   I
beseche God to blesse and preserve you, and graunt
you grace in tyme, to consydre my fyrst advertize-
mente in this letter, and maturely to occurre the present and imminente daunger.   From Yorke the 6ᵗʰ daye
of Februarie 1569-70.

> " Your Honors most humble and
> > alwaies at commandment."*

THE ARCHBISHOP OF YORK TO THE PRIVY COUNCIL.

" May it please your good Lordships to be advertised, that your letters written at Windsore the 15ᵗʰ of
October, came unto my hands on Tewsdaye at night
the 22ⁿᵈ of the same, and accordinge to his Maᵗˢ pleasure, and your Lordships order, I have with all diligencie
travelled therin, and have sent unto your Lordships
herewithall, the names and abilities of suche within
my dioces, as refuse to come to churche, usinge the
helpe of suche herein, as your Lordships in your letters
named unto me; yt was not possible for me in this
shortnes of tyme to searche owt all, beinge required by
your Lordships to returne answer within 7 daies : for
as yet I have not visited my dioces, and so canne not
come by full understandinge. of the offendours.   But

* Domestic—Addenda, Eliz., Vol. XVII.

theese are to many, whose intollerable insolencie, per-
verse and contemptuous disobedience, is with speede
to be repressed, or els hardly the state canne stande in
quiet saftie. I had in full purpose to have advertised
your Lordships herof, and for redresse praied the assistance of your autoritie, but your Lordships have
happilie prevented* me, and I truste you will bringe to
good effecte and perfectly finishe that which uppon
good & due consideration you have taken in hande.
God willeth that theese straied sheepe be called home
and be compelled to come in. And it must needs put
in daunger the publique quiet, yf they be suffered to
lyve in this sorte. I have already laboured what I
canne synce my cominge hither, as well by persuasion
as by execution of discipline to reforme them, but litle
have I prevailed, for a more stiffe necked wilfull or
obstinate people did I never knowe or heare of. Dowbt-
lesse they are reconciled to Rome & sworne to the
pope ; they will abide no conference, neither give eare
to any doctrine or persuasion. Some of them when the
praier for the Quenes Matie hath ben read unto them
have utterly refused to saie Amen unto it. Others do
glory (and that not of the simplieste sorte) that they
never knewe what the bible or Testament meant.
To some I have offered lodginge and diet in my
howse, that I might have conference with them for
their conformitie, but they chose rather to go to prison.
Thus much I write to give your Lordships a taste of

* *i.e.* gone before, anticipated.

their evill dispositions, and the most of them have ben corrupted by on Henry Comberforde, a most obstinate Popishe prieste now prisoner at Hull. While we expecte your Lordships further order, we procede here accordinge to our Commission, lest yf we shuld surceasse they would growe the stowter, thinkinge that our hands were shutt uppe.

.	.	.	.	.	.	.	.

" Thus I take my leave of your good Lordships, commending the same to the good direction of God's holy spirite. From Bushopthorpe this 28th of October 1577.

"Your Lordships at Commandment,

"E. EBOR."*

Enclosed with this letter is the following paper :—

---

* Domestic, Eliz., Vol. CXVII.

The names, sirnames, additions, and dwellinge places of suche within the diocese of Yorke as have bene detected to the L. Archb. of Yorke, and other her Maties Commissioners in those partes for their disobediences in refusinge the churche and publique prayer &c. and do not conforme them selfes; with a note of their habilities &c.

Their habilities.	Their names and sirnames.	Their additions.	Their dwelling-places.
500l. lands per annum or ther-abouts	The olde Countesse of Cumbrelande	wydowe	of Barden.
500 marks per annum or ther-abouts	The olde Ladye Wharton	wydowe	of Healaughe.
40l. in lands per annum	Lady Edith Metham	wydowe	of
40l. in lands per annum	Lady Anne Wilstroppe	wydowe	of
Her husband 100l. per annum in lands	Ladye Anne Inglebye	wieff of Sir William Ingleby, knighte	of Ripleye.
200 marks per annum in lands	William Hawkesworthe and Rosamunde his wyfe.	Esquire	of Litle Mitton.
Her husband 40l. per annum in lands	Katheryne Arthington	wyfe of William Arthington, Esq.	of Arthington.
20l. per annum in lands	Anne Weste, gentlewoman	wydowe	of Barnburghe.
40l. per annum in lands	Thomas More and Mary his wief	gentleman (sic)	of Barnburghe.
Her husband 40l. per annum in lands	Margaret Thwaites	wief of John Thwaites, gent.	of Marston.
Her husband 40l. per annum in lands	—— Palmes	wief of Bryan Palmes, Esquire	of Naburne.
Her husband 10l. in goods	Anne Lawnder	wief of John Launder, attorney	of Naburne.
Her husband 40l. per annum in lands	Anne Calverley	wyfe of Walter Claverley, Esquire	of Calverleye parishe.
Her husband 20l. per annum in lands	Alice Lyster	wief of Thomas Lyster, gent.	of Gisburne in Craven.
Her husband 20l. in goods	Agnes Foster	wyfe of John Foster, crowner	of Huntington nere York.
10l. in goods	Elizabeth Ellerker, gentlewoman		of Warter upon the wold.
	Isabell Thwenge	wydowe	of Warter aforesaide.

Their habilities.	Their names and sirnames.	Their additions.	Their dwelling-places.
20l. in lands per annum	Jane Langdaill, gentlewoman	wydowe	of Sancton.
40s. in goods	Thomas Acreth	Clerke	late parson of Catton.
40l. in goods and 20l. lands	Chrofer Monketon	Gentleman	of Lonsburghe.
20 marks per annum in lands	Katherine Thwenge, gentlewoman	wydowe	of Eastbeslertor.
20l. in goods	Cuthbert Mennell	Gentleman	of Barnehill.
100 marks per annum in lan's	Roger Toccatts	Esquire	
100 marks in goods and 100 marks in lands	Thomas Leedes	Esquire	
20l. lands in revertyon	John Mallet	Gentleman	
20l. in leases and goods	William Lacye	Gentleman	
100 marks per annum in lands	Henrye Oglethorpe	Gentleman	
Worth nothing, but very wilfull	Thomas Vavasour	Doctor in phisicke	
Worth nothinge, yet verie wilfull and a great perverter of others	Henrye Cumberforthe	Bacheler of Divinitie.	
Nothinge worth, and yet verie obstinate and infectors of others	John Bolton		22 all prisoners at Hull.
	John Alman		
	William Ustanson		
	Roberte Williamson	popyshe priests	
	Thomas Bedall, 5l. pensyon, paid by the Quenes Recevor of Notynghamshyre		
Nothinge worth, and yet altogether obstinate	John Fletcher	late Scolemasters	
	Michaell Tyrrye		
Wilfull men and nothing worthe	Geffreye Stevenson	Yeoman	
	Francys Parkinson	laborer	
5l. in goods	William Brimleye	Blacksmithe	
10l. in goods	Stephen Branton	Sadler	
5l. in goods	William Tessymonde	Tyler	
40s. in goods	Thomas Aldcorne	Carpenter	
Nothinge worthe	Olyver Walker	Weaver	
	—— Rayner		

Name	Worth	Description
Their husbands arr worthe		
Anne Weddell	20l. in goods	wief of John Weddell, of Yorke, butcher
Margaret Clitheroe	20l. in goods	wyfe of Jo. Clithero, of Yorke, butcher
Isaboll Porter	20 marks in goods	wyfe of Peter Porter, of Yorke, Taillor
Janet Geldarte	20l. in goods	wief of Percivall Geldarte, of York, butcher
Margaret Taillor	10l. in goods	wyfe of Tho. Taillor, of Yorke, tayler
Edward Teshe and Anne his wyfe	40l. in goods and leases	Gentleman
Dorothie Nevile	Her husband is worthe 100 marks in goods	wief of Henrye Nevile gen.
Agnes Taillor	Her husbande is worth 40s. in goods	late of Tadcaster wyfe of Jo. Taillor
Elizabeth Dineleye	Her husbande is worth 200l. in goods	wief of Mr. John Dineleye L. Maior of the Cittie of York
Ladye Pacocke	20l. in lands per an.	wydowe late wief to Roberte Pacocke alderman
Edwarde Beseleye and Briget his wyef		Gentleman
William Hooton and Mary his wife	20l. in goods	
Dorothie Vavasour	10l. in goods	wief of Thomas Vavasour, D. in phisicke
Emot Hallidaie	wilfull and worth nothinge ut supra	wyfe of Richard Hallidaie girdler
Janet Geldarte	5l. in goods her husb.	wyfe of Lancelot Geldarte, butcher
Francys Hall	20 marks in goods her husb.	wyfe of George Hall, Draper
Agnes Kitchynman	40s. in goods her husband	wyfe of Chr'ofer Kitchinman carpenter
Alice Cowlinge	40s. in goods her husband	wyfe of John Cowlinge butcher
Eliz. Cowlinge	nil	daughter of the said John
Jane Weste	nil	servaunt to Georg Hall aforesaide
Janet Bacheler	5l. in goods her husbande	Wyfe of William Bacheler, butcher

7   All prisoners in Yorke Castell.

2   Also prisoners in Yorke Castell.

22   All of the Citty of Yorke.

Their liabilities,	Their names and surnames.	Their additions.	Their dwelling-places.
20l. in goods her husbande	Rayne	wyfe of Christofer Rayne butcher	
5l. in goods her husband	Cockburne	wyfe of William Cockburne, butcher	
Wilfull, her husbande nothing worthe	Fysher	wyfe of William Fysher, butcher	
Yonge and wilfull worth nothinge	Anne Hewett and Margaret Hewett	Daughters of Hewett	
Brother to the late gaoler nothinge worthe, wilfull	Gregorie Wilkinson and Agnes his wyfe		
40s. in goods	Alice Abaye		
40s. in goods	William Wrighte	Hatter	
20 marks in goods her husband	Anne Cooke	wyfe of Ambrose Cooke Sadler	
20 marks in goods her husband	Alice Lobleye	wyfe of Richard Lobley Tanner	
10l. in goods	William Bowman and his wyfe	Locksmithe	
Her husband 10l. in goods	Grace Woodd	wyfe of William Woodde Gentleman	
20 nobles in goods	John Aldcorne and Eliz. his wief	Tiler	All likewise of the Citty of Yorke.
Her husb. 40s. in goods	Elizabeth Langton	wyfe of Thomas Langton Currier	22
ut supra	Alice Mashroder	wyfe of John Mashroder, potter	
ut prius	Alice Aldcorne	wyfe of Thomas Aldcorne, tiler	
nil	Ame Godfreye	his servaunte	
40s. in goods	Jane Plowman	wydowe	
nil	Margaret Plowman	her dawghter	
nil	Isabell Yoman	her servaunte	
	Katheryne Wildon	wyfe of John Wildon tayler	
Her husb. 5l. in goods vide inter prisonarios apud Hull supra	Margaret Tessymond	wyfe of William Tessymond, sadler	
Her husband 20s. goods	Alice Durham	wyfe of Richard Durham barber	
20s. in goods	John Woodd	Tayler	
Her husb. 40s. in goods	Janet Wilkinson	wyfe of John Wilkinson	
nil	Elizabeth Wilkinson		
nil	Williamson	wyfe of John Williamson	

Valuation	Name	Status	Place
20s. in goods	Thomas Wood and Agnes his wyfe	Laborer	Likewise of the Citty of Yorke.
nil	Richard Braferton, Agnes Wygan and Katherine Gills		
Her husband 5l. in goods.	Anne Hill	wyef of Robert Hill	of Tadcaster.
10l. in goods	Margaret Tailior	wydowe	of Tadcaster.
20 marks in goods	Robert Foster	yoman	of Tadcaster.
5l. in goods	Thomas Tailior	the elder	of Tadcaster.
40s. in goods	Walter More.		of Kepaxx.
10l. in goods	William Rawson		of Askham brian.
10l. in goods	Symon Charter		of Abberfurth.
5l. in goods	Agnes Rawson	wydowe	of Abberfurth.
10l. in goods	Francys Hemsworth and Jane his wyfe	yeoman	of Addle parishe.
nil	Richard Wayne	servaunt to William Arthington Esq.	of Kirkbye overblowes.
nil	Eliz. Haworthe		of Fryston paryshe.
5 markes in goods	John Lightfoote and Margaret his wyfe		of Sandall magna.
nil, and yet most obstinate and perverse	John Brettan and Fraunoys his wife		of Kellington.
40s. in goods	Edward Stele and his wyfe		of the chapelrie of Worseburgh.
10l. in lands per annum	Anne Rockeleye		of Doncaster.
Her husb. 10l. in goods	Margaret Silvester	wyef of John Silvester	of Doncaster.
40s. in goods	William Tuson		of Campsall.
40s. in goods	Giles Tailior		
40s. in goods	Nicholas Farlaye		of Kingston upon Hull.
40s. in goods	Robert Tennye		
nil	Janet Tennye		
40s. in goods	John Ruddall		
Her husband 100l. in goods	Isabell Allen.	wief of William Allen, Alderman of Yorke	of Drypoole.
40l. in goods	Christofer Watson and his wife		now remaining at Brayton.
A late rebell and pardoned	Thomas Johnsonne	Esquire	of Ryppon.
Heire to the Rebell Fulthorp attainted	Francys Fulthrope	Gentleman	of Crathorne or Hawnebye.

Their liabilities.	Their names and surnames.	Their additions.	Their dwelling-places.
Her husband 40l. in goods	Algar	wyfe of Tho. Algar attorneye	of Huntington nere Yorke.
Her husband 30l. in goods	Margaret Darbye	wyfe of Tho. Darby yoman	of Huntington aforesaide.
	Margaret Acaster	wydowe	of Huntington aforesaide.
5l. in goods	Alyce Sympson		of the same.
5l. in goods	Agnes Clerke	wydowe	of Sutton in Galtresse.
Her husb. 5l. in goods	Margaret Barker	wyfe of Christofer Clerke	of the same.
40s. in goods	Emote Wrighte		of Miton upon Swaill.
5l. in goods	Thackwraie	wydowe	of Rippon.
100l. in goods	Christofer Daye	wydowe	of Northlathe woods.
supposed to be poore	Mistres Clifford	wydowe	ot Rippon parishe.
20l. in goods	John Channer his wyfe and howseholde		of Rippon.
supposed to be poore	Peter Walworthe	gentleman	of Rippon.
nihil	Healeye the wife of Francys Healey and his daughter		of Rippon.
nihil	Snawe	wyfe of Henry Snawe	of Rippon.
60l. in goods	Thomas Harland and his wyfe		of Rippon.
300l. in goods	Thomas Hebden and his wyfe		of Rippon.
nihil	Watson	wyfe of Raphe Watson	of Rippon.
10l. in lands per an.	Richarde Fenton	Alderman	of Doncaster.
40l. in goods	Nicholas Elwes and Jane his wyfe	Attorney at the common Lawe	of Sprodburgh.
poore	William Wilkinson	priest.	of
	Sir Edward Gower and Lady Gower his wyfe	Knighte	of Stitnam.
	Edwarde Percye	Gentleman.	
	Allan Percye	Gentleman.	
	Anne Percye		
	Thomas Lacye	Gentleman.	of the towne
	Katherine Webster	Webster wyfe of	of Beverleye.
	Joan Wilberforce	Wilberforce wlef of	

E. EBOR.

The Earl of Huntingdon to Sir Francis Walsingham.

" I dyd ryde y° laste weeke 20 myles west from this towne, after I had sent my men before me, upon a soddayne, late in y° nyghte, Imedyatelye after one of my spialles had geaven me notyce y^t Wynsor was for certeyn in Arthyngton howse, w° in deede I dyd fynde trew, for Wynsor went awaye, as I may now gesse, even at y^t Instant, w° I dyd not bealeeve tylle nowe. For in truthe yt ys soche a howsse to hyde persons, as I have not in my tyme seene y° lyke, And I was assuryd by y° information of sondrye y^t theare bee vautes under y° grownde, but wheare to fynde y° waye to them I coulde not learne, And therfor after I had exemonyd y° wyddowe, who was sycke in hyr bed, or so faynyd hyr selfe, and also had sent (fower ?) of y° rest wythyr to y° prison, I was mynded to plucke uppe y° bourdes, but a priest, w° was founde after mannye searchys in a strange manner hydden, dyd confesse y° beeynge of. Wynsor theare, and sayde constantlye, y^t he was gon in to Netherdalle, and namyd too placys, in one of w°, he sayde, I shulde surelye fynde hym. And therfore I stayed my other purpose of pluckynge uppe y° bourdes, tylle I had made triall upon y° priests worde. And dyd Imedyatelye send five of my awne men y^t I was more sure of, then any I coulde send to in or nye Netherdalle, wheare they dyd not loose all theare labor, tho they gotte not y° man. But theare he was, and theare he ys. For w° cawse I mynde my selfe

to morrow to goo nye to y⁰ place, and in to y⁰ place yf
y⁰ daye wyll serve. I trust he shalle not nowe scape
my handes, as I have and wyll order y⁰ matter. Davye
Inglebye ys theare also. Yt ys soche a cuntrye as I
dyd not thynke to have fownde so nye to Yorke, And
y⁰ cheefe persons yᵗ doo inhabyte theare, have shewyd
them selfes nowe what they are in deede, wherof
Wyllm. Inglebye ys y⁰ cheefe. I praye God my labors
takyn in thys action may prove acceptable to hyr
maᵗʸ, and then I shall thynke bothe my chargys and
labors in thys well bestowyd, And care y⁰ lesse for
other matters wᶜ I knowe my dealynge in thys cause
hathe and wyll make me subiecte to, if sum heare may
yᵗ they desyre. I wyll not at thys tyme trowble you
wᵗ any particularytices (*sic*), but refer yᵗ to an other
tyme. And so abrupetlye I wyll take my leave, and
comytte you to yᵉ Lord. At Yorke thys 2d of Novem.
(1580 ?)   " Your assured frend,

                              " H. HUNTINGDON."*

MARTIN BIRKHEAD TO THE EARL OF SHREWSBURY.

" Right Honoʳ My bounden dutie humblie considered.
It maye please your good L. to be advertised that this
bearer, your L. servant cann declare particularelie, Howe
we have proceided at this assises heare at Yorke; we
have indicted and arraigned one William Lacye, and one
Richard Kirkman alias Jennyngs, either of theyme of hye
treason (who are found giltye) viz.Lacye for obtayning of
a bull and popishe orders from Gregorie the 13 pope, con-

* Dom., Addenda, Eliz., Vol. XXVII.

trarie y° statute of y° 13 yeare of y° Q. Ma^ts^, who hadd also taken upon him manie other indulgences, writings, instruments, reliques, beades, broches, laces, and tryfles brought from Rome. Th' other Kirkeman alias Jenyngs, beyng a seminarie preist perswading and withdrawing traitorouslie his Ma^ts^ poor simple subiects frome their naturall obedience to hir Majestie to y° obedience of y° pope & Romishe Religion, contrarie y° last statute made 23 of hir Ma^ts^ reign. With Kirkeman alias Jenyngs was taken masse booke, Challice, wafer cakes, wyne and all things readie to saie masse. Theye bothe remayne obstinate. Heare was also brought before y° judges five prisoners from Hull for refusing to go to y° Churche, one of theyme, John Mallott hathe yeilded to conforme himself & to go to y° Churche; th' other 4 viz: one Tocketts, one Lacy, & Harry Oglethorpe and one Leids do remayne obstinate, and have iudgment to paie 20*l.* for every moneth absente according to y° late Statute of 23 Eliz. I humblie beseich your good L..to vowchsafe (either by your L. lettres or otherwise) to give thanks to my L. Chamberlayne for his goodness towards me. Almighty God preserve your Good L. evermore in hye honor together with all yours.   Yorke the 11th of Aug. 1582.

    " Your Honors Ever bounden humble

        to command

            " MARTIN BIRKHEAD."*

---

* Talbot MSS. in the Heralds' College. For some account of the writer of this letter, see p. 44 *ante*.

THE EARL OF HUNTINGDON TO SIR FRANCIS
WALSINGHAM.

" Sr You shall understand, that since I receyved the
coppie of ye instrument of association for the preser-
vation of her Ma^{te} person, I made divers gentlemen of
this countrey acquainted therewith; and so from hand to
hand yt was made knowen in all ye parts of this shire;
whereupon divers gentlemen to ye number of 300 or
moore have of themselves desired earnestly to be ad-
mytted into that honorable societye, and have sealed,
subscribed, and sworne to performe ye contents of ye said
instrument.   The Citty of York, and divers other corporations within this contrey have don the lyke to the
number of 2000 persons and above.   And divers of the
said gentlemen within there severall wapentakes and
divisions y^t be in the Commyssyon of ye peace, and
came not to me to York, havinge sealed, subscribed &
sworne thereunto amonge them selves, dyd ingrosse
the sayd instrument in parchment, and admitted thereunto such of the meaner sort of gentlemen and of the
principall freholders and clothiers about them, as dyd
of them selves sue to be accepted into that societye.   So
y^t (especially about Hallifax, Wakefeld, and Bradford)
a great number of y^t sort have sealed, subscribed, and
sworne thereunto to the number of 5300 men besides the sayd gentlemen and corporations, and divers
others that have, as I heare, and will in other places do
the lyke, wch are not yet come to my handes.   I had
thought to have sent upp ye instruments wch I already

have, y^t be signed, sealed, and sworne unto. But finding by ye vew of them, y^t yt will be to combersom to send them by post, beinge 7500 seales at the least, I thought y^t good to reteine them heare, untill I shall heare from you againe. And in ye meane tyme I will cause a rowle to be made in parchment of all the names as well of those that I now have, as of such as shall come to my hands hereafter. Thus &c. At York the 30th of November 1584.

" Your assured frend

" H. HUNTYNGDON.

" I have sum cawse to ryde so farre as Doncaster and perhappes a lyttell farthyr, but on frydaye God wyllynge I wyll bee heare agayne."*

SIR JOHN HOTHAM TO SIR FRANCIS WALSINGHAM.

" Right Honorable my most humble dewtye remembred, may I signifye unto you that havinge receyved commaundement by letters from the Lordes of her Maties most honorable Privye Counsell, to call before me certeyne Recusants, within the Countye of Yorke, and to demaunde of eche of them, the furnyshinge of a Lyght horseman, or els to pay 25l. in monye, So yt is that the Recusants beinge dispersed into dyverse partes of the Countye, and dyverse of them not to be founde within the Countye, I cannot with such convenyent spede certyfye unto you, (as is

---

* Domestic, Addenda, Eliz., Vol. XXVIII. The signature and postscript only are in Huntingdon's handwriting.

required by there Honours sayd letters) every one
their particuler answeres, wherefore I have thought
good to signyfie unto you, howe farre my proceeding
hath bene, as here followeth, cravinge pardon for the
rest, which god willinge shalbe performed with all diligence, ceasinge to troble your honour any further, I
humbly take my leve; Yorke the 21^{tie} of October,
1585.

> "Your honours most humble
>
> at commaundement
>
> "JOHN HOTHAM.

"Roger Tocketts gent. will provide a horseman
furnyshed, or yf he be not lyked, then 25*l.* in monye.

"Thomas Leedes will provide 25*l.* in monye.

"John Britton is supposed to be in gaole in Manchester.

"Henry Oglethorpe is sayd to be in Oxefordshire with
the sheriffe of that Countye.

"William Hawkesworthe is sayd to be in the county
of Lancaster, at a place called Mitton.

"Marmaduke Redman is sayd to be at London.

"And Ingrame Thwinge is supposed to be out of the
Realme.

"There remayneth yet Frauncis Jackson George Moore
and Thomas Waterton with whom I have had no conference, neyther any certayntye of there beinge within
the countye."

SIR JOHN HOTHAM TO SIR FRANCIS WALSINGHAM.

"Right Honorable my moste humble dewtye remembred accordinge unto commandement geven unto me
by letters from her Maties most honorable pryvey
Counsell to call before me certen recusantes, to requier
them in her Maties name to furnishe eche of them a
horseman or to provide 25*l.* in money; so ytt is, that
forasmuch as their honors letters did import haste and
that the recusantes were not eselye to be founde, so as
I could not make certificat in suche convenyent tyme
as was required, I dyd signifye unto your honor, how
farr my prosedynge had ben therein : Since which tyme
I have usyd my dyligence to satisfye their Honor's
commandement; for the rest as followethe. Cesinge
to trouble your Honor I humbly take my leve. Yorke
the fyrste of November 1585.

"Your Honors most humble att
Commandement.

"Thomas Watterton, gent. consealed himselfe, that yff
my man had not mett with him by chance I should
have had noe Answer at all from him; but when he re-
seved my presepte to mete me att a place apoynted, his
Aunswer was I had nothing to doe with him, for that
he stode bounde to appere before her Maties most
honorable pryvey Counsell whereupon I was enforced
to wryte unto him their Honors pleasuer, his Aunswer
whereunto is hereinclosed.*

* Now unfortunately wanting.

M

" George Moore lyethe in Nottinghamsher as ytt is
supposed with Mr. Thomas Markam.

" Francis Jackeson dwellethe att Sharrelton within
the Countie of Yorke and concealethe him selfe and
will not be spoken with.

" So ytt dothe apere by my former certyficat and this,
theirbe tow onlye that I have had or cane have Conference with all whoe are agreed to paye money, which
some amountethe unto 50*l.* which money is readye at
Yorke to be payd to whome your Honor shall apoynte
for the reseat of the same.

"JOHN HOTHAM."

JOHN FERNE TO SIR ROBERT CECIL.

" May it please your Honor, I have enterteyned
allmost thes 2 yeares ane Espiall to lay a plott for y°
taking of one Hodgsones howse called Groman Abbey
near Whitby in Yorkshier,* & within 5 myles of y° sea :
to which place in respect of y° scituation and strenght
therof, doe resort most dangerous men, both priests
and fugitives, amongst whom David Ingleby is one.

---

* Gromond Abbey, in the parish of Egton, was a cell to the
Abbey of Gramont, in France, given by Joan, wife of Robert
de Turnham, and confirmed by King John, in the 15th year of
his reign. At the general dissolution it was valued, according
to Dugdale, at £12 2s. 8d. The site, in 35 Hen. 8, was granted
to Edward Wright, Esq., for the sum of £184 13s. 2d., subject
to a yearly payment of 18s. 10d. The next year it came into
the possession of Sir Richard Cholmley, knight, and remained
with the Cholmley family until the year 1668. From the ruins
of the convent, a spacious farm-house, with out-offices, was long
ago erected at the west end of the Priory Church. See Allen's
History of Yorkshire.

But having beene so longe deluded by this fellowe, (as
I suspected) I threatned to send him upp before your
honor; wheruppon he promysed better endevors; and
hath sent advertesment yesternight to me, y^t ye service
shalbe presently effected. The howse being stronge,
large, & many conveynyances under ground, to a
brooke running neare, I must imploy as great strenght
of people as I can from Yorke; for Sir Tho: Hobby,
being now at London, I do not knowe of any faithfull
assistance in ye cuntry: in which respect, & for y^t y^e
people are wholy defected from Religion, 20 myles alonge
y^t coste, and doe resist all warrants and officers y^t come
amongest them, I doe resolve (allthoughe it hath
seldome bene so used) to be ye same tyme within 4
myles of ye howse to prevent any Rescous to be mayd
by ye cuntrye, following Mr. Henry Cholmeley, whose
tenant Hogesonne is, for in January last one Aslaby
another of Mr. Cholmleys tenants, did rescue a prisoner,
a Recusant, from ye pursevant to ye High Commission,
& uppon the 23rd of this present ye like was done by
40 persons all weaponed against 2 men, y^t had bothe
warrant from this Counsell & ye high commission to
apprehend some Recusants; affirming y^t yf there came
never so many, with whatsoever aucthority, they shold
be stayne befor any towards (*sic*) Mr. Cholmley shold
be caryed away; and yet Cholmeley is a Justice of
peace, by what meanes I know not; & threatned
Revenge against Sir Tho: Hobby. This was done
within 3 myles of Groman Abbey; heérby your Honor

may perceave, into what conditions Religion & y⁰ state is brought in thes parts, & y⁰ iust cause I have to be in persone, at or neare y⁰ said searche, ther being no Assistance, but apparant Resistance to be expected in y⁰ Cuntrye; I humbly pray your Honor yᵗ yf this searche take not effect (as till it be done, nothing can be assured in thes cases) yᵗ all may be taken in y⁰ better parte. I may not discover y⁰ place, personnes nor service particulerly to any heare now, but onely in generall termes, & yf any hear shold take offence therin, I must relye uppon your honor. I am borne in hand* there wilbe taken David Ingleby, 2 priests, & the 4 Hodgsons, bretherne, and also a register booke a Journeall of their trecherous practises. If I had receved intelligence sooner your honor shold have had from me more tymely advertisement, and I wold be glad of your honorable advise & direction now, if it cold come before y⁰ tyme which is y⁰ 3 of May, by 10 of y⁰ clock in y⁰ morning, for yᵗ night must y⁰ search be mayd, if y⁰ appointment hold; & y⁰ place is 32 miles from Yorke, from whence I must send all y⁰ strength to guard y⁰ howse all night. Thes other letters to y⁰ Lls. do advertise them of thos gentlemen of Yorkshier, yᵗ are appointed by this Counsell to appear before their Lps to showe cause whie they have not levyed y⁰ charges of y⁰ 2 shipps sett owte by Hull in December last: And so craving pardon for this tedious letter, I do most

---

* A phrase in common use in early works, meaning to keep in expectation, persuade.

humbly take leave of your honor. At Yorke this 27 of
Aprill 1599.

     " Your Honors most humblye to be commanded,

" Jo : Ferne."*

Anon. to Sir Robert Cecil.

" Maye it please your Honor That whereas I did de-
lyver you a letter withoute my name, my m^r the Earle
of Huntington did warne me if they were matters of
state, that I shoulde not write my name, there is and
hath byn this terme so many Yorkesheire men with
youe that I durst not come to you, thoughe I have lyen
aboute London more then three weekes to attende upon
your Ho : wherein I beseech your Ho : that I maye
have some tyme with you, the matters are of greate
weight and may redowned to the Queenes hands above
tenne thowsand powndes, with dyvers of hir trators,
which she may have at hir pleasuer. All the helpe
they have is one howse called Growman Abbey, which
have dyvers tymes byn besett with 200 men and yet
they are suer (as they thincke) for it is a place, that
standith on a Ryver syde, called Eske, where they have

---

* Domestic—Eliz., Vol. CCLXX. The writer of this letter
was the son of William Ferne, of Doncaster, and a member of
the Inner Temple. In his youth he was addicted to the
pursuits of genealogy and heraldry, and published a volume
in 1586, called " The Blazon of Gentrie. Divided into
two parts. The first named The Glorie of Generosity. The
second Lacye's Nobilitie. Comprehending discourses of arms
and of gentry, &c." Hunter gives a short account of this work
in his *South Yorkshire.* Ferno was knighted in the following
reign, and died about 1610.

their conveyaunce most suer, that a thowsand men can
do no good unles they knowe them.   But I have layde
a plat so, that I will with the power of God, take the
howse with 60 men—whereof 40 men wilbe made
readie by one Mr Fearne Secreatorie to the Counsell of
Yorke, and he hymself all well appointed readie to
goe with them, and for the rest I will have readie, and
leade them all.   If I misse the takinge of the howse,
lett me dye.   Iff it please hir Matie, and your Ho : to
gyve me comforte in it, and graunte me leave to have
some secreate conferrence with youe, that youe maye
knowe me, and more playnelye understande the full
matter for if it be not rightlye handled, it will cost a
nomber of hir ma^{ties} subiects their lyves besides myne
owne lyffe.

"Blackamore I terme to be a Bushoppricke of Papists, and Growman Abbey the Headhowse, wherein the
Busshop lyeth, I meane Crawforth the Busshop, because he hath byn there ever since the death of Cam-
pion that was executed at Tïborne; and all other
Traitours that come from beyonde the seas unto that
cost, are there received, and by the meanes of that
howse, since the Earle died, three parts of the people
in Blackamore are become papystes.   So it is thought
if there be not present order taken that they will growe
to Rebellyon, the nomber is so greate.   And those that
are the preists are theis in this other paper sett downe
readie to be shewed.   I dare not for a thowsand
powndes be knowne to never a man in Yorkesheire,

but to Mr. Fearne. I have byn layinge of this platt ever since the Earle died, and now all things are fitted yf hir Highnes and your Ho : will graunte and further the same. It is more then 7 weekes sithence I came forth of Blackamore, and I have almoste twoo hundred myles home, and my monye spent, and Mr Ferne and I did thincke for to have had many of the tratours towardes London before this tyme. Thus attending your Honors answere I humblie take my leave.

"Theis are all Jesuits and Semynaries :—

" Thomas Hodgson, Ralph Ewer, Cuthbert Crawforth, Thomas Peacocke, Henry Johnson, Fraunces Nightingale, Thomas Andrewe, Martine Nelson.

" Theis are the principall men that ayde them and assist them, with many more others :—

" William Phillipps, Christofer Poskett, Fraunces Haslebye, Trynion Smythson, John Hodgson, Richard Taylford, Davy Inglebye, Richard Dutton, Henry Dutton, Henry Rydley, Richard Smyth, Alexander Cootes."*

JOHN FERNE TO SIR ROBERT CECIL.

" May it please your honor to be advertised, y^t ye Insolencye of papists increaseth still about Whitby Strand in Yorkshire ; for about 3 dayes since, I tooke ane examinacion of one Bell and Millnes (speciall Baliffes to execute proces from ye Common Place, uppon some personns dwelling neare Whitbye Strand) whoe weare

* Domestic—Eliz., Vol. CCLXX. The letter is endorsed 29 May, 1599."

wounded grevouslye, by 3 others y' charged them to be *spies for Religion* (as they termed it) but seinge them not to be suche, sayd, they weare sorye, for y' they had done, but yf they or any others came to troble them for theyre Religion or conscience, they wold kill them. But by this inclosed copye of another Examination, dothe appeare, what corage they have taken by y° remisse government heare in y' behalf. I may say noe more, but poore men can not doe y' they desyer, when y° assistance is so feeble. This insolent accion, or rather the Embrio and first concepcion of a sedition in ane assembly of so many men, weaponed in warlike manner may bewray what this sorte of people wold doe, yf tyme & occasion serve, for by the Lyons pawe, y° dimension of his whole bodye is easely knowen. God move her ma^tie to resolve spedely uppon ane Lo: President. The Report of this Affray and owtrage came to me by uncertein meanes on y° 11 of this monthe, but I stayed from advertisment, till I knew y° truthe, by y° examinacion of y° parties, yesterday, y' weare so abused. I thought my part to advertise y° same to your Honor, y' you may se y° state of thes things with us & y° fruit y' commeth, or rather y° first budds of desobedience, by want of a Religious President: and likewise least y' by complaint of Sisson, one of y° examinants (whoe as I heare is gone this day to London) some present order shold be taken, for a spedy serche to apprehend thes malefactors ; which attempt (they all dwelling neare and some of them as is sayd, in Groman Abbey) will dispache the Companye of y[t] howse, to unknown places, and hold them longer from meeting together there again ; wheras a conni-vence for a tyme will make them more secure; for in y[t] howse is y[e] whole Crue (as y[e] intelligencer told me yesterday) and there he expecteth them again, on St. Peter's day next which tyme he hath appointed for a serche, unlesse I heare further newes from him. He telleth me, he hath acquainted your Honor with his purpose, whereat I am glad, y[t] you may perceive, what course I runne in this accion. I thinke it weare fitt for a tyme to deferr y[e] apprehending of thes offendors in y[t] affray, in respect of y[e] greater service. I looke for a stronge Resistance at Groman, but I will god willing levye sufficient strenght to second y[e] watche of y[e] howse, within 2 howers after they have besett it ; and so most humbly commending my service to your Honors commandment I take my humble leave—at Yorke, this 19 Junii 1599.

" Yo[r] Honors most humble at Commandment,

" Jo: FERNE."

"The information of James Sisson, of Yarom, yeoman, and of John Corneforth of the same in the Countie of York geven upon their oathes before us Charles Hales and John Ferne Esquiers, two of her Ma[tie] Counsell in the North, the 13th daie of June 1599.

" They saie that upon Thurseday morning last being the 7th of this Instant, they came to Dunsley, nere Whitby in Yorkshire, to seaze to her Ma[tie] use the

goodes of Henry Fairfax of the same towne for his
debt due to her Matie for his Recusancye, they being
aucthorised togither with one Richard Tankard so to do
by severall warrants, vizt one from Sir John Fortescue,
an other from the High Sherif of Yorkshire and an
other from Mr. John Gate & Nicholas Girlingtone, to
levye certen somes of money of the goodes of certen
recusantes, named in Scedulls thereunto annexed,
whereof the said Henry Fairefax was one. And they
further say that they at there first comming to the said
Henry Fairefax did shew him his name in the inquisition, and the goodes found in the same to be his, and
by them to be seazed to her Maties use; and demaunded
delivery of those goodes accordinglie to her Maties use
in peaceable manner. Wherunto the said Fairefax
aunswered that they should have none of his goodes,
neither would obey any aucthoritie that they carryed.
Wherupon these Ex's (examinants) offred to go into
his fould yard, into which he had dryven all his Cattell,
& ther kept them, with 18 or 20 persones weaponed,
with staves, pytchforkes, bowes and arrowes, and himself with a long staffe & a calliver, and the said Fairefax and his companie would not suffer them to enter,
but bent all their forces against them. Insomuch that
these Ex's and the rest of ther companie viz. Richard
Tankard, Richard Lythe, & John Harker, which Lythe
and Harker came in aide of the other three, being not
able to gett those Cattell, from so great a force went
into the Towne, to crave assistaunce of ye Cunstable &

inhabitants, but could gett none neither would the
Cunstable John Camplyn be found, this being betwene
fower and fyve of the clock in the morning, and then
these Ex's and the said Tankard Lythe and Harker
purposing to go to Whitbye or some other place nere,
for better ayde were mett a little waie of Dunsley
Towne, upon the moore, by about 20 horsemen and
ten fotemen, dyvers of them weaponed with bowes and
arrowes, halberds, fowling peeces, callyvers, javelinges,
staves, swordes and daggers, and as sone as those Ex's
and their fellowes, came within arrowes shott of these
horsemen and fotemen they shott at these Ex's, and
the rest, and cryed "Downe with them, kyll the
villaines; And 6 of them pulled Tankard from his
horse, and when they had him under his horse, they
wounded him twise in the head with his owne dagger.
And then the rest of them sett upon these ex's and
Lyth and Harker, and took their weapons from them,
and gave them drye blowes wth staves, and asked them
for their aucthorytie, which the said Sisson did shewe
unto one James Roos, using M^{ris} Katherens Ratclifes
howse at Ugthorpe and after the said Rosse had reed
those Warrantes, he gave them againe unto this ex'
Sisson. And he saieth that there was emongst that
disordred compenie, one James Bowes, using at M^{ris}
Ratcliffes, Symon Rydley and William Rydley, her servantes Thomas Readman of Newton, William Bartram
of Stokesley, John Marshall of Biggyn howse, Christopher
Fernabye of Stokesley, John Foulthorpe of Barmby, &

William Ratcliffe brother to Katherin Ratcliffe. The rest of that companie they could not learn what they were. After which that companie parted from these ex's and their fellowes, and gave them their weapons againe, and bad them gett them awaie threatning them that if ever they came there againe they should dye for yt. And then these ex's and their fellowes went awaie, taking their waie towardes Pickeringlythe, which they tooke to be the safest waie to gett some help for Tankard which was hurte and before they had passed half a myle, some of the first disordred companie, together with dyvers others to the number of 40, weaponed with bowes, arrowes, shott and long staves, swordes and daggers did a fresh sett upon these ex's, the said Tankard, Lythe & Harker and shott at them with arrowes and discharged one peece, and came to them with their swordes drawn, and sett upon them all except Tankard who fled awaie upon his horsback, and did wound this ex' Corneforde upon the arme and in the head, and gave him many blowes upon the bodye with swordes and staves, which did not wound him but brust* him sore, and did likewise wound the said Lythe upon the head with his owne dagger, & over the mouth, & did beat him so crewellie with a staffe, untill they broke the staff with striking him. They did likewise sore beat Harker and this ex' Sysson, and still as they stroke a blowe at any of these ex's, or their fellowes they said, take this for Phillipes, and this for

* *i.e.*, bruised.

Hawkrigge, and this for Fowthropp, and this for Richard Lecke, and so for dyvers others Recusantes, whose goodes had bene hertofore seazed by these ex's. And whilest these disordred persons weare beatyng these ox's and their fellowes, one of them which bett this ex. Sisson, being a young man pale faced, in a vyollet collor Jyrkin, and a pare of whyte clothe britches, took the warrants frome the said Sisson, and putt them in his pockett and carried them awaie. And after they had sore beaten these ex's and their fellowes, and geven them many vile wordes, threatning them, that if they came any more into that cuntrye about such busines, they would kyll them, and taking their pistoletts and swordes and breaking them in peeces, they went from them, and whilest most of them were beating these ex's and Lythe & Harker, the rest of them sett upon Tankard as he fled, shoting at him with arrowes, and the said Tankard and his mare, falling in a myre, they houghshyned the mare, and cutt Tankards legg in two places very grevouslie and wounded him in the arme, whereby he ys in perill of death, and threatned to cutt his tonge, and putt his eyes out, and the like threatning they used to Sisson, and afterwardes they cutt of all y° mares legges from her body, as she lay alyve in y° myre, as these ex's have hard; but the names of these disordred persones they know not.

" CH. HALES.   Jo : FERNE.

" Concord. cum originali,

" Jo : FERNE."

J<small>OHN</small> F<small>ERNE</small> <small>TO</small> R<small>OBERT</small> B<small>EALE</small>, <small>OF THE</small> C<small>OUNCIL OF</small>
THE N<small>ORTH</small>.

. . . "I had intelligence of a notorious lewd howse
y^t receveth priests & fugitives from beyond seas; and
ye Lo. Sheffield lying then by chance at Mulgrave
Castle in Yorkshier, 3 miles from this howse called
Groman Abbey, a place well known to Mr. Topcliff,
I did send commission to his Lordship to besett &
serche ye howse which he did with great celeritye &
secrecy, & alighted from horseback half a mile from
the howse, & came on foote with great speede leading
36 of his servants & ye Queens pursevant to ye howse
& compassed it rounde about in a moment, but all was
discovered, as I think, by my espiall, for I have many
reasons of suspicion. Y^e insolency of Recusants is
such in this place, being neare Whitbye in Yorkshier
where of late hathe bene great owtrage offred to Baliffs
y^t came to seeze one Fairfax goods, a recusant, y^t I
commanded thither in person also to restreine their
insolencye in this serche. My Lord took great pains
& gave that testimonie of his affection to Religion, y^t
not any of his cote have done ye like in thes partes: it
were not amis y^t her ma^{tye} knew of his care of this
her service, it would be a good incoragement to him,
when he understood y^t it had been commended to her;
you may boldly say y^t he will undertake any service
against ye Papists, for God hath called him to a very
zealous profession of Religion. . . .

"At York this 3 of July 1599.

"J<small>O</small>. F<small>ERNE</small>."

JOHN FEENE TO SIR ROBERT CECIL.

"May it please your honor, The Intelligencer for
Groman Abbey having, as I writt by my letters of
y⁰ 19 of June, appointed a serche upon St. Peters day
at night, did still continew y⁰ same resolucion, so
yᵗ y⁰ serche was attempted on y⁰ next morning at 2 of
y⁰ clocke, as he had appointed. And because y⁰ Recusants have many eyes in this place, I could by noe
meanes take from hence suche a number as was sufficient to compass y⁰ howse and able to resist their vio-
lence, but it wold discover y⁰ attempt. And therfor
I did send bothe letters and warrant to y⁰ Lord Sheffield for his assistance in y⁰ service, for I durst hazard
uppon his Lp. a service of farr greater moment, god
having called him to a most sincer and zealous profession of Religion. His Lordship lay then by chance at
Mulgrave Castle, 3 myles from Groman. I acquainted
him by my letters, with your Honors warrant, which
coming to him about 10 a clock in y⁰ night did presently take y⁰ kayes of his castle gates into his owne
handes; and prepared him self and his people, and
came in personne to y⁰ howse with 36 of his servants.
He left his horses half a mile of y⁰ howse, and came
with great speed to y⁰ howse, on foote, compassed it
round presentlye; within half hower after, I came to
y⁰ howse, but y⁰ back doores weare open at my Lords
first coming; the fresh stepps of a horse & of y⁰ bare
foote of a man was perceved when it grew light. But
as I verelye thinke y⁰ espiall had discovered before, for

it is knowen y^t Hodgson who dwelleth in ye howse, did feare a serche ye day before. My reasons of suspicion ar thes, 1. He delivered me a fals plott of ye howse. 2. He promysed to conduct in ye night. 3. That he wold stay during ye searche in a secreat place near ye howse, to give advise where to serche; but he fayled in bothe. 4. His contrariety of intelligence, for on Thursday evening I receved a letter to procede, and at ye same tyme he sent another letter to one in York whom he knew was not at home to open it, y^t I shold stay till Sunday night (as appeared at my retorne from Groman by conferring of bothe ye letters together), and uppon Sunday he knew I cold not come, ye sitting beginning ye next day : I will doe my best to fynd owte his evill dealing, & therof your Honor shalbe advertised, hoping he shall receive punishment fitt for such a deludor. But certeinlye it is of great difficultye to performe a serche in y^t cuntrye, for the Recusants keepe scouts & watches day & night, that theyr Cattaill shuld not be seised, as they pretend, & they ryd all with Calivers petronells or frenche pistolls; very miserable is ye case of poore ministers & protestants in y^t place. There was found in this serche, all things for ye furnishing of A masse, and divers popish bookes, but nothing els could be founde, allthough all floores seelings pavements double walls were broke upp and divers valts of strange conveyance weare found owte. Amongst which one at a staire head, within a thick stone wall, was covered with a

great post of y⁰ bignes of a man's body, which semed
to beare y⁰ howse, but in deed did hinge onely & was
removeable to & froe, being locked beneath with Iron
worke, did stand fast, but being unlocked, wold remove
from the hole which it covered at y⁰ nether end, at
which hole a man might easely descend: my Lord took
great paines in his busines & is muche greved
yᵗ y⁰ service was defeated: yf your Honor wold make
this his Lordships care of her Matⁿ service knowen to
her highnes, it wold be a great incoragement to his
Lordship when he understoode so muche. . . .

" At York this 3 of Julye 1599.

" Your Ho: most humble
at Commandment,
"Jo: Ferne."

Thomas, Lord Burghley to Sir Robert Cecil.

" My honorable good Brother, I thought good to lett
you understand that this Christmas tyme I have taken
in one howse near a towne callyd Ryppon within sixe
myles of my howse at Snape, two notorious semy-
naryes, th'one of them callyd Nellson that was once
taken before, and upon his recantation had hys pardon.
Th'other is one Myddleton, verry well learnyd and a
very stowte and resolute fellow; this man was
appointyd to have rydd sowthward with fyve or sixe
others in his compayny all lyke gentillmen and had
appointyd every one to have had ledd spare by them a
swyft runnyng geldyng. Th'yntellygincer yᵗ told me

N

of this was one that was made privy unto it by this
Myddleton the semynarye for whome he shold have
provyded this runnyng geldyng. The party fearith
ther was som further matter then a common journey.
If the party that I employed in y⁰ takyng of these
prests be not dyscloosyd by this apprehendyng of
them, (he) is such a one as I had rather loose fyve
hundred pounds then he shold be knowne, for he is one
in great trust with them, and one nere a kynne to
Davye Ingelby, with whome I have delt to gyve me
Intellygence of his being, but he hath sworne unto me
yᵗ he hath not bene here almost this two yeares; I
askyd hym if he cam over whythar he wold give us
knowledg of hym but he made great (cursey) at it
and sayd he was his nere kynsman whome he wold be·
looth to betraye, but you know what reward may doo·
and he yᵗ wyll betray one may be brought to betraye
another. . . .

"8 January 1599—1600.

"Your faythfull and trew lovyng Broother

"THO : BURGHLEY.

"I have receyved yᵗ yong man yow signifyed by
your letters yᵗ he offryd to be employd, & I have
commytted him this thre wekes to y⁰ Castell to gett
credytt amongst thes Recusants, and within this two
or thre dayes I have given hym leave to breake owt,.
who promyseth me he wyll give me notyce where I shall
take hym with a seminary or Jhesuyt—he is a lyttell

to yong to be trusted but y⁰ fellow hath a good crafty wytt."*

" My honorable good Broother. I had not thought to have had anny occasion to have wrytten unto yow by this messenger, but onely upon some accydent that fell owt of his staye and his compayny, for that I had Intellygence uppon the takyng of the two laste prestes, that abowt that tyme certayn suspectyd persons shold have passyd that waye with ledd horses in the compayny, wheruppon I wrott my lettars to Sʳ Rychard Mallyvery, one of the Councell here, to have a watch when anny such compayny passed by Boroughbrigg and to staye them. Itt fell owt that these compayny lay at Borowbrigg whereof he havyng Intelligence, apprehended them at one of the Clock at myddnight, and y⁰ next mornyng brought them from thence to Yorke to me, and so fyndyng what they were and perusyng their pastportes, wherin ther names as also ther horses wos descrybed, I thought fytt to lett them passe withall the favour I cold. They were very wyllyng to be stayd, and fownd me ready to goo to dynner when they cam, so being myself very well acquayntyd with Mr. Ashton I invyted them all to staye dynner with me? Thus leavyng further to trouble you I rest as ever I wyll doo.

" Yor ever faithfull and trew lovyng Broother.

(unsigned)

" From Yorke, 10th of January, 1599-1600."*

* Domestic—Eliz., Vol. CCLXIV.

" 8 February, 1598-9.

".A note of such monie as hath bene receaved by Sir John Stanhope knight, Treasurer of her Maties Chamber from Mr. Skydamore receavor of Yorkeshier for these Recusants following for the providing and furnishing of light horses in Ireland. Viz. —

John Inglebie of Rudbie, esquier . . 30*l*.
Gilbert Medcalf of Hudgrange . . . 15*l*.
Margaret Scroope of Danby Ewer, widowe . 15*l*.
Elizabeth Pudsey of Barford, widowe . . 15*l*.
Petter Witham of Ledsame, gent. . . 15*l*.
Katherin Ratclif of Ugthorp . . . 15*l*.
Thomas Leedes of Melford, gent. . . 15*l*.
Thomas Gayle of Wilberford . . . 15*l*.
Christopher Conyers of Hutton uppon Wiske, Esq. . . . - . . 15*l*.
John Saer of Worsall, esquier . . . 15*l*.
Anthonie Holtbie of Marrick, gent. . . 15*l*.
Robert Bowes of Apleton, gent. . . . 15*l*.
Thomas Mennell of Kilvington, gent. . . 15*l*.
John Talbot of Thorneton in the streete . 15*l*.
Richard Talbot, gent. . . . . 15*l*.
Anthonie Catherick of Carleton, gent.. . 15*l*.
Henrie Blenkinsoppe and Thomas Peckering 29*l*. 6/8
Peter Knaresborne . . . . . 15*l*.
Frauncys Ratclif 29*l*. 13/4
George Anne esquier. . . . . 15*l*.
Anthonie Witham esquier . . . 15*l*.

Sum 359l.

Katherin Sutton	15*l*.
Richard Fenton	15*l*.
William Mydleton	15*l*.
The Ladie Ratclif	15*l*.

Paid more by Thomas Barnabie of the same
Countie who was bounde to pay his
monie here at London . . . . 15*l*.

Sum 434*l*.

" The names of dyvers Recusants assessed by the Councell at York towardes the payment of monie for the providing of Light Horses for Ireland, who refuse payment thereof; for which they desyer to knowe their Lordships' pleasure what course shall be taken with them. Viz. :—

Comit. Ebor

Elizabeth Yorke late wife of Peter Yorke of Goldwhayte	15*l*.
Richard Danbye of Sowthcove, esquier .	30*l*.
Thomas Conyers of Danbie wiske, gent. .	15*l*.
John Hodgscone of Gowman Abbie, gent.	30*l*.
Frauncys Aslabie of Ligh, gent . .	15*l*.
Mris Thuresbie of Marrick, widowe . .	15*l*.
Henrie Scroope of Danbie yewer, gent. .	15*l*.
Grace Lambert of the same, widowe . .	15*l*.
Brydgett Crathorne of Nesse, widowe .	15*l*.*

* Domestic—Eliz., Vol. CCLXX.

CHAPTER IV.

YORKSHIRE REPRESENTATIVES AND THEIR CONTEMPORARIES, 1603—1628.

THE foremost Yorkshireman in the early part of the reign of James I. was undoubtedly Sir John Savile, of Howley. The father of this notable character was Sir Robert Savile, also of Howley, an illegitimate son of Sir Henry Savile, of Thornhill. Sir Robert died in 1585, at which time his son and successor was twenty-nine years old. Sir John seems to have spent the early years of his life in Lincolnshire, with which county his mother, a sister of John, Lord Hussey, was connected. In 1587 he is mentioned as captain of one of the trained bands for Horncastle Sessions, and in 1589 he served the office of High Sheriff of Lincolnshire. It does not appear that he took any prominent part in Yorkshire affairs in the reign of Elizabeth. His stately house at Howley is said to have been completed about the year 1590; and it is likely that he shortly afterwards took up his abode there. This establishment of himself in the heart of the clothing districts of Leeds, Halifax and Wakefield gave him a favourable opportunity for gaining the good graces of the inhabitants of those towns; and throughout his life he retained their attachment, and loved to regard himself as their patron. Secure of the support of the most thickly populated parts of the West Riding, he sought the representation of the county in the first Parliament of King James, and was successful.

So far as one can judge from the meagre details of the sessions of this Parliament given in the Commons' Journals, Sir John made a very active and efficient member. His name frequently occurs amongst the members of different committees appointed; and not unusually does he figure as chairman. The clothiers, the tanners, the shoemakers and others had all their grievances to be redressed, or their monopolies to be restrained; and the prominent part which Savile took in the discussions on these matters shows him to have made commercial interests his especial study.

In June, 1607, his eagerness to protect his friends, the clothiers, brought him into collision with the most powerful man of the day, none other than Robert Cecil, Earl of Salisbury. This is shown by a letter from Edmund, Lord Sheffield,* President of the North, to Salisbury, in which the writer "understands that at the Committee this afternoon there fell out some sharpness between you and Sir John Savile." Sheffield went on to express his regret at this, and to explain

---

* Created Earl of Mulgrave in 1625; he died in 1546, aged 80. This unfortunate man lost all his sons by accidents, except Charles, who died young. John, Edmund and Philip were drowned in crossing the Humber at Whitgift Ferry, in December, 1614; William was drowned in France, and George killed when exercising in a riding-house.

that he had chosen Savile to attend to the passage of the Clothiers' Bill through the House, as the man best acquainted with the subject.

On the 20th May, 1614, a debate arose about a new patent for dyeing and dressing cloth, which led to numerous complaints of the stagnation of the cloth trade by different members of the House. Sir John Savile helped the discussion with a few statistics of the trade in his own neighbourhood. He told his hearers that some thousands of pounds' worth of cloth remained upon the hands of the manufacturers in his country, the buyers being so few; that 13,000 men were occupied with this kind of work within ten miles of his house, 2,000 of whom were householders, and the value of whose respective stocks varied between 5*l.* and 20*l.*; there were also 800 householders, makers of cotton, who were not worth 30s. each. He thought this state of the country could not endure a month.

For some years previous to the year 1615 he held the honourable office of Custos Rotulorum of the West Riding; but some unpleasantness with his brother magistrates led to his resignation or displacement. The first intimation we have of this is in a letter from the President of the North to the Lord Chancellor, in which the writer, to use his own words, "desired much to have waited upon you myself to present an Information, lately made unto me, of the evil Carriage of one Sir John Savile, a Gentleman of Yorkshire, one of the principal Commission, that

maketh Use of his Authority to satisfy his own Ends, if
sundry Complaints be true, which of late have been
made unto me, touching one Particular, which in my
Opinion is a Matter of foul Condition, and which I am
bold to intreat your Lordship to give me Leave to make
known unto you by the relation of Sir Thomas Fairfax,
a Gentleman of good Worth, to whom the Particulars
of that Matter are well known."

The date of the letter from which the above extract
is taken is 13th February, 1613-4. Nearly two years
afterwards—that is, on the 6th of December, 1615—Sir
John Saville writes to the Lord Chancellor in the
following terms:—

"Though out of my Duty and good Respect always
born unto your Lordship, I am very desirous to attend
your Lordship before my going out of Town, yet knowing how I march attired at this present, and how
noted, since my last Censure and Imprisonment, I hold
it good Discretion to forbear, and think that rather
over Boldness than good Manners to press unto your
Lordship, into whose Presence, I confess, I cannot
come without blushing : Not that I am either guilty
in myself, or unsatisfied in your Lordship's Justice,
but to see my Discretion and Credit thus cast upon the
Rock by the subtile Prosecution and injurious Pro-
vocation of a malicious and mean Adversary, which I
could not prevent ; wherefore, my good Lord, fearing
that there is something besides my own Fault which
draws on these Troubles, and that the Service of forty

Years under the late Queen of gracious Memory, and now under his Majesty, with my no small Charge and Trouble, cannot gain any better Opinion, but that I am held averse to his Majesty's Proceedings, and to use my Place rather to execute my private Malice than publick Justice; I hold it Wisdom to give Way, and Stubbornness to strive with those Occasions, which may daily draw on such Offence, and therefore, I humbly beseech your Lordship, to free me of this Charge I hold in the Commission, my Resolution being no more to execute, the same; but to withdraw myself, where I may more peacefully pass this Life in Expectation of a better."

To the above letter the Lord Chancellor adds—

"There is nothing but his own Fault and his disorderly and passionate Carriage of himself (ill beseeming a man of his Place and Calling) that draws on these his Troubles, for which I am sorry: And therefore I commend him in making this Suit, which I had rather should be done upon his own Request than otherwise.

"Th. Ellesmere, Canc.

"9th Dec., 1615."*

* The above extracts are taken from the *Letters and Despatches of the Earl of Strafford*, 2 vols., published in 1739. A third, addressed to Sir Thomas Wentworth, also printed there, runs thus:—

"May it please your Worship,—Since the end of the last Term, Sir John Savile, by earnest suit to the Lord Chancellor, procured himself to be put forth of the Commission of peace, and his Lordship gave him leave to nominate whom he would have to succeed him in the office of *Custos Rotulorum* for this

SIR THOMAS WENTWORTH TO THE EARL OF BUCKINGHAM.

" Right Honorable and my very good Lord. Thes are to give your Lordship humble thanks for your respective letters dated from Warwicke the 5 of this instant September, which I receaved the 13 of the same; the messinger told me your Lordship expected a speedy answear, in observance whearof I must crave your patience in reading a long letter.

" Your Lordship was pleased therin to lett me understande, that whereas his Majestie is informed that Sir John Savill yealded up his place of Custos Rotulorum voluntarily unto me, his Majestie will take itt well att my hands that I resigne itt up to him againe, with the

West Riding; whereupon he, out of his love, named yourself, who by his Honour's warrant, was thereupon so placed in the Commission. At which time also his Lordship was pleased to give order that I should continue Clerk of the Peace, which I humbly intreat your Worship that, with your favour and good allowance, I may do, and (God willing) I shall be ever ready and willing to do you the best service I can. The next Sessions are appointed to be holden at Wetherby upon Tuesday, the 9th of January next; at Wakefield on Thursday, the 11th of the same month; and on Tuesday after at Doncaster. Thus resting upon your Worship's good favour, I humbly take leave, &c.,   " W. CARTWRIGHT.

"Newland, 26th December, 1615."

The writer of this letter was appointed clerk of the peace for the West Riding about the year 1610. He is so described in the Heralds' Visitation of Yorkshire in 1612 (see Harl. MS., 1487), when he obtained a grant of arms. He married a daughter of John Clay, of Clay-house, in Elland. John, his only son, a Feodary of the Honor of Pontefract, under the Duchy of Lancaster, bought the manor of North Wheatley, co. Notts, about 1623, and settled there. Newland, near Wakefield, is the place from whence the above letter is dated. It was then the seat of Francis Bunny, Esq., who was Cartwright's son-in-law.

same willingnes, and will be mindfull of me to give me as good prefermentt upon any other occasion.

"My Lord: I am with all duty to receave and with all humble thankfullness to acknowledge his Majesties great favours hearin: both of his espetiall grace to take the consentt of his humblest subject, wher it might have pleased his Majestie absolutely to command, as alsoe for soe princely a promise of other prefermentt.: and itt wear indeed the greatest good happ unto me, if I had the means wherby his Majestie would be pleased to take notice how much I esteem myself bownd to his princely goodness for the same.

"Wher your Lordship is informed that Sir Ihon yealded up his place of Custos Rotulorum willingly unto me; under favour, I have noe reason soe to conceave; for first, he had noe interest to yeald, and further, I imagin he would not have done the same willingly att all, wherof this his desiring it againe is a sufficientt argumentt. Butt, howsoever, voluntarily unto me I cannot be perswaded, both in respect he never acquainted me with this motion, which would have been done, had I been so much behoulden unto him as is pretended, and in regard I had then some reason to misdoubt (which I have since found) he was not soe well affected towards me.

"But if itt please your Lordship to be satisfied of the truth, you shall find Sir John brought into the Staire-Chamber for his passionate carriage upon the benche towards one of his fellow commissioners; upon a motion in that Court for his contempts committed to the Fleet, and, upon reading of an affidavit, thought unfitt to be continued in the Commission of Peace, to which purpose my late Lord Chancelour gave his direction about the 3 of December shallbe tow years; which Sir Ihon getting notice of, to give the better coullor to his displacing, writt some 8 dayes after to my Lord desiring his Lordship would be pleased to spaire his service in respect of his years; wher indeed he was in effect out of the Commission before, by vertu of that direction: and so consequently ther was nothing in him to resigne, aither voluntarily or other wayes. This will partly appear by a coppy of Sir Ihon's letter, and my Lord's answear under the same, which this bearer hath to shew your Lordship.

" Presently hearupon itt pleased my Lord Chancelour, I being att that time in the cuntry, freely of himself to conferre that place upon me, and as his Lordship did fully assure me, without any motion made unto him, directly or indirectly, by any frend of mine whoesoever.

" Being thus placed I have ever since, according to that poore talent God hath lentt me, applied myself, with all paines, dilligence, care, and sincerity to his Majesties service, both according to the common duty of a subject and the particular duty of my place, wherin if any man can charge me to the contrary, I wilbe ready to justifie my self.

" Allbeitt I doe infinittly desire to doe his Majestie

service, I may truly say that I am free from ambition to desire places of imploymentt whereby ether his Majesties service might not be soe well performed, or my owne ends better effected; yet, my Lord, to be removed without any misdeamenour, I trust, that can be alledged against me, the like I thinke hath not been heard of; but thatt Sir Ihon should supply the roome in my place, the worlde conceaving generally and I having felt experiencedly to be very little frendly towards me, itt might justly be taken as the greatest disgrace that could be done unto me, and being that which his Majestie never offered to Sir Ihon during all the time of his displeasure against him, I might well conceave his Majestie to be (to my greatest greef) highly offended with me by some indirect means of my adversaries.

" Thes reasons give me assurance in my hope that his Majestie out of his accustomed goodnes to all sort of persons willbe pleased to deale graciously with me, espetially when his Majestie shallbe informed of these reasons, which I humbly desire he may by your Lordship's good means, as alsoe if Sir Ihon be soe desirouse to doe his Majestie service (which is all our duties) he may doe itt as effectually, being Justice of Peace, as if he wear the Custos Rotulorum.

" Howsoever with all due reverence and observance shall I waite his Majesties best pleasure, and willingly and dutifully submitt myself to the same, yett humbly crave to be excused if, out of thes reasons, I say plainly as yett I finde noe willingnes in myself to yeald up my place to Sir Ihon Savill.

"Thus much am I bold to signifie to your Lordship to give you satisfaction, which I doe very much desire, and withall to move your Lordship very humbly that ther may be noe further procedings hearin, till I attend your Lordship, which shallbe, God willing, with all convenient speed.

"Lastly, my Lord, myself never having nourished a thought that might in any sortt draw your Lordship's hard conceitt towards me, I fully rely upon your Lordship's favour, in a matter of this nature, that soe deeply concerns my creditt in the cuntry whear I live, which makes me now therof the more sensible ; and shall give me just occasion still to indevour myself to doe you service, and beseeche God to bleese your Lordship with longe life and all happiness.

"Your Lordship's humbly to be commaunded,

"TH. WENTWORTH.

"Gawthorp,

this 15th of September 1617."*

* The letter of which the above is a copy has only quite re-cently been found amongst the papers of the Hon. G. M. Fortescue, of Dropmore, Maidenhead. The discovery of it and of other important papers in the same collection is owing to the labours of the Historical Manuscripts Commisssioners. Mr. S. Rawson Gardiner has since edited the Fortescue Papers for the Camden Society ; and to that edition the writer has to express his best acknowledgments for enabling him to make his story so much more complete. Another letter relating to the same subject from Thomas Savile, the third son of Sir John, and his suc-

The last letter introduces us to one who was destined to play a far greater part in the affairs of England than Sir John Savile. The leading features of Sir Thomas Wentworth's life are too much a matter of common history to need mention here. A brief account of his origin and early years will be sufficient. He was the son and heir of Sir William Wentworth, of Wentworth Woodhouse, near Rotherham; his mother was the daughter of Robert Atkinson, a lawyer, at whose house in Chancery Lane, London, Thomas first saw the light. Little is known of his early years and education, beyond the fact that he spent some time at St. John's College, Cambridge.*

-cessor at Howley, better known in later life as Viscount Savile and Earl of Sussex, forms a part of the collection. It bears no date—a portion runs as follows : " For Sir Thomas Wentworth's allegations, I can saye no more then this, that if Mr. Bond, who was then my Lord Chauncelloures Secretarie and the messenger to me from his Lorde, do not justifie that my Lord was unwilling to put in anie to the place which my father had resigned, but whome he wished wel unto ; and therefore he de-sired me to name one, and I named Sir Thomas Wentworth : let me forfeit for ever my creditt with youre Lordship, which I would not doe for all Wentworth's estate.

" I could alledge my father hath beene in it this forty yeeres and done the King continuall service ; I could allso alledge that his deservings to the King (setting aside the wrangling in the Parlament which you, my noble Lord, I hope have reconciled) would farr outweigh his. . . . The doing of this concernes me so much in my estate, as if your Lordship should give me two or three thousand pownd a yeare."

* It is pleasant to notice that he was not forgetful of his college days, even towards the close of his active career. In 1639, when Dr. Beale and the Fellows of St. John's wrote him a letter of congratulation on his appointment as Lord-Lieutenant

He married, before he was nineteen, Lady Margaret Clifford, of the Cumberland family. Soon after marriage he travelled abroad, having as his tutor and companion, Charles Greenwood, afterwards rector of Thornhill, who was long honoured with his friendship and confidence. On his return he lived at Wentworth, and occasionally at Gawthorpe.

Between the period of Wentworth's appointment as Custos Rotolorum and his appearance in a still more public character, he was noted for the most splendid hospitality. His ordinary household consisted of sixty-four persons, and he was rarely without numerous guests. A household book is still extant in which an account was entered of the provisions consumed daily, and of the arrival and departure of all strangers. The allusions to him in letters of his contemporaries amply testify to the consideration in which he was held as almost the leading gentleman of Yorkshire, and his friends regarded it as a matter of course that, when he was of sufficient age, he should take his seat as representative of the county in parliament.

of Ireland, he replied : "So mindful I am of the ancient favours I received in that society of St. John's, whilst I was a student there, and so sensible of your present civility towards me, as I may not, upon this invitation, pass by either of them unac-knowledged. And, therefore, do here very heartily thank you, for renewing to me the sense of the one, and affording me the favour of the other. And in both these regards, shall be very apprehensive of any occasions wherein I may do any good offices, either towards that house or yourselves." This extract has been taken from a note in Hartshorne's *Book Rarities of the University of Cambridge*, published in 1829.

Before endeavouring to describe the great Yorkshire
election contests in which Savile and Wentworth fought
so keenly for supremacy, we will give some account of
another remarkable man of this period. Sir Arthur
Ingram was not a Yorkshireman by birth; he was a
wealthy citizen of London,* who acquired large interest in the county by the purchase of various manors
therein, amongst which may be mentioned those of
Temple Newsome,· Leeds, Kirkgate cum Holbecke,
Altofts, Warmfield cum Heath, and Halifax. It was
he who built the mansion at Temple Newsome,—an
evidence to future generations of his splendour and
magnificence. In March, 1612, he was appointed one
of the Secretaries of the Council of the North; and
about the same time undertook a large contract in
connection with the alum works in the county, which
he carried on for many years at but small profit to

* Lansdowne MS. 92, in the British Museum, contains a copy
of a paper signed by the Earls of Cecil and Northampton, and
Lord Chancellor Ellesmere, to the effect that certain malicious
and evil-disposed persons having spread abroad in derogation
of the good name and credit of Arthur Ingram, of London,
Esquire, that he hath lately obtained protection against his
creditors, they, the undersigned, knowing from their positions
and places the falseness of the report, declare the same. It is
added that the said Arthur Ingram hath also humbly desired
it may thereby be likewise published to all persons that can
claim any just debt, that if they will come on the following
Saturday to his dwelling-house in "Fanchurch streete in London," they shall then and there receive full payment in ready
money, &c. The concluding sentence runs thus, " This malicious
bruit deserveth punishment being without other ground than to
disgrace an understanding officer, a good citizen, and an honest
man." The date of this paper is 19 Nov., 1611.

himself.* When occupied with the affairs of the Northern Council, he lived principally in a large house in the Minster-yard at York. Some amusing court gossip from which we are about to quote, shows him to have been no favourite at court, except with King James. The honour of knighthood was conferred upon him in the year 1613, and the king's liking, no doubt, had its cause in the liberal nature and love of lavish expenditure for which Sir Arthur was noted, and which possibly led him often to place his purse at the service of our needy monarch.

John Chamberlain writes to Sir Dudley Carleton, March 2nd, 1614-15 :—

. . . . "I had almost forgotten our greatest newes that on Saterday Sr Arthur Ingram was sworn coferer of the kinges household, which was caried so close that yt was not vented till the very instant, but the sodainnes did no way better the cause, but rather put all into such a combustion, that the

---

* Harleian MS. 6115, which contains a few notes on the City of York, &c., has the following entry : "One Mr. Atherton began to practise the making of Alum about Gisborough in Yorkshire, with whom Sir John Bourcher, knt., did join. The king in the 4th year of his reign granted certain conditional letters patent to the Lord Sheffield, President of the North, Sir Thomas Challoner, Sir David Fowles, knts., and the said Sir John Bourcher, knt., for 21 years, for the sole making of alum in Yorkshire ; in 2 years' time they were 33,000*l.* out of purse. They had new workmen out of Germany. Other letters patent were granted for 31 years for all England, Scotland, and Ireland without conditions, and then were they out above 40,000*l.* and no alum made to benefit." Some further information on this subject will be found in Graves' *History of Cleveland.*

officers of the greencloth excepted mainly against yt, and produced the kinges promise and hand to the contrarie, wherby he assured that those places shold passe orderly and in succession; but say what they could he was sworne in the presence of the Lords Treasurer, Admiral Chamberlain, Knolles and Wotton, having agreed with old Sir Varney (Vernon) to resign his place to him in consideration of 1,500*l.* redy monie, 600*l.* a yeare during his life, and 200*l.* a yeare to his wife after his decease; but the storme was not so soone pacified, for all the officers in court even to the blacke garde seemed to take yt to hart, that such an indignitie shold be offered, and such a scandalous fellow set over them as they paint him out to be, whereupon the green-cloth and some others pressed to the king and had audience, where they behaved themselves very boldly or rather malapertly toward some Lords.'' The king, we are told, gave them "goode words & gracious," but remembered none of his promises. The Queen and the Prince took their part, saying it was a pity that one man should bring such general discontent into the King's own house; "but for all this," adds Chamberlain, "he was established in his place." Writing again on the 16th March, Chamberlain says, " Sir Arthur Ingram is in a sort *desurçonné*, for Sir Marmaduke Darrell is appointed to kepe the table and discharge the busines of the coferer, and he only to retain the name till Michaelmas that the accounts may be made up, and in the mean time order taken that he may be reimboursed of such monies as he hath lawfully laide out or can challenge in this cause." On the 6th April he writes, " Sir Arthur Ingram with much ado is removed, and all his brave furniture caried from the Court, there were many tricks and cunning passages used to kepe him in, or at least to have won time, but the houshold was so mainly bent to have him out, and found so many goode frends that there was no abiding.". Under date of 7th April, the same informant tells us that Ingram is yet very unwilling to throw up his post, " now having furnished his lodging at court with rich hangings, bedding and silver vessell, on friday last he sent for his diet, which beeing refused him by the officers, complained, and by the assistance of some great Lords prevayled thus far that yt was to be allowed him till this day,·by the Kings owne appointment, who said he had deserved better of him than to be sent away utterly discountenanced : the next weeke he is to go into Yorkeshire about the allam (alum) busines for the King, and at his return he pretends to go to the Spaw for his health." . . . "yf this busines of Ingram's had not ben, I know not how we shold have entertained ourselfes for this whole moneth together, yt hath filled both court and citie with dayly newes and discourse."*

* For the following notes on Sir Arthur Ingram, Dr. Thomas Birch (Birch MS. 4460 in the British Museum) is responsible. "He was a rich merchant in London, and of an overgrown estate, purchased much, and his way was to pay the one half down fairly and fully, but the second half by a chancery bill, y^t is, he would find some flaw, some incumbrance or other to

A great variety of correspondence has been preserved relating to the general election of 1620. It throws, of course, considerable light on the method of conducting elections in those days, so a few extracts from it will prove not uninteresting. Sir Henry Savile, of Methley, took a prominent part in it. He was the eldest son of Sir John Savile, Baron of the Exchequer, one of a family wholly distinct from the Saviles of Howley. Sir Henry was created a baronet in 1611. He was several times Vice-President of the North, and seems to have been a man held in universal esteem. He sat for Aldborough in the two previous parliaments of James, but feeling by no means secure there for a third election, wrote to Sir Thomas Wentworth for help in gaining a seat. Wentworth, in his reply, says, "I have written effectually to Mr. Secretary for a Burgess-ship for you at Richmond; but I will amongst them work out one, or I will miss far of my aim. So soon

baulk the second payment, and so call the seller into and hold him in yᵉ Chancery. He often invited another person to dine with him, wᶜʰ he always refused, at last Sir Arthur met with him, pressed him hard, but still he would not promise, Sir Arthur would needs know yᵉ reason, 'Why,' saith yᵉ Gentleman, 'because I will not sell my land,' wᶜʰ he thought was the thing Sir Arthur aimed at in his repeated invitations. Afterwards Sir Arthur built an Almshouse and carrying Mr. Garbut (of Leeds, as I think 'twas he) to see it, would needs have his opinion of it, wᶜʰ tho' he was loath to giv, yet being urged, he told him, it was too little, 'Why,' said Sir A., 'yᵉ rooms are big enough, and it's in every man's choice what number he will admit.' 'However,' said Mr. G., 'it is too little to hold those yᵗ you have undone,' with which true and biting 'Reperté,' we may imagine how he was pleased."

as I hear from Mr. Secretary, I will give further certainty
herein; in the meantime methinks it were not amiss,
if you tried your ancient power with them at Aldborough,
which I leave to your better consideration, and in the
mean time not labour the less to make it sure for you
elsewhere, if these clowns chance to fail you. The
writ, as I hear, is this week gone to the Sheriff, so the
next County Day, which must, without hope of alteration, be that of the Election, falls to be Christmas Day,
which were to be wished otherwise; but the discom-
modity of our friends more upon that day than another
makes the favour the greater, our obligation the more,
and therefore I hope they will the rather dispense with
it. If the old knight should but endanger it, faith, we
might be reputed men of small power and esteem in the
country, but the truth is, I fear him not. If your
health serve you, I shall wish your company at York,
and that yourself and friends would eat a Christmas
Pie with me there, &c. Nov. 28, 1620."

Sir Thomas Wentworth had arranged to stand for
the county with Sir George Calvert,* the Secretary of

* Descended from a noble family in Flanders, and born at
Kiplin in Yorkshire about 1582. In 1593 he entered as a
Commoner of Trinity College, Oxford, and in 1597 took the
degree of B.A. On his return from his travels he became
Secretary to Sir Robert Cecil, afterwards Earl of Salisbury.
He was made one of the Principal Secretaries of State, 16th Feb.,
1618-19, but resigned in 1624, frankly owning that he was become a Catholic. The King, however, who, in projecting an
alliance with Spain, was suffering his vigilance against Papacy
to sleep, created him in 1625 (by the name of Sir George
Calvert, of Danbywiske in Yorkshire, Knight) Baron Baltimore,

State, and was busy at this time writing to various influential friends and others, soliciting their support. To some he thought it necessary to hold out other inducements than those suggested by friendship alone. Thus he writes to Christopher Wandesford :* "And now, lest you should think me forgetful of that which concerns yourself, I hasten to let you know that I have got an absolute promise of my Lord Clifford† that if I be chosen knight you shall have a Burgess-ship (reserved for me) at Appleby, wherewith I must confess, I am not a little pleased, in regard we shall sit there, judge, and laugh together." To Sir George Calvert, writing on Dec. 5, he says, " I find the Gentlemen of these parts generally ready to do you service. Sir Thomas Fairfax stirs not, but Sir John Savile by his

co. Longford. He was at that time member for the University of Oxford. After the death of James he successively planted colonies in Newfoundland and Maryland. He died in 1632. A portrait of him, from the Duke of Devonshire's gallery in Bolton Abbey, was in the Leeds Exhibition of 1868.

* Of Kirklington in Richmondshire, the son of Sir George Wandesford. He was born at Bishop Burton in 1592, and was educated at Clare Hall, Cambridge. He accompanied Wentworth to Ireland in 1633 as Master of the Rolls. He became Lord Deputy of Ireland in 1640, when he was created Baron Mowbray and Viscount Castelcomer; he died shortly afterwards. A portrait of him, in the possession of his descendant, the Rev. H. G. W. Comber, of Oswaldkirk, was exhibited at Leeds in 1868.

† Henry, fifth and last Earl of Cumberland, born at Londesborough in 1592, Wentworth's brother-in-law. He died at York in 1643, after rendering active service to the King at the beginning of the Civil Wars. Two portraits of him, in the possessions respectively of the Duke of Devonshire and of Edward Akroyd, Esq., M.P., were exhibited at Leeds.

instruments exceeding busy, intimating to the common sort under-hand, that yourself, being not resident in the country, cannot by law be chosen; and being his Majesty's Secretary and a stranger, are not safe to be trusted by the country; but all this according to his manner so closely and cunningly as if he had no part therein; neither doth he as yet further declare himself than that he will be at York the day of the election, and thus finding he cannot work them from me, labours only to supplant you."

Sir Henry Savile to Sir Richard Beaumont.*

. . . "I am absolutely of opinion that Sir John (Savile) will not stande when ytt comes to the upshott; but ys content to make the worlde believe he will, to trye what the countrie will say or doe; but I thinke when he shall well understand his frendes' and neighbours' engagements, he will thinke ytt more wisedome and safetie for his reputation to goe to his grave with that honor the countrie hathe alreadie caste upon him, than to hazarde the losse of all att a farewell. Hallomshyre is made so firme to our partie, of my knowledge, as all his interest can make noe breache there. And att this

* Of Whitley Hall, born in August, 1574, created a knight in 1603, and a baronet in 1627. He was the owner of Sandal Castle, and in October, 1617, petitioned the King for a grant of " Hall Lathes, part of the manor of Sandal," to be impaled with his small park adjacent; which petition was granted. Sir Richard was a Justice of the Peace, and a Treasurer for lame soldiers in the West Riding, 15 Jas. I. He was never married, and died in 1634. A portrait of him, belonging to H. R. Beaumont, Esq., M.P., was exhibited at Leeds in 1868.

tyme, as the case standeth, Agbrig and Morley dis-
tracted in themselfe can not make a Knight of the
Shire. I would not have you soe curious to refuse a
Burgeshipp of Lancashyre, for I myselfe must be contented with one more remote, and out of our own
countie: and I am soe well acquaynted with the
scrupule, that in the Parliament house ytt makes
neyther difference of matter or reputation, the best
men in the kingdome servinge many tymes (without
touch of creditt) for the obscurest places, and farthest
from theyre dwellings in the kingdome.

"Aldburgh playd the knave with me ; and trustinge
to him I had lyke to hav gott noe place att all.

"For Mr. Kaye, ytt ys not possible for him to waver:
for I have his letter under his hand, of engagement,
first to parson Greenwood and after to myselfe. But
I expected to heare what my cozen of Langley* doth

---

* Sir Henry's father, Sir John Savile, Baron of the Exchequer, married a daughter of Robert Ramsden, of Longley,
near Huddersfield, Esq., William, grandson of Robert, and
therefore Sir Henry's own cousin, held Longley at this time.
He married Rosamond, daughter of Thomas Pilkington, of
Bradley, Esq. To the subsidy levied in 1595 Wm. Ramsden,
Esq., and John Ramsden, gent., were the largest contributors in
Almondbury—the former being assessed at 20l. in lands, the
latter at 6l. 8s. 4d. in lands. The manor of Huddersfield was
purchased by William of the Queen, 30th August, 1599, as appears
by an entry in the Docquet Book of that date. There was an inquisition of his estates taken at Halifax on 28th August, 1623,
shortly after his death, before Thomas Lovell, Esq., the Escheator for Yorkshire, and a jury. It was certified that
"William Ramsden nuper de Longley Armiger" was seised of
the manors of Saddleworth or Quicke, &c., formerly parcel of
the possessions of the Priory of Kirklees ; of the manor of

resolve; who yf he leave his blood for a matche att cockinge I shall be sorie I am his kinesman, whether it be the yonge or olde. Sir Tho. Wentworth hath gott a slippe of the ice on horseback, which will make him keepe in a weeke or tenn days. Soe with my kynde remembrance to all our frendes with you, I rest

"Your assured loving cosen,

"H. SAVILE.*

"4 Dec., 1520."

CHRISTOPHER PEPPER TO SIR HENRY SAVILE.

"Sʳ,—All respective compliments premised. *Solamen miseris, &c.* It is both your happe and mine to be unworthily respected, you for your Burgeshipp at Aldbrough, I for my recordershipp heare, you where your former imployments had given iust cause to expect continuance, I where 20ᵗʸ· yeares service might have procured one halfe dayes Respitt for my presence and advise in the Election. For my appoined tyme of home-coming was knowne and by me observed yet the choyse was made and Indentures drawne the afternoone before. It was Sir Tho. Wharton's predominant power with our Alderman seconded with earnest sol-

---

Huddersfield, and all houses, buildings, lands, tenements, meadows, pastures, rents, reversions, hereditaments whatsoever belonging to the same; of a capital messuage in the town of Almondbury called Longley Hall, &c., &c. Sir John is declared to be the son and heir of William, and to have been 28 years old at the time of his father's death.

* Additional MS. 24,475—a copy by Hunter from Dr. Bandinel's collection at Oxford.

licitation of other the Burgesses and an undertaking to free the Town from all checke of my Lo : President and Mr. Secretary Calvert, who had both written severally to the towne for nomination of one of ther Burgers y^t (as you have rightly conceived) hath brought the election to be questionable in respect of some clause in the late proclamation.   My hope was y^t considering the severall answeres to the fornamed ho^{able} persons I myself should have had the offer before any forreyner, wch if it had so happened, or y^t I could in any way have effected what you require, I esteeme your worth to be such & acknowledgeing my selfe to owe so much to the memory of your late worthy father and to the meritt of him who hath beene pleased so friendly & fervently both by word & writing to further your desires heerein, as I would right willingly have yielded you the place.   But good Sir let that which is past cure be past care for *nescit vox missa reverti*.   And so in hast being sorry my readines to gratifye both Mr Justice Hutton & your selfe could take no better effect, I rest

> "Yours to be com. to my litle utmost
>> " CHR. PEPPER.*

SAVILE RADCLIFFE TO SIR RICHARD BEAUMONT.
" Most worthie Sir,
> " I received your letter when I was with Sir Thomas Wentworth whom I acquainted with such contents of it as you desired.   My Cosen George

* Harl. MS. 7,000.

Radcliff and I had talke about a Burgeship for Clitherowe, who was verie willinge to asist with the
best,meanes he could to procure it, and to refer it
to your dispose. But nowe all hope of prevaylinge is
extinct; for Mr Chancelor of the Duchie hath verie
latelie written a letter to the baylives and burgesses
thereby challenginge a right in the election for
everie corporation within his countie, and hathe named
for Clitherowe one Mr Shelton. The Corporation
dares not denie him; and the other was longe agoe
disposed to Sir Thomas Walmesley. Sir thoughe I
fayle to procure the place for you it is not throughe
defect of anie love or respect unto you, but because
the Burgesses of Clitherowe fayle with me in the
performance of that which diveres of them both prof-
fered and promised which they are constrayned by
greatnes to fayle in. And this in haste with remembrance of my respect and service unto you I ever
remayne

> " Your loving frend and cosen
> > " SAVILE RADCLIFFE."

" Todmorden December 16."

" To the right wor. my most worthie frend and
cosen Sir Richard Beaumont, knight, at
Whitley or Longley."

> THE SAME TO THE SAME.

" Honored Sir,

" I was at Clitherowe upon Tuesday
when I did understand that Mr Chancelor his letter

for Mr Shelton or Sheldon would not be denied; and
withall I did heare that Mr Auditor Fanshawe had
made great meanes for the place, but some said that
it was thought Mr Auditor was provided. If you
had bene resolved when I last did see you to desire
the place I thinke I could then have obtained it; but
whilst I did labour to keepe it in suspense Mr Chancelor & Mr Auditor's potencie prevayled, soe that
nowe I ame perswaded if ether of them will have it
the proffers which some of the Burgesses did make
me will not be performed. I ame sorie it faleth soe
forth but howsoever I desire you will accept of my
unfained respects and love unto you, wherein I will
not fayle ever to remayne

>   "Your assured cosen and frend

>   " Savile Radcliffe.*

" Todmorden December 30."

Writing to Sir Arthur Ingram, Wentworth complained that Sir Arthur, in an address to his friends at
Halifax, had desired their voices for Mr Secretary and
himself, " the rather for that Sir John Savile stand
not ;" " so, say they, if he stand, we are left to our
liberty." He therefore begs him to clear that doubt
by another letter, or he fears that they will give their
second voice to Sir John. Savile's influence in the
more densely populated clothing districts was very
great, and the letter just quoted from speaks of the

* Additional MS. 24,475.

crafty manner in which he describes himself as the
patron of the clothiers, and therefore their fittest
representative. On the 8th December, Wentworth
wrote to Fairfax that the "old gallant of Hooley"
certainly would stand. How anxious he was to secure
the return of Sir George Calvert, as well as his own, is
shown by the following extract from his letter to Sir
Henry Slingsby, of Scriven :—

"The certainty I have of Sir John Savile's standing, and the various reports I hear of the country
people's affection towards Mr. Secretary, make me
desirous to know how you find them inclined in your
parts. For this wapentake, as also that of Osgodcross
and Staincross, I certainly persuade myself, will go
wholly for us. In Skirack I assure myself for a
better part, and I will perform promise with Mr. Secretary, bringing a thousand voices of my own besides
my friends. Some persuade me, that the better way
to secure both, were for me to stand prime, cast all my
second voices on Mr. Secretary, and put him first into
the indenture. I pray you consider of it, and write me
your opinion ; I would not lose substance for such a
toyish ceremony. There is danger both ways ; for if
Mr. Secretary stand first, it is much to be feared the
country will not stand firm and entire against Sir John.

"At a word we shall need all our endeavours to
make Mr. Secretary, and therefore, Sir, I pray you
gather up all you possibly can. I would gladly know

how many you think we may expect from you. My
Lord Clifford will be at Tadcaster upon Christmas Eve
about one of the clock : if that be your way, I am sure
he would be glad yourself and friends would meet him
there, so that we might go into York the next day.
And thus desiring your answer, I remain

" Your most assured and affectionate
Friend and Kinsman,

" TH. WENTWORTH.*

" Wentworth Woodhouse,
    Dec. 8, 1620."

The eventful Christmas Day arrived, and after what
must have been a very severe struggle, Sir Thomas
Wentworth and Sir George Calvert were declared to
be returned. At the first meeting of the Parliament
Sir John Savile presented a petition against them.
Wentworth was charged with having threatened the
free-holders, and with an " unlawful preparing them "
to elect himself and his kinsman; two warrants were
produced, written in Wentworth's name as justice of
the peace, and signed by Bartin Allott† and Richard
Micklethwaite,‡ two of the High Constables; one warrant requiring, the other requesting, the freeholders of
such a place or parish to be at York on Christmas Day;
there to make election of him and Calvert; the free-

---

* *Strafford Letters and Dispatches*, Vol. I., wherein may be
found some other letters of like tenor, written by Wentworth
about the same date to different Yorkshire gentry.

† Of Bentley, in Emley, and Bilham Grange, son of Robert
Allott, of Bentley, and Jannet Charlesworth, of Totties in
Holmfirth.   ‡ Of Beilby.

holders were also informed that the high constables would certify to Wentworth all the names, as well of those giving as of those refusing their voices. An attorney named Johnson deposed to having read in Wentworth's own hand, and to having twice heard read by others, a letter of similar purport to a third high constable named Stanhope.

In the debate which arose out of this petition, Mr. Mallory, the member for Ripon, said he was an " eye and ear-witness of the discontent of the gentlemen at these constables' doings, and that thousands in the town, who were for ' a Savyle ' were excluded." Wentworth took the accusation very loftily at this debate. He declined then to enter upon the charges, as he should meet them all in due season. Nevertheless the opinion was strongly and generally expressed that, although a man might write to his friends to induce electors to give their voices, it was unlawful to require or to threaten, or to order the names of refusers to be reported; for in such case, when a man was " powerful in his county," the election ceased to be free.

The Committee appointed to inquire into the matter met, and the interest and excitement created appear to have been extraordinary. A complaint was made to the House that the committee-room was so crowded by those not on the Committee, that a proper hearing of the case was almost impossible. The evidence brought forward implicated the High Sheriff, Sir Thomas Gower, as well as the Constables, as several witnesses

P

swore that he had excluded great numbers who came
to vote for Savile, and had never troubled himself to
inquire whether they who shouted for Savile's opponents
were freeholders or not. Three persons swore stoutly
that on the day of election about "a thousand persons
crying *a Savile!*" and pressing to the town-hall, had
been refused, the door being kept by halberds, and that
one of the party who attempted to force his way inside,
had his head broken. To this was opposed the fact
that the place in York where the knights were chosen
was at the prison, and that armed men were placed
there, not to overawe the electors, but to keep safe the
prisoners. The greatest importance was attached to
the evidence of the high constables. Allott and
Micklethwaite, who were first examined, declared that
they were themselves responsible for the wording of the
warrants of which complaint had been made. What
they understood from Wentworth's instructions was,.
that he only desired the freeholders to come and choose
him and Calvert if they thought them fit men and
esteemed them; and they declared that there was nothing
unusual in the language transmitting those instructions.
The third high constable, Stanhope, produced the
letter to which the attorney Johnson had testified, and
it turned out to be, not a command, but an entreaty
to the high constables to desire the petty constables to
set down the names of all freeholders within their
townships, and which of them had promised to be at
York and bestow their voices with Wentworth, that so

he might possess a testimony of their good affections, and know to whom he was beholden. Practically there was no great difference between this and the language complained of; but there was no expressed threat, and the law had not been directly violated. The result was, that the election was declared good; but the constables were left to the censure of the House; the proposition to exonerate Wentworth from all blame in the preparations being only passed by a small majority.

Another violent debate occurred on the conduct of the high constables. There was a strong personal feeling on the part of some members against Wentworth, from his having not only excluded the old popular member, Sir John Savile, from the representation of the county, but also from his having used his great personal influence in forcing into his place a stranger, a minister of state, a man having neither property nor connections there. The member for Oxford, Sir John Brooke, aiming at Wentworth through the constables, declared it fit that they should go to the Tower, for forestalling freedom of election by their warrants. It was urged in these unfortunate Yorkshiremen's defence, that they were poor, and that they had been put to great charges, in having been five weeks from home entirely at their own expense. The House at length determined that two of the constables, namely, Allott and Micklethwaite, should make a public submission of their offence at the next Yorkshire Sessions, and that they should be called in and severely reprimanded at the bar of the House; Stanhope escaped with a small fine. The two constables, accordingly, kneeling at the bar, made the required submission, and received the Speaker's severe censure "for meddling with what belonged not to them, for undue preparation, for warrants of command to petty constables, and for menaces, by requiring the names of refusers to be delivered."

Wentworth, though confirmed in his seat for Yorkshire, still professed dissatisfaction at the proceedings. He made a vigorous speech, insisting that Savile's charges had been made against himself, and that they had failed in proof. Against him personally nothing whatever had been established, and he therefore desired judgment upon Savile also. A less haughty, determined, and pertinacious spirit than Wentworth's would hardly have claimed such absolute acquittal while any sound still lingered in the House of the debates above sketched; but his was a temper that rose in proportion to the resistance it provoked, and, short of everything, counted nothing gained.* On this point, however, the Commons would not give way. It was considered that Savile had produced matter of grave import to the charge, and had vindicated freedom of election.

On the 26th March, during this sitting of the

* See Forster's *Life of Sir John Eliot*, to which work and to the *Journals of the House of Commons* the writer is indebted for some of the particulars of this election, and of the subsequent one in 1625.

Parliament, Sir Edwin Sandys* moved that the ancient privilege of sending Burgesses should be restored to Pontefract, and a Committee was appointed to consider the matter. This Committee reported that Pontefract had first sent Burgesses to Parliament about the year 1297, and continued to do so for a good while afterwards; that, by reason of the Barons' Wars, it grew poor, and about the year 1432, a return was made that they could not send Burgesses, on account of their poverty. King James, it further appeared, had granted them, in the fourth year of his reign, all their former liberties and customs, notwithstanding they had been forfeited, or lost. The Committee thought, therefore, it was consistent both with law and justice, that a writ should be issued. Sir Edwin Sandys was duly rewarded for the pains he had taken, as the electors of the revived borough gratefully returned his son, also named Edwin, as one of their representatives, the other being George Shellitoe, Esq.†

* The second son of Dr. Edwin Sandys, Archbishop of York. He was admitted Fellow of Corpus Christi College, Oxford, in 1579, and was collated to a Prebendal stall in York Cathedral in 1581. This he resigned before being knighted in May, 1603. He was High Sheriff of Kent in 1616; was employed by the King in several affairs of great trust and moment, and was a leading man in Parliamentary matters. He died in 1629. Anthony à Wood, in his Athenæ Oxoniensis, speaks of him as "ingenio et gravitate morum insignis."

† Of Heath, near Wakefield, son and heir of Francis, one of the Attorneys of the High Court of the Star Chamber at Westminster. He purchased the lordship of Seacroft, near Leeds, of Charles Blunt, Lord Mountjoy and Earl of Devonshire, to whom it had been granted by King James for his services in Ireland. He married Elizabeth, the daughter of Sir

There was another general election about three years later, of which but few particulars can be gleaned. There can be no doubt that Wentworth again contested the county, but this time the Savile interest was too strong for him, and Sir John amply revenged his previous defeat by securing the return not only of himself, but of his son, Sir Thomas. Wentworth had to content himself with a much less important constituency. On the 23rd January, 1623-4, he writes to Lord Clifford, "The town of Pontefract (notwithstanding all labour made against me) hath returned myself and Sir Henry Holcroft their Burgesses; so as I see it is my fortune to be of the House, albeit upon the reading of your Lordship's last letter I was much doubtful I should have been turned to grass here in the country."

Sir Henry Holcroft had, however, been chosen to sit for another constituency (Stockbridge) also, which suited him better than Pontefract, so a new writ had to be issued. Sir John Jackson* and Sir Richard

---

Richard Bulkley, of Beaumaris, knt., and, having no family, left her all his lands. The widow married Sir Ralph Hansby, of Tickhill Castle.

* Of Hickleton, knight. His father, also Sir John, was a Bencher of the Inner Temple, and practised as Attorney before the Council of the North: he married Elizabeth, eldest daughter of Sir John Savile, of Methley. This Sir John was Justice of the Peace and Treasurer for lame soldiers for the West Riding in the 6th year of King Charles. His son was created a Baronet by Charles II., and married for his second wife Lucy, the daughter of Henry Tindall, of Brotherton, Esq., relict of Sir William Jobson, of Heath Hall, near Wakefield.

Beaumont came forward as candidates. In a few days it was reported to the High Sheriff by the Mayor and certain Aldermen that Sir John Jackson had been elected; a day or two later other Aldermen and Burgesses declared that the choice had fallen upon Sir Richard Beaumont. A petition was presented from the borough, alleging that before the writ came, the Mayor of Pontefract had undertaken that Jackson should have the place, and had shut the door against all coming to vote for Beaumont; he had also made Burgesses of 40 recusants and papists, in order to carry the election. The Committee appointed to investigate the matter decided that all the inhabitants, householders and residents there ought to have voice in the election, and that upon the last writ no Burgess had been duly returned. Sir John Jackson ultimately secured the seat.

The dissolution of this Parliament, consequent upon the death of King James, which occurred 27th March, 1625, again brought Wentworth into the field for the representation of the county. With him was joined Sir Thomas Fairfax. Arrayed against them were the formidable Saviles, father and son. "For the advantage of these," wrote Fairfax to Lord Scroope, President of the North, "scandalous and seducing letters are written; a copy of one of them I here inclosed send to your lordship, that you may perceive, if strength do fail, policy (though with untruths) must supply them. And by these means, as if the state of religion did lie upon the stake, they will no doubt accumulate such a multitude of people in those well-disposed towns of trades, as they will be powerful; neither can the falsehood of the suggestions appear; for at the days of election shouts, not reasons, must be heard."

Sir George Wentworth,* the son-in-law of Fairfax, reported to him that all the gentlemen in his part of the country were very firm both for his election and for Sir Thomas Wentworth's, "save only Sir Francis Wortley,† who hath something wronged you and your

---

* The second son of Michael Wentworth, of Woolley, Esq. He succeeded his brother Michael in the Woolley estates in 1642. Sir George sat for Pontefract at the beginning of the Long Parliament. The remainder of his history may be gathered from the Royalist Composition Papers in the Public Record Office, wherein his "delinquency" is thus stated—"that he was sometime a member of the House of Commons, deserted the Parliament, and was in arms against it, being a Colonel under the Earl of Newcastle; went to Oxford, and sat in the assembly there; went from garrison to garrison held against the Parliament, as to Leeds, Wakefield, Halifax, Pontefract, Sheffield, York, and last to Newark, where he was at the time of the surrender." For this Sir George was condemned to pay 4,302*l.*, being one-third of the amount at which his estates were valued. This heavy penalty Sir George petitioned the Commissioners to reconsider, "being the greatest fine that hath been set upon any beyond Trent." A reduction of 250*l.* was all that was gained by this appeal.

† Of Wortley, near Barnsley; studied at Magdalen Hall, Oxford; created a Baronet in 1611. Antony à Wood describes him as "treading in the steps of his worthy ancestors in hospitality, charity, and good neighbourhood," also as "well learned in the Greek and Latin authors, of a ready, quick wit, a good speaker, and well seen in poetry." He was taken prisoner during the Civil Wars at Walton Hall, near Wakefield, and imprisoned in 1644 in the Tower. A petition presented to the commissioners for compounding with the estates of delinquents in February, 1648-9, shows Sir Francis to be still in confinement there.

cause, but himself more. He hath entreated all his neighbours and friends for Sir Thomas Wentworth, but not one for you, Sir."

Sir Thomas Wentworth, however, mindful of his fate at the previous election, did not neglect his old friends at Pontefract. After writing a friendly letter to his late colleague there, Sir John Jackson, he communicated in the following manner to " Mr. Cowper, Mayor of Pontefract " :—

" Mr. Mayor,

"Understanding of a new Parliament and of the consequence thereof, a new election of Knights and Burgesses, I have thought good to desire your self and the rest of my good friends of Pontefract that I might still stand one of their Burgesses, since I will serve for no other but them, unless as Knight of the Shire, whereby, your particular included in the general, I shall be equally bound to serve you as well as the rest of the Country. I do likewise much wish, that the difference risen by reason of the last Election may be composed, your town have in itself by that means love and good agreement, and abroad all friends to the welfare thereof; and therefore considering the ability and capacity of the person, and my particular re-

---

This petition was on behalf of Sarah, his only daughter, the wife of Roger Brettridge, of St. Martin's in the Fields, Esq. (also described as of Newhall, co. York), stating her right to the manor of Carleton, the manor-house or capital messuage called St. Ellenwell there, &c., which had been settled upon her in lieu of 1,000l. in money, plate and jewels, at the age of 21 years, or on the day of her marriage.

spect unto him, I do exceeding much desire Sir
John Jackson may bè my partner in that service ; and
in case I should serve in the other place, that you then
would join Sir Richard Beaumont with Sir John Jackson. All which, in good faith, I principally think fit
to put you in mind of, so that all breaches may be thus
timely made up, and that yourselves and all your
neighbours, knit and woven together in perfect solid
love and peace, may with one united strength apply
yourselves to the good and avail of your corporation.
And for my own part, I assure you I will not be found
ever to be wanting in my best and readiest help towards so good a work. Therefore I must intreat you
to favour me so far as to deal effectually herein, and
if you find any otherwise addicted, yet that from me
you would intreat them to keep themselves unengaged
any other way until I come to your town myself,
which shall be, God willing, within five weeks. For
albeit I am now upon the point of going to London,
yet I resolve, God willing, to make so short a stay
there, as that I will be back again in time to be at
the Election of the Knights at York, and to take
your town too in my way, to speak with you and the
rest of my friends concerning this business. So with
my love to yourself, desiring you to remember me to all
my good friends in your town,

"I remain, your very loving friend,

"TH. WENTWORTH."*

* *Strafford Despatches, &c.,* Vol. I.

Sir Richard Beaumont writes to Wentworth on the 9th June, 1625 :—

"My occasions are, and have been such, as with no convenience I can come up to London, for which I am very sorry, that I shall not enjoy your good company this summer, and give what assistance I could to make good our York election, which I hold as clear as the noon sun, for if it be tolerated that men shall come six, seven, nay ten apprentices out of a house, this is more like a rebellion than an election : the Gentry are wronged, the Freeholders are wronged. For Ponte-fract, Sir, I do not intend to serve in that rank ; I am much beholden to them for the matter, but not for the manner : I should have been willing to have kept your place for you, or for any friend of yours, and served in it, and yielded it up of an hour's warning to have done you service ; but as it is, I pray, acquaint my kinsman that I would have him get a new writ from Mr. Speaker, which he is well acquainted with, that the Town may chuse another. I would have Sir Henry Savile, or Mr. Shilletoe have the place. Sir, I do acknowledge to yourself an obligation of friendship, which on my part shall never be concelled, and I wish that my love and service may ever give you an accept-able interest, which at this time I commend unto you, wishing you a happy success in all your own desires, and so I take leave and rest."*

* *Strafford Despatches, &c.,* Vol. I.

This time the Saviles lost their seats for the county; but the manner in which the decision was arrived at seems to have been anything but satisfactory. Directly after the first meeting of the Parliament, which occurred on the 21st June, 1625, a petition was presented against the return of Wentworth and Fairfax, signed by about 1,050 freeholders. It was alleged that Savile had a majority of voters on his side; that Sir Christopher Hillyard, now the member for Hedon, had demanded a poll; that the Sheriff, "wholly Wentworth's," had, after some hesitation, granted it; that whilst it continued, he took measures to exclude all freeholders who had not been present at the reading of the writ; and that, after about thirty-five had polled, and the Sheriff saw the chances were in favour of Savile, he abruptly closed the voting, and declared for Wentworth. The evidence in favour of the petition went to show that there had been unusual excitement; the emulation in the choice for Parliament, always strong in the county, had risen to unexampled height; and never had so large a concourse been brought together in the County Court at York.

Wentworth met these allegations with a high spirit. He denied every statement made; but even admitting their truth, he considered that they in no way concerned him. The Sheriff alone was the person implicated, and he ought to be summoned before the House. Wentworth's great object was to gain time, in the expectation that inquiry would be stayed by subjects of more national importance. But the House was resolved upon a complete investigation into the matter, and the Sheriff was summoned to come up, a fortnight being allowed for his appearance.

Nothing, remarked Sir John Eliot at this point, could equal the vexation exhibited at this display of a fixed determination not to drop the inquiry. The spirit continued to show itself that had impelled the first daring attempt to force adjournment of the subject by adjourning the House itself. But it was north against north, he adds significantly; and Savile had the older experience. All the arts that northern policy could invent, therefore, to gain advantage in the carriage, met in the end but their own likeness. The care and diligence that opposed them were no less than theirs, and the craft was more. Savile knew too well those paths of subtlety not himself to follow the hunter on his track, and, being more beaten in the way, he was able in his own trap to ensnare him.*

Two days after the time fixed the Sheriff made an unwilling appearance, and tried to justify his conduct. Immediately after eight o'clock, he said, he made proclamation, and read the writ, at the usual place. Then, the gates according to custom being shut, he took a view of the freeholders; and returning, declared his opinion that Wentworth and Fairfax had double the voices to Savile. He owned to having at first objected

* See Forster's *Life of Eliot*, Vol. I.

to grant a poll, as it had been demanded after the
proper time ; and declared Savile himself to have been
the cause of its abrupt termination. He charged
Savile with having attempted to bring unqualified
persons up to the polling-booth, and with having
frightened or driven away by improper representations
qualified persons who had come to vote for Wentworth.
The Sheriff's evidence gave very general dissatisfaction ; but little truth, said Eliot, could be gathered
from his words, and less content and satisfaction from
himself. He excused himself for not having brought
up witnesses on his behalf by declaring that he had
interpreted the House's order as requiring his own
attendance simply ; and claimed additional time for his
defence in the event of his statements being disputed.
A further examination made him give a more detailed
justification of his conduct. Holding, he said, those
only of the freeholders qualified to vote who had been
present at the reading of the writ, he had caused them
to be drawn by the foregate into the Castle-yard, and
there enclosed between that gate and the postern ;
with provision that each freeholder, as he was sworn
and numbered, should be let out at the postern-gate,
where the polling clerks were stationed. His object
in this was not merely to prevent confusion and
disorder, but to avoid the abuse and scandal, not
unfrequent on such occasions, of the same electors presenting themselves more than once, and under divers
names getting themselves each counted for several.

Savile had good reason, he continued, to regard this as an objectionable precaution, and his resistance became so determined that it led to the breaking open of the foregate, and numbers of those whom the Sheriff had pronounced disqualified had rushed in. Savile had also circulated a report that the poll was to be kept open for several days; and numbers of Wentworth's supporters, fearing a long attendance, and the crowding and excitement around them, left the court disheartened. Under these circumstances, the Sheriff considered it his duty to close the proceedings, and being convinced, both by view and hearing, of Wentworth's majority, at once decided in his favour.

After the examination of the Sheriff was concluded, a strong effort was made by some of the members, under various pleas and pretences, to delay the proceedings. Sir John Eliot, however, moved that the Sheriff's statements should be dealt with by the House as they stood, without giving further time for examination of additional witnesses; and he carried this in Committee by a majority of 25 to 17.

When Wentworth came back into the House, from which he had retired during the discussion, he declared that he had never sought to delay his cause, but that he only wished to have it heard in a legal manner. He insisted that a large majority of the freeholders were for himself and Sir Thomas Fairfax. And as for their position and rank, he had been supported on the day of the election by the greatest number of men of

quality that had taken part in any return these twenty
years. On the other, Sir John Savile had brought with
him numbers not entitled to take part in the election.
The demand for the poll had been made after eleven
o'clock, with no intention that it should proceed; and the
poll had been interrupted by the unlawful act of Sir
John Savile himself. In the recent case of Pontefract,
where the election was void, the poll had been broken
off by the parties returned. His own case differed
altogether, and he desired that his counsel should be
heard at the bar of the House on the following day, to
maintain in that state of facts the law to be on his
side. If this view of the case were denied, he claimed
the right to prove it by witnesses; and time must be
given him to bring up those witnesses.

A long debate followed on this speech. There were
many technical points at issue, and it would be tedious
to reproduce here all the intricacies of the discussion.
It was eventually settled that the circumstances of the
disturbance of the poll, according to the version of
Wentworth, should be taken as the case of the sitting
members; that this case should be submitted to Savile
in writing, and that Savile should present himself at
the next sitting to give an answer.

On Tuesday, the 5th of July, Savile presented
himself, and desired "in some few things" a hearing.
He apologised for the trouble he had occasioned. He
grieved that any concerns of his should so long have
been an interruption to their business. His anxiety

now was to prevent their further vexation in the matter. The written statement of the sitting members, he went on to say, having been handed to him without any signature, he requested that Wentworth's name might be subscribed to it; and next, that Wentworth might be called upon to avow, upon his reputation in that House, that so much therein as came within his knowledge was true, and the rest he thought so.

Wentworth now saw that he was outwitted by the " sly old fox," as he calls Savile in one of his letters. His policy was delay, but by stating his case in writing, he had put into a feasible shape what the House had to decide. Besides, Savile, by not contesting the case even as so put by his adversary, had barred all further possibility but of immediate decision one way or the other. " Nothing he first doubted less," Eliot remarks, "than admission of his case; supposing the jealousy of his adversary would have made him fight at distance. But he, that was his countryman and equal, seeing the advantage readily, closed presently upon him in that grant, and, by concession of the case, surprised and disarmed him." The upshot of it all was, that after one or two more complicated discussions, the election was declared void, and Fairfax and Wentworth returned to York-shire to try their fortune once more with the electors.

On the 16th of July Wentworth, writing from his seat to Sir Thomas Fairfax at Denton, tells him that the day of their election is fixed for the 1st August,

Q

on which day the Parliament would re-assemble at
Oxford. He says it should be handsomely infused
into the gentry how much it concerned them to maintain their own act, and that the whole kingdom looked
not only whether Sir John be able to carry it against
Fairfax and himself, but indeed against all the gentlemen besides. He proposes that. they should join
their forces at Tadcaster, and concludes: " The freeholders must be thoroughly dealt with, not to stir
out of York before they be polled. It were very fit,
in my opinion, that two hogsheads of wine and half
a score of beer were laid in within the Castle, for the
freeholders, who will be forced to stay long, to refresh
themselves with this hot season."

The same candidates were successful, as appears by
an entry on the Commons' Journals that on the 8th
August they again took their seats for Yorkshire.
Their triumph was very short-lived; for the King,
finding the present Parliament by no means inclined to
favour his schemes, abruptly dissolved it on the 12th.
This movement was followed up by an ingenious
device, the exclusive merit of which belonged to the
Duke of Buckingham. Wentworth and others, the
principal leaders of the popular party, unexpectedly
found themselves pricked for Sheriffs of their respective counties, and so were debarred from serving
in the Parliament which was shortly afterwards called
together. Sir Arthur Ingram, writing to the new
High Sheriff in November, says, "Noble Sir, God

give you joy, you are now the great officer of York-shire; but you had the endeavours of your poor friend to have prevented it. But I think, if all the Council that was at Court had joined together in request for you, it would not have prevailed. . . . . For your being chosen, my poor opinion is, that there did not anything befall you in the whole course of your life, that is, and will be more honour to you in the public, who speak most strangely of it. There is now no more to say to it, but to undergo it cheerfully."

To Sir Christopher Wandesford Wentworth thus discloses himself: "As concerning the future election, I have thoroughly weighed all the circumstances, and find in my judgment Sir John Savile stronger than formerly. For, besides his own number most assured unto him at the last, it will be impossible to draw so great a part from him out of this country—nay, I fear not possible to keep them at home. Besides, it is to be doubted, except Sir William Constable stand, a great part of the East Riding will voice with Savile, in opposition of the President, whom they persuade themselves he would question in Parliament; so as where the hazard is so great, augmented too by reason you have not had as yet the means to be known hereabouts, I should not counsel you in the quality of so dear a friend as you are to me, if I should persuade you other than altogether to desist for to declare yourself at this time. Yet, I confess, I wish Old

*Hooley** were put to it, so it were not at your cost, out of the interest only I protest, which I conceive the gentry have in it. Now, as that noble Baronet of the East hath declared himself to you, so hath Sir Francis Wortley to me, that he intends to stand: from which good purpose I did not study his conversion; for, I foresaw if he gained it, Savile were lost for ever; and if he failed, the other got no conquest much to brag of; besides, being his countryman, these parts would be more easily drawn with him than a stranger, and consequently more weaken the old fox in his own earth, than any other I can think of. So as conjunction between them would, in my opinion, most strain him, and betwixt them be easily embraced upon the first motion, as I persuade myself: so as I will give my neighbour a touch of what I hear of Sir William Constable's intention. In which choice, albeit there is no great good, the harm is the less, in regard those few good Parliament men we have will all be returned burgesses; and that Sir Thomas Hobby will be sure, however, to be mindful of the great man. Thus shall we at ease see the skirmish beat upon other men's shoulders, the sweat and difficulty of their labour work towards our ends, and yourself in a season of more advantage (when you shall have gained by your service that as a merit, which these men compass by their alliance) carry the place with much more

---

* An allusion to Sir John Savile's place of abode, Howley, which is pronounced in that manner.

honour and safety. For, if Sir John be put by again this time, it will be, without fail, a work of an easy wit, to make you one the next Parliament after this, whensoever it happens. Neglect not your means, I pray you, in no case for Richmond, wherein if the Sheriff can any ways further you, I persuade myself you have him sure on your side. But if you should chance to miss, you may be sure I would strain all the points of my hose before you wanted a place, albeit it were with the exclusion of the Bull Segg, you know whom I mean. And, in good faith, so stands the case that I cannot provide you both, and therefore let me not be put to it, except of necessity."*

About the time of the dissolution of the last Parliament at Oxford, the Duke of Buckingham made advances to Wentworth, and assured him of his good esteem and favour. Wentworth, on his part, expressed himself ready to serve the Duke in the quality of an honest man and a gentleman. However, in spite of these overtures made him, he found himself pricked for Sheriff the next year, as we have seen. The Duke assured him afterwards that it was done without his knowledge, as he was in Holland at the time. Wentworth had certainly faith in Buckingham's professions, or he would hardly have made the following request :—

. SIR THOMAS WENTWORTH TO LORD CONWAY.

"My much-honored Lorde,

"The duties of the place I now hold, not ad-

* *Strafford Despatches*, Vol. I.

mitting my absence out of thes parttes, I shallbe bold
to trouble your lo^p wth a few lines, wheras otherwayes I
would have attended you in person.   Ther is a stronge
and generall beleefe wth us hear, that my Lord Scroope*
purposeth to leave the Presidentshippe of Yorke;
whearupon many of my frendes have earnestly moved
me to use sum meanes to procure itt, and I have att
last yealded to take itt a little into consideration, more
to complye wth them, then out of any violentt, or inor-
dinate desire therunto in my self: yet as on the one
side, I have never thought of itt, unlesse itt might be
effected wth the good liking of my Lord Scroope; soe
will I never move further in itt, till I knowe allsoe how
this sute may please my Lord of Buckingham, seeing
indeed such a seale of his graciouse good opinion would
comfortt me much, make the place more acceptable;
and that I am fully resolved, not to ascende one steppe
in this kinde except I may take alonge wth me by the
way a spetiall obligation to my Lord Duke, from whose
bowntye and goodnesse I doe nott only acknowledge
much allready; but iustified in the truthe of my owne
hartte, doe still repose and rest under the shadow and
protection of his favoure.   I beseeche your Lo^p therefore
be pleased to take sum good oportunity fully to acquainte
his Grace hearwth, and then to voutchsafe, (wth your accustomed freedom and noblenesse) to give me your coun-

---

* Emanuel, the eleventh and last Baron Scrope, was made
President of the North in 1619. In June, 1627, he was created
Earl of Sunderland, and died the same year.

sell and direction, wch I am prepaired strictly to observe, as one allbeitt chearfully imbracing better meanes to doe his Matie humble and faithfull service in thes parttes whear I live; yet can wth as well a contented minde rest wher I am, if by reason of my many imperfections I shall not be iudged capable of nearer imploymentt and trust. Ther is nothing more to adde for the pre-sentt, save that I must rest much bounden unto your Lo^p, for the light I shall borrow from your iudgmentt, and affection hearin, and soe borrowe itt too, as may better inable me more effectually to exspresse my self hearafter.

"Your lo^{ps} most humble and affectionate
kinsman to be commaunded,
"T. WENTWORTH.
"Wentworth this 20th of January 1625(-6)."*

This application was not successful. The favourite felt more secure of his position now that the Parliament was dispersed; and he perhaps thought that Wentworth's friendship would be more disastrous to him than his enmity. Indeed, he converted him soon afterwards into an open foe by striking a blow which was witnessed by all Yorkshire. Even as he sat in public court as Sheriff, a writ was put into his hands removing from him the office of Custos Rotulorum, and giving it back to his old opponent, Sir John Savile. "I could wish," he exclaimed to his countrymen who observed this insult, "they had forborne this service

* Domestic—Charles I., Vol. XVIII.

this time : a place in sooth ill-chosen, a stage ill-pre-
pared, for venting such poor, vain, insulting humour!
Nevertheless, since they will needs thus weakly breathe
upon me a seeming disgrace in the public face of my
country, I shall crave leave to wipe it away as openly,
as easily ! Therefore, shame be from henceforth to
them that deserve it."

For some time after this, Wentworth seems to have
led a quiet country life, patiently awaiting the next
Parliament. But he had not to wait so long for an
opportunity of placing himself in open antagonism to
the Court. During the year 1626, the proclamation
went forth for a general forced loan. A sudden exi-
gence was pleaded, and a promise given not only that
the present measure should not be drawn into a prece-
dent, but that a Parliament should be called as soon as
possible, and repayment made out of the first voted
subsidies, of all that was now advanced. Commissioners
were named in every county, with direction to take the
last subsidy-book for their guide, exacting from each
person in that precise ratio, and with a commission
almost unlimited to deal with the refractory. The
remonstrances which this method of raising money
drew from all parts of the country is a subject of common
history, and we need give no further illustration of the
matter than the following report from the Yorkshire
Commissioners* to the Privy Council :—

* The following is a complete list of them : The Lord President of the North (Lord Scrope) ; the Earl of Cumberland, Sir

"Right Honourable, according to the purport of your honourable Lettres to us and others directed to call before us some who refused or did not readilye contribute to his Majesties occasions by the late Loane according to his Maties Commission and Instructions, whose names wee had sent in a list with your lettres from the Board with direction to treat with them to expedite that busynes, or to take them bound to appeare before your Lordshipps; we sent particular lettres to everye person in that list to be before us att Yorke this day, where divers appeared and were persuaded to pay, some were out of the countrye, and divers others made severall aunsweares, whose particular aunsweares paymentes and defaultes wee send in a schedule herewithall, subscribed under theire severall names, which is all the satisfaction wee cann effect att this present, wherefore leaving them and our indeavours therein to your Lordships consideration wee take leave and alwayes rest, &c.

"H. SAVILE.

"W. ELLIS.   JO. LOWTHER.

"Att Yorke this 29th of May 1627."

To this is attached the following schedule:—

Thomas Wentworth, Bart.; Sir Henry Savile, Bart.; Sir Richard Tempest, Sir Richard Darley, Sir Thomas Norcliffe, High Sheriff, Sir Christopher Hillyard, Sir Richard Beaumont, Sir Edward Stanhope, Sir Thomas Fairfax, of Denton, Sir Ferdinando Fairfax, Sir John Lowther, and Sir William Ellis (two of the learned Council), knights; William Mallory, and John Kaye, Esquires.

"West Rydding—Ebor:

Sir John Wood of Beeston,* knight, in lands 13*l.* 6 8

    He received our letters and appeares not.

Henry Savile of Skircotte, in lands 2*l.* 0 0

    He hath payde.

Jervase Hatefeild of Stanley, in lands 3*l.* 0 0

    He hath payde.

Arthure Pilkinton of the same, Esquire in

    lands 6*l.* 13 4

    He received our lettres but appeares not.

Sir Thomas Wentworth of Wentworth

    Knight and Baronett in lands........ 40*l.* 0 0

    He hath made aunsweare unto us by

      letters which we have herewith

      sent in the packett.

Sir Edward Osburne, † Knight and Baronett,

    in lands 25*l.* 0 0

---

* He was descended, according to Hopkinson, from a family of that name in Cambridgeshire, and held considerable lands in the county. These he sold, and purchased with the proceeds the manor of Beeston, near Leeds, of Ralph Beeston, Esq. He lived there, and was Justice of the Peace and Treasurer for lame soldiers in the West Riding] of Yorkshire in the 18th year of King James. His third son, Thomas, who succeeded to the estates, was twice married, and had two daughters, who died without issue. "Thomas Wood, of Beeston, Esq.," figured among the Royalists who had to compound for their estates. According to the petition he presents, he was "misled" into accepting the captaincy of a troop, and only remained in the service one month. His estate was valued at 120*l.* per annum; his fine was 120*l.*

† Of Kiveton, grandson of Sir Edward Osborne, Lord Mayor of London in 1582, son of Sir Hewit, knighted by the Earl of Essex in Ireland in 1599, and father of the first Duke of

He is not in the Countrye, for that our
    lettres could not be delivered to
    him.

Sir Francis Fouliamb,* bart.; in lands 25*l.* 0 0
    He hath received our lettres but ap-
    peares not.

Richard Burrowes of Tinslawe in goods ... 5*l.* 0 0
    He hath received our lettres but ap-
    peares not.

William Viccars of Scawsbye, in goods ... 10*l.* 0 0
    He hathe nowe payde.

George French of Stainton, in lands......... 3*l.* 0 0
    He is verye poore and wee suppose not
      able to pay.

Leeds. He was created a baronet in July, 1620, and in 1629
was appointed Vice-President of the North under the Earl of
Strafford. He took an active part for the King in the Civil
Wars, and is thus reported upon by the commissioners for
compounding with the estates of delinquents :—" Sir Edward
Osborne of Kiveton was a Commissioner for leavying moneyes
to maintaine y° forces raysed against the parliament. Hee
render'd in November 1645. His estate in fee in possession per
ann. 578*l.* Alsoe a Rectory in fee per annum 100*l.* For his
wives life per annum 293*l.* 13s. 4d. for which his fine at a tenth
is 1649*l.* But if hee settle the Rectory of Seaton Rosse valued
at 100*l.* per annum upon the minister there and his successors
for ever, then to be abated 1000*l.* and the fine to remaine 649*l.*
If but 50*l.* per annum then 500*l.* to bee abated."

    * Foljambe, of Walton, Derbyshire, and Aldwarke, co. York.
He was created a baronet in July, 1622 ; was High Sheriff of
Derbyshire in 1633. He married first, Elizabeth, daughter of
Sir William Wray, of Glentworth, in Lincolnshire, who bore
him a daughter, whom he disclaimed ; secondly, Elizabeth,
daughter of Sir George Reresby, of Thribergh, by whom he
had no issue. Sir Francis sold the lordship of Walton to Sir

Francis Stevenson of Wadworth, in goods.   3*l.*   0   0

     He hath nowe payde.

Richard Scott of Ecclesfeild in lands 4*l.*   0   0

     He showeth his Maties Privye seale for

        10*l.* by him lent, dated the 14th

        of Aprill 1626, and thinketh that

        his Maties instructions will there-

        fore discharge him of this, and

        offereth to pay if your Lordships

        will not allowe thereof.

Thomas Wormeley of Sprodbrough in lands   6*l.*   0   0

     He hath now payde.

William Rowse of Haughton parva in goods   3*l.*   0   0

     He payd 20s. elswhere as a Bearer and

        hath nowe payd to this Collector

        20s. more.

Sir Francis Wortley, knight and bar. in lands 30*l.*   0   0

     He is not in the Countrye and sayd to

        be att London.

Robert Rockley, of Rockley, Esq.,* in lands   9*l.*   0   0

     He showeth his Maties privye seale for

        13*l.* 6s. 8d. lent by him, dated the

        14th of April 1626, and thinketh

Arthur Ingram, who demolished the house there. He died at
Bath in December, 1640.

   * Son and heir of Gervase; was Justice of the Peace and
Treasurer for lame soldiers in the West Riding, the eighth year
of the reign of Charles I., and a deputy-lieutenant. He had a
numerous family; Thomas, his eldest son, who was captain of
a troop of horse in Ireland, died unmarried. Francis, who succeeded to the estate, was a fellow of University College, Oxford.

that his Maties instructions will
therefore discharge him of this,
and offereth to pay if your Lordships will not allowe thereof.

Robert Bladwin, of Himsworth, in lands... 3*l.* 0 0
 He is not in the Countrye, and sayd
  to be att London.

Sir Richard Saltonstall of Huntwicke,*
 knight, in lands 13*l.* 6 8
 He is not in the Countrye, but said to
  be att London.

George Ward, of Upton, in goods 3*l.* 0 0
 He received our lettres, but appeares
  not.

William Stable of Allerton per aquam, in
 lands..................................... 2*l.* 0 0
 He did appeare before us, but refused
  to pay the money, or to enter bond
  to appeare before the Lordes.

James Murgetroyde of Morton in lands..... 1*l.* 10 0
 He hath payde 6*l.* in another weapon-

---

* Huntwick Grange, in the parish of Wragby; son and heir
of Samuel Saltonstall. He was a Justice of the Peace and Treasurer for lame soldiers in the first year of King Charles; married Grace, daughter of Robert Kaye, of Woodsome, Esq., and
had several sons and daughters. After his wife's death, says
Hopkinson, "he sold his lands and went with his children into
New England where he lived and (as was said) married the
daughter of the Lord Delaware, and in the troublesome times
came into England and resided at London." Some of his
descendants lived at Rogerthorpe, in the wapentake of Os-
goldcross.

take and therefore not to be
charged with this.

Wydowe Thompson of Oshald in lands ... 3*l* 6s. 8d.
    She received our lettres and appeares
    not.

Sir Edward Stanhope of Grimston,* knight,
    in lands................................... 20*l*. 0 0
    He annsweareth by his lettres that the
      money is alreadye sent upp to
      London and doubteth not but that
      itt is before this time paid.

George Shillitoe of Scacroft, Esq.,† in
    lands 10*l*. 0 0

George Broadbelt of Alwoodley, in goods.. 3*l*. 0 0
    These were in the List sent downe sayd
      to be in London, and still there
      remayne, not being in the Coun-
      trye, for any thing wee knowe."

Enclosed with the report is the letter of Sir Thomas
Wentworth therein alluded to; it runs thus:—

SIR THOMAS WENTWORTH TO THE COMMISSIONERS.

"May itt please you. I have to day receaved your
letter, dated the tenthe of this instant: whearin I am
required to be with you att Yorke, on tuesday next;
the occasion is as I perceave, concerning the late loan
to his Matie by me as yet unpaid. I should precisely

---

  * Near Tadcaster. He was Knight of the Bath, Justice of the
Peace, and High Sheriff in the 14th year of King James.
  † Late of Heath, see p. 213.

have observed your time, if infirme bodyes weare as
readye ministers of the minde, as pens, out of which
reason I trust, my absence willbe rightly interpreted,
and held excused by you. This gentle proceeding of
the Lordes of the Counsell (whear they might have
sent for me up by Pursevant) I humbly acknowledge;
and therfore to apply myself unto ther commaunds in
the dutifullest manner, I shall desire, that with your
good leaves, I may present my own answeare att the
borde, which I will hearby by Gods helpe undertake to
performe, in as short a space, as the moderate care of
my healthe will well admitt, and ease you therby of
any further trouble or burthen. But if itt soe fall
forth, as you shall not thinke good to grant me this
request, I will then waite upon you before the end of
tho weeke, allbeitt I be carried in a litter. Thus
desiring to understande by the bearer your good
pleasure hearin I rest.

    "Your very affectionate freinde

       " T. WENTWORTH.

 " Thornhill, this 27ᵗʰ of May, 1627.

   "To my Honorable good and much respected
    freindes, Sir Henry Savile, Barronet, Sir Tho.
    Fairfaxe, Sir Wm. Ellis, Knights and Wm.
    Mallorye, Esquier, att Yorke."*

The conciliatory tone of the letter just quoted would
lead one to expect that Wentworth meant to comply with
the demand made upon him. But he shortly afterwards

   * Domestic—Charles I., Vol. LXV.

courteously, but determinedly, refused to contribute.
For this act he was committed to the Marshalsea
Prison for a time, and afterwards remitted to detention
at Dartford in Kent, and its vicinity.

In the meantime his old rival, Sir John Savile, was
rapidly rising into the favour of the ruling powers, and
seems to have become quite a skilled courtier.   So
confident was he of his present influence with the
Duke of Buckingham, that upon the death, just at this
period, of Sir John Suckling, Comptroller of the
King's Household, he addressed his Grace in the following terms, beseeching his appointment to that office :—

SIR JOHN SAVILE TO THE DUKE OF BUCKINGHAM.

"May it please your grace,—I have received advertisement from my sonne of the death of Mr. Comptroller,
and cannot but a litle augnowledge my owne un-
fortunatenes, to be absent at this time, yet I do the
less doupt anie misfortune by it when I consider the
noble opinion I iustlie ought to have of your graces
honorable dealing wth your true frendes, and particu-
larlie wth myself.   And in troth my lord I must ever
reckon my self amongst the number of your truest
servantes; whilst I am conscious to my self y^t I beare
as unfeigned, constant, & reall a hart unto your
grace against all the world, as anie man in it, wch I
assure my self will now plead for me to your grace, in
my owne absence, wthout anie further outward pro-
testations at wch I never was cunning : and the rather
in regard my absence, is now occasioned by his Maties

most especiall service; for having procured all this
Countrie to subscribe, I was desirous (y^t I might give
a more effectuall accompt of this service to your grace
than everie bodie did) to see the money paid allso &
returned into the exchequer before I myself parted
from hence; wch will by the next weeke be accom-
plished; I have allso sitten a commission for the dis-
forresting of Dichmarch, & compounding with the
tenantes, a matter of much importance to his Maties
revenew, lastlie I have taken some paines for the sending away these souldiers wch are to go from hence, to
see them well apparailed, well chosen, well provided for
by the Countrie, so as they may be an example hereafter
to other shires, for 100 of these are in service worth
200 of such as are ordinarily pressed, commonlie the
scumme & dregges of the people; this accompt I
thought fitt to give your grace of my absence,
hetherto, lest my owne ease might be pretended, and
this request (for the Comptrolle's staff) I presume to
make unto your grace, as beleiving it verie fitt for me,
& ever whilst I shall be able to beare it, my continuall
desire shall be to deserve it & then rest.

" Your graces ever faithful & contented Servant

" John Savile.

" Haigh hall this 4th of April 1627.

" To the illustrious & excellent Prince &c."*

Buckingham lent a more gracious ear to Savile's
request than he did to the one preferred a few months

* Domestic—Charles I., Vol. LIX.

R

before by Wentworth; for shortly after the date of this letter, it is announced that Sir John Savile has been formally installed as Comptroller of the Household.

None of the indignities heaped upon Wentworth, in these two or three years—the loan, his imprisonment, his forced seclusion from the last Parliament, nor this last preferment of his old rival—seems to have touched him so nearly as the insult put upon him by Buckingham in his own county. Even in the open court-house, as we have seen, whilst attending to his Sheriff's duties, "amid," to use his own expression, "justices, escheators, juries, bankrupts, thieves, and such kind of cattle," an ancient Yorkshire dignity was taken from him to be conferred on Savile. He saw that he could only rise to power when the power of Buckingham should be broken, and he determined at once and finally to avenge himself upon the Court. An opportunity was soon afforded him by the issuing of writs for a third Parliament early in 1628. He pitted himself once more against Sir John Savile on the hustings at York, and beat him, backed though Savile was by local interest of unexampled strength, and by all the powers of the northern presidency employed without scruple. A petition, as usual, was presented against him; and the principal question raised in it was, whether claimants to vote who refused to declare their names were not thereby disabled to be electors. It appeared that during the days of the election men presented themselves at York, who, having braved the displeasure of the officers of the northern presidency in refusing to vote for the Saviles, had, at the polling-booths, after offering proof of their possession of forty-shilling freeholds, of their residency, and of their not having before polled, refused to give their names. Their votes were nevertheless held good, on the ground that, as it might be inconvenient to have them set down their names, "because notice might be taken of them to their prejudice," it was not necessary to insert the names in the indenture. Sir Henry Bellasis was the other representative of the county.

Neither through the stormy session of this Parliament nor indeed through his subsequent career do I propose to follow Wentworth. His vigorous support of the Petition of Right, and his sudden transformation into the King's most ardent adherent, are too much matters of universal knowledge to be enlarged upon in a work which endeavours to trace out the more forgotten bye-paths of history.

It is somewhat remarkable that the two old Yorkshire rivals received their grants of baronies upon the same day—namely, the 21st July, 1628. Shortly afterwards Wentworth received his patent as Lord President of the North, and from that time forth bent his wonderful genius to the oppression of the people for whose rights he had just ceased to fight. "A man," exclaimed Pym, on his impeachment, "of great parts and contrivance, and of great industry to bring what he designed to pass; a man who in the memory of many present had sat in that House an earnest vindicator of the laws, and a most zealous assertor and champion for the liberties of the people ; but who long since had turned apostate from those good affections, and, according to the custom and nature of apostates, was become the greatest promoter of tyranny that any age had produced."*

SIR HENRY SAVILE TO LORD WENTWORTH.

" My Honourable good Lord,

" Your Lordship hath now, by your own great Merit, no less than by the gracious Favour and good Opinion of your Sovereign, completed the highest Pitch of northern Honour, which no Man wishes may longer continue yours than myself, who have never been revered other than yours. I hear your Lordship will shortly make your Entry into York, the Seat of your Government, and, to that End, I may not fail according to my Duty to attend you, I desire to know your Lordship's Time. And withal, I have

* " Strafford's first inclinations and addresses to the court were only to establish his greatness in the country, where he apprehended some acts of power from the lord Savile, who had been his rival always there, and of late, had strengthened himself by being made a Privy Councillor and officer at court : but his first attempts were so prosperous, that he contented not himself with being secure from that lord's power in the country, but rested not until he had bereaved him of all power and place at court ; and so sent him down a most abject and disconsolate old man into his country, where he was to have the superintending over him, by getting himself at that time made Lord President of the North."—Clarendon's *History of the Rebellion.*

thought it Part of the same to acquaint your Lordship, that I know not well how far I may be induced by the Persuasions of some Well-willers to go up to this Parliament for the County; and to enter. upon your Lordship's Remains without your Privity were, in some Measure, to injure the Love and Service I owe you. What I shall resolve in the Business depends rather of my Friends than myself. My Motives are, Hope of better and more free Times; a Desire to see my honourable Friends in the South, from whom I have been long absent, and may well be forgotten, if I return not thither in some reasonable Time; a Desire to keep this Honour deposited for this Time in that Name, which hath often enjoyed it, until your Lordship's Nephew and my young Cousin Sir William* be more capable thereof. For, my Ambitions as they are not easily kindled, so care I not how soon they are quenched; a private Life being most suitable to my natural Disposition, and best agreeing with a Body too subject to Infirmities and Indisposition of Health. And I have most Reason of all, in this very Season to fear myself, who am constantly taken with the Gout at or after Christmas infallibly, and so have been for divers Years last past. So what may be the Issue of this Conceit rests in his Hands, that is the Disposer of Health and

---

* Savile, of Thornhill, whose father, Sir George, married Wentworth's sister. He was returned for the county in 1640; was colonel of a regiment of foot raised for the King in the wapentake of Agbrigg and Morley; and then Governor of York, where he died.

Sickness at his Pleasure. The last of my Motives is an Ambition to serve my Country with a good Heart, which must serve to supply all other Defects in a Man not qualified for such an Assembly. The Day for the Election, some say, is the Monday after Twelfth-Tide, which is sooner than I expected. My Opinion was, that the House must first sit before any authentic Notice could be taken of your Lordship's Remove; yet on the other Side your Lordship's Great Seals of Several Kinds, are signal Demonstrations thereof, and properly called Patents, which may alter the case. So, desiring by this Bearer to hear of your Lordship's Welfare and further Pleasure, I rest ever

" Your Lordship's

"Humbly to be commanded,

"H. SAVILE.*

" Methely, Dec. 23, 1628."

---

* *Strafford Despatches*, Vol. I. Another letter to Wentworth from the same correspondent is also printed there, referring to the election in the spring of the year. It is dated 12th March, 1627-8. Sir Henry says, " I could do no less than congratulate with you in your triumph even over my own great kinsman, of whom, for anything I can hear, you and your company made small reckonings by your usage of him on all sides. He sent divers particular messengers, as namely his son Bland, and others to see whether I was ill of the gout in good earnest, and sent me word that howsoever it was a good excuse. I hear the city murmurs and petitions against the son's election. If we be cast out both of town and country, in good faith our case will be lamentable, and I fear without your pity." By the " we " of the last sentence are meant, of course, Sir John Savile and Sir Thomas, his son, who contested the county and city of York respectively. Sir Thomas was returned for the city with Sir Arthur Ingram, but was dislodged on petition by Alderman

John, Lord Savile, died 31st Aug., 1630, and was buried at Batley. There was an inquisition of his estates after his death, taken at Leeds on the 31st March, 1631. The jurors—John Midgley, John Harrison, Benjamin Wade, Francis Jackson, Alexander Metcalfe, George Killingbeck, William Simpson, gentlemen, and others—certified that he held the manors of Headingley, Burley, Morley, East Ardsley, West Ardsley, Woodchurch, and Gildersome, with their appurtenances; also that part of the manor of "Christal *alias* Kirstall," which lies on the north bank of the river Aire; also the capital messuages, Howley Hall, Haigh Hall, Finchden, Scolecroft, with all lands, tenements, and hereditaments thereto belonging; also, certain lands known by the name of the New Park of Wakefield, situate in the several parishes, towns and places of Wakefield, Dewsbury, Alverthorpe and Ossett, &c., &c.; the Rectory of Woodchurch; " a Fabrica ferraria, *Anglicé*, the Iron forge," at Kirkstall, with the buildings, &c., flood-gates and streams, connected with the said forge, Savile also held six corn-mills and one fulling-mill in connection with his several manors.

Wentworth was appointed Deputy and Governor of Ireland on the 12th January, 1632-3. Two letters of

Hoyle, by a resolution of the House of the 23rd April, 1628. "Son Bland" was Sir Thomas Bland, of Kippax-park, who married Katherine, daughter of Sir John Savile, of Howley. Sir Henry Savile represented the county in this Parliament. He died in 1632, aged 53. His children, all having died young, he was succeeded at Methley by his brother John.

his are here appended, written during his Presidency at York, which will bear comparison with the best of the compositions of that character. The first describes the course of an epidemical disease which, breaking out simultaneously in Lancashire, and, in a severer form, in Lincolnshire, approached York on both sides, and ultimately attacked the suburbs of the city. The second letter is in every way valuable. The definiteness, force, and even, in a certain sense, the grandeur of Wentworth's character, never appear so striking as in his professions of devotion to kingly authority, and the scorn with which he treats opponents.*

LORD WENTWORTH TO VISCOUNT DORCHESTER.

"My very good Lord,

"It is full time in my iudgment to give your Lo^p a shortt accompt of our presentt condition in thes parttes, wch as it shall seeme good in your better wisedum, may be made knowen to his Ma^{ty}, or my Lords of the Counsell in case you would directte us, any thing more to be dun then is allready.

"True itt is (that leaving our neigboures of Lancishire and Lincolnshire miserably distressed with the pestilence) that now wthin thes sixe weeks, the infection is cumd to our selves in divers partts of this County, and last of all into this Citty. Upon the edge of Lancishire, ther is the toune of Heptonstall,

---

* See the late Mr. John Bruce's Preface to the Calendar of Domestic State Papers of Charles I., 1631–3—from whence the modernised version of the second letter has been taken.

wch hath neare forty howses infected ; Mirfeild a little
toune not farre of itt, hath lost ninescore persons, and
both thes tounes wthin four miles of Hallifax, wch yet
God be praysed, stands sownde, but much indangered,
by reason of the great number of people, and lardge
wade of clothing theraboutes.   It is likwise in the
tow tounes of Beeston and Holbecke, wch are wthin
one mile of Leedes, and if it should please God to
visit either of thos greate tounes, Hallifax or Leedes,
wch tow allone trade more then all the cuntry besides,
in good faithe it would mightily distresse and im-
poverishe all that side of the Cuntrye.

   " Againe on this side, ther is the toune of Rednes,
and Armin, both seated upon this river, furiously infected, at the least fourscore howses infected, and a
hundreth persons deade within thes five weekes, besides sum four or five little villages besides; this
being brought to us forth of Lincolnshire, as on the
other parte it was forth of Lancishire, and of the tow
is observed to be much more taking and deadly.

   " Finally, it was brought heather by a lewde
woman who brake forth of Armin, wth the sore running
upon her, lodged in an outside of the toune and ther
ungratiously left itt behinde her ; sinc ther are deade
in that street sum fourscore persons, and hath not as
yet God be praysed gott wthin the walls, saving in tow
howses, forth of wch all the dwellers are removed to the
Pesthowses ; but is broken forth wthout the walls at
tow other ends of the toune, and into Huntington.

and Acam, tow little villadgs w^{th}in tow miles of us. Thus wee stande expecting what God will doe for us, I trust we are yet safe w^{th}in the toune, and that winter cumming one wee may by Gods blessing recover ourselves; The toune takes much comfortt in our stay heare, and would fall into affrights and confusion if wee should leave them, soe as wee as yet hold on our ordinary sitting, and we dispence of his Maties accustomed justice to his people; and in good faithe, I should for my partte bé very loathe to leave them in this distressed case, seeing they conceave they are much the better for my stay amongst them, and that intruthe I thinke they are now much more orderly then they would be under the government of the Maior alóne.

" All the meanes wee can thinke of have been used to preventt the spredding of itt, by inhibiting all the publicke faires hearabouts, wch might drawe a concourse of people togeither; our watches are very well and strickly keept in every place; all passadges betwixt us and Lincolnshire by water stopped as much as may be, to the intent that cumming by lande they may be a little better aired before they cum into any partt of this County; and the visited persons well provided not only for the necessities of nature, but of all such druggs and other medecins as the Phisitions advise to be good to preventt and correctt the malignity of this contagion, soe as the better halfe of thos that have had itt in this toune, is, thanks be to god, escaped.

"I feare I growe troublesum, but I am more particulare in my relation, that knowing the truthe of our case wee may by your Lo^{ps} meanes, be bettered by the wisedum of his Ma^{ty} and the lords, if ther be any other thinge wch they shall commaunde for our good or greater safety, amidst soe much danger. My lord, the uttermost of the paines I will give you for the presentt, shall be only to write myself

"Your Lo^{ps} very humble servantt,

"WENTWORTH.

"Yorke this 22th of Septemb. 1631.

"Even now they bring me worde of the plague broken forthe in another little toune tow miles of."*

LORD WENTWORTH TO THE EARL OF CARLISLE.

"My very good Lord,—The excess of your favour in sending your footman so long and wearisome a journey, I must acknowledge, and contemplate your Lordship's nobleness to your absent servants so truly and so thankfully as to keep myself in an equal temper (wherever God and his Majesty shall bestow me), to receive your commands with all cheerfulness, and to fulfil them with all readiness and care. That his Majesty rests satisfied in the course I hold in this Government, is my chiefest exaltation before men, and my fullest contentment in my inmost retirements. And, surely, I will never omit continually to serve him his own way, where I once understand it, and where that beam leaves me, serve him the most

Domestic—Charles I., Vol. CC.

profitable way the dimmer lights of my own judgment shall, by any means, be able to lead me unto.
In this truth I will live and die; all the devils of hell,
all their ministers on earth, shall never be able to
impeach or shake it.

"For Sir David Foulis, the unfortunate subject of
part of my letters of late, when I consider him as a
gentleman that hath received some respects from me,
never the least injury, I pity him; when I consider
him your Lordship's kinsman, in that relation I am
heartily sorry for him, and for myself too, that being
so cordially an honourer of yours and all that depend
on you, should thus misadventurously light upon a
man that hath of your blood running in his veins, yet
cannot, without much comfort in myself, without
much injury to you, but observe the vigour of your
respect towards me, in thus passing him over to a
course of justice, which liberty you bestow upon me,
and which I will nevertheless exercise with such
modesty and moderation as shall show you that I am
as far from drinking *à la confusion des personnes,* as
the Frenchman the last summer.

"When I read his letter (which of your goodness
is communicated with me), I find that insolent vanity
of his, which hath brought forth all this trouble,
written in capital letters. He saith it was to the
admiration of all men I would not hear him. Alas!
I did hear him, and used him with all civility; but
there was a wonder (catholic enough, indeed,) in all

men, to see him so poorly and meanly humble himself, in the same town where, within a few weeks before, he had as insolently demeaned himself, I dare confidently say, more insolently, than ever any of his Majesty's Council here, and a deputy lieutenant, had done to the President and King's Lieutenant.

"But, good man, here is the jest: he tells us that by taking this business into his own hand, his Majesty shall make a purchase of him; a purchase with a witness! so clogged with wretched, woeful incumbrances as makes it nothing worth. He will lead and persuade others; he will by his example much better the King's service; leaves it to be considered by the best affected how much his disgrace might hurt his Majesty's service.

"Lord, with Æsop's fly upon the axletree of tho wheel, what a dust he makes! Where are those he can lead or persuade? Take him out of the commission of the peace (the instrument of terror by which he pulled them on along with him by the noses), he governed himself with such exact pride and distemper amongst them, that in good faith I verily believe that there are not half a score that would either follow or be persuaded by him. As for his example of life, it was so virtuous, or so vicious, as I believe we might find hundreds scandalled, sooner than one bettered by it. And surely if he leave it to be considered by the best affected, their verdict will be, his Majesty shall contribute more to his own authority by making him an example of his justice, than can possibly be gained by taking him in again. But this is an arrogance grown frequent now-a-days, which I cannot endure.

" Every ordinary man must put himself in balance with the King, as if it were a measuring cast betwixt them who were like to prove the greater losers upon the parting. Let me cast then this grain of truth in, and it shall turn the scale. Silly wretches! Let us not deceive ourselves. The King's service cannot suffer by the disgrace of him, and me, and forty more such. The ground whereupon Government stands will not so easily be washed away, so as the sooner we unfool ourselves of this error, the sooner we shall learn to know ourselves, and shake off that self-pride which hath to our own esteem represented us much bigger, more considerable, than indeed there is cause for.

" But the world will speak of his sufferings, who hath done so much service for the Crown, and that a submission, with a sure promise to amend, will be more honourable. His sufferings are not like to be other than such as shall be measured forth unto him by the equal and straight rule of Justice, and then who can he fault but himself? What he hath merited of the Crown in former times I know not, but I am sure it is visible he hath served himself to a fair fortune by the means of the Crown, and that of late since I came hither, I have heard of many disservices, but not any one service he hath paid back unto the Crown. It is true, indeed, he hath been content to bag up five or six thousand pounds of the King's money, kept it close in his stomach this twenty years, in plain terms cheated the King of it, and now it seems, that spirit being conjured forth of his pocket again, he bound to pay it in hath occasioned all this foul weather which he hath blown upon other the innocent Ministers of his Majesty in other remote quarters, not daring to breathe the least blast of it upon those taller cedars that had so over-looked him as to find him out when he least dreamt of it. And for his sure promise of amends, trust him that list, for he that hath falsified all those great obligations, let himself loose from those strongest bonds of love and thankfulness, I shall never flatter myself to hold him fast by the slippery ties of fear and strained professions ; and so I leave him, and buy or purchase him that lists ; for my part he shall never cost me a farthing or a line more labour. Your Lordship's most faithful, most humble servant,

" WENTWORTH.*

" York, 24th Oct., 1632."

* Wentworth married for his third wife, Elizabeth, daughter of Sir Godfrey Rodes, of Great Houghton. A few letters from him to this lady are in the possession of Lord Houghton, and preserved at Fryston Hall, with many other interesting relics of the Rodes family, of which his Lordship is the representative. Lord Houghton kindly placed a privately printed copy of these letters at the use of the editor of this volume, who takes the opportunity of acknowledging the courtesy. The letters are of a private nature, but a short specimen of them may not be out of place :—

" Sweete Hartte,—I shall doe more for you this morning, then

I could have dun since I was your husbande, write you a letter
from woodhouse ; whether now I am cum in healthe I humbly
praise god, and to the abode of my fathers.   my businesse here
is much and intricate, yet that doth not affright me.   I have
begun and a little paines and patience will sett all I trust. . . .
heare is the hudgest abundance of fruite I ever saw, and veni-
son in abundance ; wee keepe excellent cheare, and have passing
good wine, and that finds Southworth, faithe, he banges it
soundly.

"God allmighty take vs all into his blessed protection, and
send me and this company well at dublin againe.

  " Your very loving husbande,
           " WENTWORTH."

. Lord Houghton thus brings this interesting little collection of
Wentworth papers to a conclusion:—

"There is a letter extant, dated from the Tower, February 4,
1640-1, in which the Earl informs his wife that ' the charge is now
cum inn, and I am now able I prayse God to tell you, that I
conceave there is nothing capitall ; and for the rest I knowe at
the worste, his Ma^ty will pardon all, without hurting my
fortune, and then we shall be happy by God's grace.'   And in
another, dated April 19th, he writes that his trial as to fact is
near at an end, and there remained only matter of law to be
spoken to; that the king continued very gracious to him, and his
friends increased rather than lessened : he concludes by trusting
all will end well, and bidding her be of good cheer.   On the
12th of May he was no more ; but the day before his execution
he solemnly enjoined his son, ' Be sure you give all respect to
my wife, that hath ever bore a great love unto you, and therefore will be well becoming you.'"

CHAPTER V.

TOWNS AND THEIR TRADES.

THE letters and papers which are here collected in order to illustrate this department of our county history, are of too varied a nature to admit of being made any clearer or more connected by means of a general introduction; so it will be better to leave each one to tell its own story. The first contains particulars relating to the town and castle of Scarborough, drawn up about the year 1565 with a view to show the importance of maintaining the pier at that port.

"1. The towne of Skarbroughe is an auncientt and a large towne scituate upon the Sea coste of the Northe este parte of Yorkshier, and at this daye is muche in decaye.

"2. The same towne haithe bene maynteyned heartofore onelie by fishynge.

"3. And for the mayntenance of the fishynge there haithe bene kepte and contynued a peare or keye for the makinge of a haven or harborowe for defence and safetie of Shippes and bootes frome the raging sea, which is theare often so tempestious that no vessell maye abide it, withowte the ayde of the same pere, and especiallie the wynde bearinge este or northeste.

S

"4. The same peare beynge mayntened makithe before the said towne a haven and save harboure for all the fishers and shippes that passe frome Scotland, Barwicke, or Newcastle southwards, and likewise for suche as passe the contrarie waye, and so for all others shippes that be on that costes in any tempest, and withowte the said pere be maynteyned it is thought the fishynge and takynge of the Lyngs and Saltfishe of this coste will muche decaye and be impayred.

"5. Theare is adjoynynge to the same towne an auncientt Castle sett upon a highe hill environed thre partes with the sea, and the fourthe a verie greate and steape hill and within the walle of the same Castle there is by estimation fourtie or fiftie acres of good medowe and pasture, and verie fayre freshe water, and the same is environed so with the Sea that it cannott be entred unto but throughe the castle, and if any shuld take the same beynge once well vitayled that ground woulde kepe Beffe and mutton to revitayle the same for a good nombre of men.

"6. The moste store of this coste, Lynge and Haberdyne * is there made and dried, by reason the Fyshers, straungers and others that fishe in thies northe seas do theare unlade theire fishe new takyn and fishithe agayne of newe once or twise and un-ladith theare before they departe awaye ladyn.

"7. As they alledge, there haithe bene in that towne at once fiftie smalle shipps for fishynge of 20

* *Ling* is a species of cod-fish, *haberdine* is salted cod.

or 30 tonne the pece, wherein weare 16 or 20 men in the pece that traded fishynge, and at this presentt there is but onelie sixe.

" 8. Theare was also as they alledge in that towne crayres * used for merchandise and nowe not past foure, so that bothe their trafficke and fishynge is decayed.

" 9. In the begynnynge of thies late warres abowte 24 yeares paste the Bootes and Shipps of that towne were takyn by th'ennymyes, and the towne as well therbye muche impoverished as also by the mayntennance of the said pere which in that tyme th'ynhabitants of that towne haith sundrye tymes to their great charge repaired, so that nowe by meanes therof they be neyther able to furnyshe y° said towne with shipps and botes nor to repaire and mayntene the said porte.

" 10. The custome of that towne haithe bene for wynes and other merchandise, as they of that towne saithe it will appeare by bokes, fourescore or one hundredth pounds by yeare, and nowe the same is litle or nothynge, for they onelie trade for salte for the saltynge of their fishe, and no other merchaundise comythe thither excepte by chaunce.

" 11. The Inhabitants there is moste maynteyned by fishinge, and by the dryenge and makinge thereof into Saltfishe, so that if the pere be not repaired whiche maynteyneth the fishynge and resorte thider, the towne will shortlie be uninhabited, but when the

* Or *craier*, a kind of small ship.

peare is well maynteyned the fishermen as well
straungers as others when they have takyn good
store of fishe do unlade and sell the same at Skarbroughe once or twise before they carie awaye any.

"12. The Quenes ma^tie haithe for the fee-ferme of
the towne yearelie fourescore and eleven poundes, the
whiche all butt 24*l*. risithe of fishynge.

"13. Her Matie haithe the parsonage per annum
40*l*. the moste commoditie whereof arisithe of tithe
Fishe and offeryngs of the towne.

"14. Her Matie haithe also howses in the towne
perteyned to Abbeys, Colledges and Chauntries by
yeare fiftie pounds.

"15. When any 10th or 15th is graunted the Rate of
that towne is 33*l*. 6s. 8d. for any 10th and 15th.

"16. Her Matie haithe had there yearlie for provision
of her house foure thousand fishe much undre price
that others payeth.

"17. This contrie and many others be there served
of saltfishe.

"18. All the premysses arisithe chieflie upon fishinge,
the whiche cannot there be contynued withowte the
pere be maynteyned, for that the same is in all stormes
and rage the safetie and defence of the Shippes and
Botes.

"19. So that if the pere be decayed and not maynteyned it will not onelie be a greate losse of that
commodious harboure, but a decaye of th'afforsaid
towne and revenewe, and a decaye of fishermen and

marryners, of provision of fishe, and a desolation of the towne and the Castle to serve to no purpose.

"20. The Countrie heare is presentlie so muche to be charged with buyldinge and repayringe of Bridges takyn awaye and brokyn by the late rage of waters wherunto they be bounden by lawe, that their charitie wilbe smale to the Repaire of the pere, wherunto no lawe byndithe theym.

"21. If the quene's Maiestie be not pleaced for the presentt nede to help with some money to repaire the said pere, the Ruyn of that towne and decaye of th'afforsaid commodities is like to ensue.

"22. King Richard the third for the bettre mayntenance of that towne hade incorporated theym, and made a Maior there, and also a Sheriff, and made the towne and liberties a shier of itself.

"23. He had also graunted unto them houldinge of pleas, and libertie to shipp and carie the wolls and shepe fells of Allertonshier, Cleveland, Blakamore, Whitbystrond, Pickerynge, forest of Galtresse, Birdfurthe, Ridale, Pickerynge Lithe, and Hertfurthlithe.

"24. It was thought by us that viewed the pere that the well bestowynge presentlie of one Thowsand pounds at the moste, would make the pere in suche a case as it shulde be like to contynewe forever withowte muche more helpe, but it must be in other sorte made then it nowe is, and withowte any tymbre, but onelie of greate stone to be caried with tonnes. There is stone sufficient verie nyghe to be carried with tonnes at every full water.

"25. The makinge of 20 or 30 tonnes with their Iron worke and the makynge of 2 or 3 stronge wyndlesses and their Iron works wilbe a great charge, and if they had those, the reste of the charges is thought woulde be undre a thowsand pound.

"26. Theare is no kynde of merchandice to be had nyghe unto that towne mete to be shipped frome thence for mayntenance of the towne oneles it shulde be fishe, corne, wolle and fell of shepe for it joynythe to Yokswoalde, Blakamore and Pickeringe lithe, beynge of no great fertillitye.

"27. If the quenes Matie graunte any money to ayde them at this presentt it woulde be putt in the hands of some of creditt and knowledge that shulde se it well bestowed withowte wastinge.

"28. After the pere once repaired, if it woulde pleace her highnes to lett the towne for mayntenance of their pere, have the Parsonages of Skarbroughe and Fylaye in fee-ferme, with such orders as the same and the profitt thereof above the Rentt to her highnes shulde not be mysused nor Imployed to private gayne nor other purpose, but onelie to repaire the pere as nede shall require; it is thought the same shuld not Impayre ye quenes Revenewe nor hereafter charge her Matie and successors, and yett shulde sufficientlie for ever maynteyne the peare, beynge once made, as it nowe is devised and thought mete to be done.

"29. Wheare the same pere is nowe and heretofore haith bene all the owtesides made of tymber framed like two housesides and filled within with stones, and stondithe upright as brode at the topp as at the bothome. So that when the tymber faylythe whiche longe cannott continewe againste the raginge of the sea, then the stones fallithe downe on both sides and so the breake is made.

" 30. Nowe it is thought good to make the pere much broder in the bothome as Twentie yardes brode on the grounde, and at every course to be narrower untill it come to the height, & there to be at the topp at the leaste four or five yeards brode, and so to make it with stone upon stone to the height, muche like the fashion of the Rouffe of a house, and beynge so well layde with greate stones at the owtsides thereof, and well filled with stones in the middeste, It is thought that it can never be moved, nor much impaired by any Rage of water, for the one side will beare so agaynste the other that it will hardlie be removed.

" 31. All suche places of ye pere as yet stondethe may stand still, & have on both sides stones layde therunto of slope, which will cause it stand still, and there is muche stone remaynynge in the places of the breache which maye serve, in the place wheare they lye, and there is stone sufficientt to be had in places adoiynynge.

" 32. The haven within the pere at full water is as they alledge 20 foote water, and if the pere shoulde be made further into the sea as it was begon and mentt to have bene in the tyme of our late Sovereigne Lorde

Kinge Edward the sixte, the haven then within the
pere woulde have bene tenne fathome depthe but that
wilbe the more charges to make the pere in a new
place by reason of removinge the Stones. Butt if it
myght be so made the havyn and pere woulde then
serve any shipp as well at lowe water as at other.

"33. Theare is no other save herborawe betwix
Humber and Tyne but onelie Scarbroughe.

"34. The lengthe of the peere is eighte hundred
foote and the height therof is twentie foote or thereabouts."*

Answer of the Bailiffs and others of Scarborough
to certain Articles concerning the re-edifying of Dover
Pier:—

" First we say that we have no tonnes that we can
fitly spare for we must be forced to make moe this
yeare; but we have willingly sent you the best cowper
we have, named William Newby, and lykewise two of
our best workmen for your purpose, named Henry
Petch and Robert Petch. And also you have alredy
William Forde an other of our best workmen.

" Item.—We say that we have no platt† of our pere
redy at this present to be sent, but the true forme therof
ys thus: First in length yt conteyneth 267 yards; in
bredth at the bottom 20 yards; and at the upper part
or toppe therof 7 yards and a half; in depthnesse, on
the uttermost part therof towards the sea, 10 yards,

* Domestic—Elizabeth, Vol. XXXVIII.   † A map or plan.

and on the ynner syde or part 9 yardes. The founda-
cion of our pere under the sand ys upon claye.

"Item.—We say that said pere hath cost us over
and above the 500*l.* by her Matie gyven, synce the
beginnynge of that work 2000*l.* or more. And the
repayringe therof ys yet yearlye unto us 40*l.* charge
or therabouts, with very small help of the contry
now, or afore.

"Item.—We say that yt ys true that we first proved,
with planked woodworks to make the said pere, and by
experience found that course and cost altogether vayne,
and this of stone to be much better.

"Item.—We say that for the rearinge up of the
lesser stones to the upper part of the work we used a
crayne, with a pare of wyndlesses within yt with a great
rope, and two pare of lesser wyndlesses, and a bridge
made of planks, and therwithall reared the stones up,
as our workmen can more perfitly shew you.

"Item.—We say that some of the rocks which we
fetch with tonnes ar half a myle or therabouts distant
from our said pere, lyinge on the backsyde of the
castle, others of the stones beyng smaller ar brought
on handbarowes, and do lye nere hand on the backsyde
of the pere.

"Item.—We say that the cheif workman for the
settinge of the stones, whom we named the master of
the work, had for his hyre 8d. a tyde, and 16d. a day.

"Item.—We say that sometymes in great stormes,
some brech ys made in the pere, which, with all expedition we presently repare agayne.

" Item.—We say that we receyve to the mantenance of our pere by the name of Jutty monye of every shippe havinge a toppe 12ᵈ, of every crayer 8d., and of every fisherman for the whole yeare, 2s.

" Item.—We say that there ryseth at the sprynge 18 foott water, and at the nepe eleaven foot water. And we have a great seagate in a storme.

" Item.—We say that one pece of our pere laitt bett downe and now builded agayne, conteyninge in length 35 foott, and in depthnesse and bredth as ys aforesaid did amount in charge unto 92*l.* 10s.

> " Neccollas Woollff balleff
> John Fisher Deputye baylyf for Thomas Williamson*
>
> Robart Lacy,   Wylliam Fysher,
> Mathew Pacoke,   Wylliam Conyers,
> George Thomson, Wylliam Pacok.

Endorsed " 8 May, 1584."†

---

* Thomas Williamson was at this time under a cloud, as appears from a paper in the British Museum (Add. MS. 28,223), endorsed " Articles sett downe concernynge Wylliamson by Sir Henry Gate," from which we gather that he was a prisoner in York Castle on a charge of recusancy. One article runs— " Willm. Taylior, curate of Scarbroughe by his letters enformed Sr Henrie Gate as followithe :—That Thomas Williamson being Bailief of Scarbroughe sildome cam to the churche and his wief never . . . . and when any sermon or communyon was in the tyme of his Bailiffwik, he used to shifte himselfe into the countrey the mornynge before." Also " Williamson perswaded a widowe that if shee shuld marry a mynyster shee shuld loose hir creditte." And finally " Williamson hath of late procured his dwellinge upon or nere unto the Sea coast, to no good purpose at all, as yt seemith unto the said Sir Henrie Gates.

THE BAILIFFS, &C., OF SCARBOROUGH TO SIR ROBERT
CECIL.

"To the R. Honorable Sir Roberte Cecill, knight,.
one of Her Ma^{ls} moste Ho: Privie Counsell.

"Humblie besiche your Ho: your poor supplicants.
the Balifs, Burgesses and Comunaltie of her ma^t
towne of Scarborowe; That wheras her ma^{ls} said
towne being greatlie annoyd, impoverished & decaid
by reason of a market latelie erected by Sir Henry
Gate knight disceased, & now contynued by Edward
Gate esqr. sonne & heire of the said Sir Henry at
Seamer being within thre miles of Scarborowe aforesaid, in y^t respecte, for suppressing the said market,
your supplicants did exhibit there bill of complainte
into the Checquer chamber, wherunto the said Sir
Henry answered. And afterwards the cause was by
the R. honorable the Lorde highe threasurer of
England, referred to the determination of the right
Ho: the Earle of Huntington, Lo: President of the
northe partes, and his L. taking paines therin cold
not determyne the same by reason of the deathe
of the said Sir Henry who died the said suyte de--
pendinge. In consideration wherof, & forasmuche as
the artificers of her ma^{ls} said towne ar utterlie decaid

And for that he is a man of a verie shrewde wytte, great
willfullnes and evillie affected in Religion, the said Sir Henry
Gate thinoketh yt necessarie that the same Williamson shuld be
removed from his said dwellinge, and from bearinge any rule as.
Bailif there," &c.

† Domestic—Elizabeth, Vol. CLXX.

by the contynuance of the said market as dothe appere in particularities by certen articles exemplified under the seale of her ma^{te} said towne redye to be shewed.

"Item.—The navigation, pere, & whole force of her ma^{te} said towne dothe utterlie decay by reason of the said markett, notwithstandinge y^t the same is the best harbor for passingers uppon the sea, as also a great helpe unto the cuntrie thereabouts, if the said market were suppressed.

"Item.—The said towne dothe yerelie paie unto her ma^{tie} for fee ferme the annuell rent of foureschore eleven pounds 15s. 8d., over and besides taxes and other benefits accrueing unto her ma^{tye} of great value, wch to satisfie they ar no longer able, excepte the said market maie be suppressed.

"Item.—Heretofore were erected thre severall markets nere to Scarborowe aforesaid, viz. one at Filay, an other at Shierburne and the third at Brompton, every of them being muche furder distant frome her ma^{te} said towne then Seamer ys, as also of lesse nusance to the same, then Seamer ys; And yet in regarde of the maintenance of her ma^{te} said towne, all the said thre severall marketts were suppressed, *anno quadragesimo nuper Regis Henr.* 3.

"Item.—All manner of victualls ar continuallie caried from her ma^{te} said towne to Seamer aforesaide.

"For wch causes & diverse others, your humble supplicants do humble besiche your Ho: to be an honorable meanes y^t the said market maie imediatlie be suppressed, or at the leaste wise that your poor supp^{lts} maie have your Ho: lettres & commission to be directed to the said ho: Earle, to procede to the finall determination of the said cause betwene your supp^{lts} and the said Mr Gate, or els to certifie what his L. dothe fynde to thend your Ho: and others her ma^{ts} moste Ho: privie Counsell maie censure the same. And your humble supp^{lts} shall dalie praie &c.* .

"Reasons to shewe that the market of Seamer is not hurtfull to the Town of Scarb.

"Imprimis—yt is to be proved that the Towne of Scarb. was about 60 yeares agoe inhabited wth 700 houshoulders, and so appearethe by their Records, wherof within 30 yeares folowinge ther were decaied 400, and by the same Record yt is manifest, that ther were in tymes past as many moe buildings w^{th}in the Towne.

"Item; ther hathe bene in Scarb. at once fyftie smale shippes for fishinge & those of 20 and 30 Tunn apeece, wherein were 16 or 20 men, that traded fishinge; and 30 yeares and more before Seamer market was renued, when the survey of the Towne & Castle was taken, ther were but six, wch was in ye 7th yeare of her Ma^{ts} raigne.†

"Item; ther was in the Towne belonginge to ytt, as ys and hathe bene reported by th'auncient men and by

---

* Domestic—Addenda—Elizabeth, Vol. XXXII.
† *i.e.,* the Survey already given at length.

the custam y^t then ye prince had may appeare, 20
crayers for marchantdize, & at the said survey taken
(as aforesaid) ther were but fowre, so as bothe their
trafficke and fyshinge was then decayed.

"Item; the custum the Towne yeilded to the Prince
in those dayes for wines & other marchaundize, as
hathe bene sene by their books amounted sometime to
80*l*. sometime to a 100*l*. by yeare, and now & 20 yeare
before the renuynge of Seamer market yt is litle or
nothinge—for ther speciall trade for these 30 yeares &
more hathe bene for salt and coale and for corne,
wch they cary owt in verie aboundant & to intolerable
measure.

"Th'inhabitants of the Towne of Scarb. when the
merchaunts traded fishinge & other merchauntdize
were mayntayned some by travaile & imploym^t at sea,
some by dryinge & makinge of saltfishe, some by nett-
inge, some by spinninge, some by makinge of ropes &
diverse others by other misteries, all which since they
left the sea and applied themselves to maultinge &
ingrossinge of corne, are mightelie decayed, and the
Towne impoverished almost without hope of recovery.

"Item; th'inhabitants of Scarb. havinge the Towne
in fee ferme at 92*l*. per An. did in those tymes pay the
same or the most therof by the fishinge, and made
great proffits of their grounds and pastures more than
a 100*l*. yearly above the feeferme; beside that the
fermer of the parsonadge ther, beinge of the yearelie
Rent of 40*l*., raysed the most part therof of his tythe

fishe, all wch is now and was 40 yeares before the renewing of Seamer market utterly decayed and raysed
hardly upon the grounds and offerings in and about the
Towne.

" The Towne being thus brought into decay by their
owne insedulity longe before the renewinge of Seamer
market, manie of the best sort of Scarb. gave their
consent undre their hands to Sr Hen: Gate to renue the
market in Seamer, wch was done to thende they might
receave some comfort & reliefe by that market, as indeed thei do.

"Item ; ther are at this daye moe ritche men in
Scarb. then was 30 yeares agoe, wherby yt may appeare that the market in Seamer is more beneficiall,
then hurtfull to them.

"Item ; the poore of Scarb. have secretlie complained to their frendes for their restraint in cominge
to Seamer market for that thei have gayned, some
12d., some 8d. a daie, some more and some lesse accordinge to the quantitie and qualitie of the commodities thei brought to Seamer market by retaylinge
saltfishe, heringe, onyons, salt &c., wch duringe the
suspendinge of Seamer market thei lacked to their
great impoverishinge.

"Item ; the bettre sort y^t came thither to sell other
grocery or mercery wares have confessed that thei have
made great gaine by that market.

" Item ; Many that dwell farre of do come to Seamer
market, wch never did nor ever will come to Scarb. by

whose repaire thinhabitants of Scarb. receave muche benefitt by contractinge ther wth them.

"Item; th'inhabitants aswell of the more as the woulds do repaire in as populous sort to Scarb. as when Seamer market was not renued.

"Item; the commodities w[ch] bothe the wouldes and the mores afford are so plentifullie brought to Scarb. notwithstandinge Seamer market, that oftentimes the countrimen are forced to sett up their corne & somtyme dryven to carry yt home or to the next towne to their great losse, for that the m[rs] of Scarb. have layd paines upon th'inhabts. of Scarb. not to geve them housroome for yt, and have imprisoned some of their neighbors, and taken grievous fines of others for intertayninge the Countrymens commodyties in their howses, w[ch] they could not sell.*

"Reasons shewinge the presente decaye of the Towne of Scarbroughe.

"Imprimis—thei have made a practise to buy houses and pull them downe to sell the slate and timbre to foreine Townes.

"Item; their exactions are so great, that y[e] sett upon suche merchants and fishermen as come in wth any comoditie, that thei have made all seamen weary, w[ch] is done, for that a fewe of them may have the whole trade amonge themselves to sell at what price thei will. By w[ch] meanes bothe Flemings French men Devonshere

* Additional MS. 28,223.

men Cornishe men Dorcetshere men & Sussex men y^t
in tymes past & of late yeares have by a 100 sale (sail)
at once repayred to them have now utterly forsaken
them but in tyme of distresse of wether.

"Item; Wheras they have graunted unto them the
feeferme of the Towne, the fines, amerciaments and
the fees due for anchorage and perage specially for the
maintenance of the peere wch is and hathe beene the
lyfe of ye Towne, the Baylives have divided the same
yearlie amongst themselves & their consorts consult-
ing together to procure some meanes from tyme to
tyme, y^t her ma^tie (as her highness of late yeares hathe
done) and ye country should repaire the same.

"The peere and town of Scarb. was so decayed A° 37
Hen. 8 that y^t was provided for by an act of parliament A° pred., and an order ther sett downe for the
continuance therof, wch thei notwithstanding contynue
not.

"Item; ther was petition made to ye Archb. of
York for releefe to be had of the country for repare of
there pere before Seamer market.

"Item; by petition moved by Sr. H. Gate to her
ma^tie thei were releved from her highnes to the value
of 200l., wch decay grew before Seamer market."*

* Additional MS. 28,223.

T

The Privy Council to the Lord President and Council of the North.

"After our verie hartie commendations to yor good L. and the rest, wee fynde by yor lettre of the 13th of September that you have not been hable to do any thing for the compounding of the difference betwene those of the towne of Scarborough and M^r, Edward Gate, con-cerning the preiudice and hindrance wch those of the said towne do pretend to receyve by the markett established at Seymer, in respect of the absence of Mr Gate out of the contrey. And for that wee have also cause to thinke in regard of his like sudden departure lately also from London, that he doth purposly absent himselfe to the end to avoyde that the matter may not (sic) receyve examynation. And hathe also lately as wee understand, for further caution conveyed the estate and right of the said towne of Seymer to a very yong sonne of his, to have the more cullor to excuse hymselfe not to satisfy any order that should be taken therein; wee have thought good upon the complaintes which have ben rendered in that behalfe unto us by the Inhabitants of the said towne of Scarborough to praie and req^r yor L. to take presente order that the said markett be agayne suspended until Mr Gate shall attend us, and satisfy us wth sufficient reasons against the same. And so we wishe yor L. and the rest heartelie well to fare. From the Court at Richemond the 8th of October 1599.*

* Additional MS. 28,223.

THE MAYOR, &C., OF HULL TO THE PRIVY COUNCIL.

" Right Ho^r our verie humble duties remembred. By vertue of your Ll^{ps} letters frome Whitehall the laste of March last, we have called before us the subsidie men, and others supposed to be of abilitie within this Towne & the liberties thereof : And have moved theme to contribute towardes his Ma^{ts} chardges in recoveringe the patrymonie of his children in Germanie. It may please your good Ll^{ps} to be advertised, that we have found theme verie willinge in all dutifull respect to yeild towards the same, manie of theme beyond their abilities, whose names with the sommes by theme given, amountinge in the whole to 132*l.* 6s. 2d., we have in a scedule or note hereinclosed made bold to returne unto your good Ll^{ps}, humblie craveinge your Ho^{rs} favourable acceptance of the same, and due consideration and comiseration of the sudden and great decay of this Towne, happenynge, as well by the generall decay of trade, as also by the late losse of many of our shipps & men at sea, and by the present pynchinge dearth with us, and all the countries here-abouts. Of which we have presumed to gyve notice to your good Ll^{ps}; as also that Robert Legard of Anlabie within this countie, esquire, beinge Justice of peace in the Eastriddinge of Yorkshire, denieth to contribute heare, alleadginge that he will pay their where he is justice, and in Commission. And so desyringe to knowe your Ll^{ps} further pleasure to whome the monie should be paide, and craveinge pardon for our boldnes herein, we humblie take our leaves.

" Frome Kingston upon Hull the 6th of June 1622.
" Your Ll^{ops} humble at commaundement

     " Josua Hall maior
     Joseph Feild
     Thomas Swan
" Thomas Raikes, vic. Edw. Richardsonn
     Thomas Ferres
     John Preston.".

The Lord Mayor and Corporation of York to the Privy Council.

" Maie it pleas your Honors to be advertised, that accordinge to, your Lo^{ops} letters of the last of March to us directed, towchinge the yeildinge unto the kings most excellent Matie A present supply of moneys by waie of A voluntarie contribution within the Cittie of York and liberties therof towards his highnes urgent occasyons for the recovery of the patrimony of his Maties children in Germany, we at severall daies and tymes called before us all the Knights, Gentlemen, Subsidiemen and all others of knowne Abillity within the saide Cittie and liberties therof, and used our best indevors to move them to ioyne cheerfully in the said contribution, which they willinglie yeilded unto accordinge to ther abillities the names of whom with the sumes by them offered, togethers with our owne contribution we do humblie certefy to your Lo^{ops} in A

schedule hereinclosed, which contribution, though it
be not so much, as in our most loyall and affectionate
dueties to his Maᵗⁱᵉ we could wish it were, and cheer-
fullie, and hartelie, condiscend unto, yet we hope his
maᵗⁱᵉ wilbe gratiouslie pleased to accept therof, beinge
by your Loᵖᵖˢ good meanes informed, as the truth is
of the decayinge estate of this Cittie for want
of commerce and tradeinge, the Artificers therin haveinge much Ado for to get bread to susteyne them and
ther families in this tyme of scarcety of corne and
money the like wherof hath not fallen owt in the
memory of man; And further maie it please your
Loᵖᵖˢ we have appointed James Boyes, of the Cittie of
York, gentleman, to be collector of the said moneys
and have given hym a schedule therof, accordinge to
that which we herewith inclosed certefy to your
Honors, and required hym spedely to collect and make
payment therof, And so with our humble dueties and
services' to your Loᵖᵖˢ remembred we take our leaves
and rest ever

" Your Honors to be comaunded

" Elias Micklethwayte* William Brearay maiorr

Willm. Greenbury   Robt. Myers

Thomas Hoyle†   Jo: Vaux.

"Yorke this of June the 26ᵗʰ 1662."

* A merchant in York, twice Lord Mayor; died about 1632.
His descendants settled at Swine in Holderness.. See Hunter's
South Yorkshire, II., p. 253.

† One of the leaders of the Puritan party in York. He was
returned for the city.in 1628, Sir Thomas Savile having been

THE MAYOR, &c., OF YORK TO THE PRIVY COUNCIL.

" Maie it please your Honors to be advertized that your Lo^{pps} letter of the 19th of October 1621 wee receyved in the behalf of the Bakers of the Citie of York towchinge the graunting unto them such libertie and allowance in exercisinge of ther Trade that is allowed unto the Bakers of London and other corporate Townes by force of A booke published in the late Quene Elizabeth tyme by allowance or commaundement of some of the then Right honorable privy Counsell; or ells to showe the reasons of our refusalls. Upon the receipt of your Lo^{pps} saide letters we called diverse of the principall Bakers before us, And upon conference did think that we had given them such satisfaction as that they should not have bene further troblesome to your Honors, yett perceiveing by your Lo^{pps} letters of the 23th of October last, that the saide Bakers have petitioned your Honors therein againe, which is done by the meanes of some turbulent and factious persons of the same companie, and some others ill-advisers therin as we have iust cause to conceive and therefore humblie pray your Honors pardons for our neglect in that we did not upon the receipt of your Lo^{pps} first letters, give answere as we were required which was for the reason aforesaide, And nowe for the dischardge of our

unseated on petition; and succeeded Sir William Allanson as Lord Mayor in 1634. He reaped the reward of his attachment to the parliament by getting the office of Treasurer's Remembrancer of the Exchequer, worth some 1,200l. a year. On the first anniversary of the king's execution he committed suicide in his lodgings at Westminster.

dueties and your Honor's satisfaction, we offer thes
reasons and causes followinge why they should not have
the same allowances. First for that in ancient Books
& Registers of this Cittie it appeareth that the Cittizens & Inhabitants in the same have bene served and
furnished with bread not onely by the Bakers of this
Cittie but by Countrie people and others commonly
called bowle* Bakers, which bowle Bakers did give in
everiepeny white lofe 6s. in weight, which is in everie peny
lofe above thre ounces in weight more then the Bakers
in this Cittie did give, or were to give by the Statute
Lawes of this Realme, thereupon the Bakers of this
Cittie, (not) being able as they pretended to live
upon ther occupations in regard that the countrie and
bowle Bakers did give greater weight then the saide
Bakers did give, petitioned in that behalf in the tyme
of King Philip and Quene Marie, and therupon by the
then Magistrates of this Cittie the saide Countrie
and bowle Bakers were withdrawn, for that the Bakers
of this Cittie did undertake to furnish the Cittizens
and inhabitants of this Cittie at the Markett Crosse in
giveinge the same weight that the said Countrie and
bowle Bakers did. And within some fewe yeres after
they petitioned againe to the Magistrates of the saide
Cittie, that they were not able to performe ther agre-
ment wherupon they had th'one half of the 6s. weight
abated and were to add onely 3s. in weight to everie
peny white lofe. And within a short tyme after that
they againe compleyned and had th'one half of the

* Boulte bakers ?—*i.e.,* bakers of sifted or boulted bread.

saide 3s. released and were to add onelie 18d. in weight
over and above the assize to be given them by the
Statute Lawes of this Realme,* which they performed
by the space of 40^{tie} yeres. And nowe the saide Bakers
in this Cittie perceiveinge that they onelie have the
benifitt of the saile of bread, and not anie countrie or
bowle Bakers of long tyme permitted, and nowe quite
owt of use, demaund allowance of 6s. in everie quarter
of wheat accordinge to the said booke published in
the late Quene Elizabeth tyme, which we the magistrates of the Cittie have not thought mete to allowe
them, in regard ther is nowe no other breade brought
to this Cittie by the countrie or bowle Bakers for the
serveinge of the poore Artificers as was of auncient
tyme used, and as is used in other Citties and Corpo-
rato Townes. And we demaund no further of them,
but that they should bake ther bread of the assize, and
accordinge to the Lawes of this Realme without in-
forcing them to make any further allowance accordinge to ther saide former agrements, and to bringe the
same to the Crosse on the markett daies as formerlie
was used, which we hold, under your Lo^{pps} reformation
verie reasonable and necessarie, knoweinge they maie
verie well afford so to doe, haveinge the sole saile and
provision of bread for the Cittie, the saide bowle Bakers
beinge by the meanes aforesaide quite discontinewed
and after so long tyme not to be recontinewed. And we

* One law in force at this time was that "No baker should
sell his bread of less weight than the due assize, viz., proportionable to the price of corn in the market, as it is regulated by
a printed assize-book, set out to that purpose."

further certefy unto your Lo^{pps} that we well knowe that
the Bakers of this Citty do nowe live in as good and
plentifull sorte of ther saide occupation, as they have
done at anie tyme within the memorie of man, and
never had anie other allowance but as aforesaide; and if
they should have anie allowance as they desire, it would
prove verie preiudiciall to the poore of our Cittie, for
that this Cittie is not served with bread at the Markett
Crosse, as formerlie it was, and as other Cittie and Corporate Townes be. And moreover the saide Companie
of Bakers have showed themselves so remise and dis-
obedient in not bakeinge of mayn* bread beinge an Auncient mistery used in this Cittie and in no other Citties
of this kingdome, Although his Matie did at his last
beinge here give in chardge the continewance therof,
which, without imposeinge of great fynes we cannot
bringe them to the performance thereof, insomuch as
the said misterie is in dainger to be lost ther beinge
verie fewe Alive that can make it, and none trayned
up or taught in the makeinge thereof. All which we
do humblie leave to your grave wisdome and iudg-
ments and shall rest ever.

" York, this 27th of November 1622.

" Your Honors most humblie to be commanded

"WILLIAM BREARAY, maior.

ROBERT ASKWITH,
WILLIAM GREENBURY,   ROBERT MYERS,
LEONARD BESSER,   ELIAS MICKLETHWAITE,
THOMAS AGAR,   CHRISTOFER DICKINSON."

* Maint, mixed (?).

THE MAYOR, &c., OF HULL TO THE PRIVY COUNCIL.

" Right Ho^r our verie humble duties remembred.

" It may please your good LL^ps to be advertised, that by vertue of his Ma^ts proclamation for puttinge in execution of certaine Orders, made by his Matie to be observed for remedie of the dearth of Graine & other victualls, and of your LL^ps letters to us delyvered concernynge the same, We have proceded therein as followeth, namely; We called together a competent nomber of the most honest & meete persons of the three severall parishes lyinge within this countie,* and gave theme charge to enquire of the severall Articles mencioned in the said booke of Orders, who at the day fixed theme by us, returned to us their severall answeres in wrytinge. And we fynd by their said answeres, that in the same our Countie, which consisteth of three parishes, Their is not so much in Corne or grain (the same beinge for the most part barlie) as will serve to sowe their landes and fynd their howshould people wherewith they are chardged. And the presentors do also say, their are no Badgers, Brogers or Kydders† of corne within the same countie; And

---

* *i.e.* County of the Town of Kingston-upon-Hull. By Charter granted by Henry VI. (1440), the jurisdiction of the town, then made a county, extended over many adjoining parishes, reaching from Garrison-side to westward of Swanland, being 9 miles long and averaging 2 miles in breadth.—See Sheahan's *History of Hull.*

† A variety of north-country expressions for hucksters or small dealers.

that their are fower Bakers who bake at the most all
of theme not two quarters of corne in the weeke; And
that their are in the same countie but three maultsters,
and that their are noe buyers of corne on the grounde;
And that their are in all the said County neine Aile-
brewers & Victuallers allowed, whome we have caused
to enter recognizances with sureties for keping the
Assices lymitted by the lawes, the saide booke of
orders, and other usuall & necessaries poynts.

" And as touchinge our procedings within this our
Borough or Towne of Kingston upon Hull, we make
bold to signifie unto your good LL^{ps} that we have not
anie tillage nor corne or graine growinge in or about
the same or the feildes neare adioinynge; But have
at this present, in the hands of divers marchants &
others, within this towne, by theme broughte frome
beyond the seas, reasonable store of Rye and other
graine to the quantitie of two thowsand quarters and
above, for service of the Inhabitants heare, and the
Countree, of which their is dailie some parts sould and
delyvered oute, at such reasonable rates as they may
be afforded, that is to say, whyte rye aboute 32s. the
quarter, Black forraine Rye aboute 30s. the quarter,
Barlie aboute 27s. the quarter, beanes about 24s. the
quarter, and wheate aboute 3l. the quarter, of which
last kynde of graine we have litle or none at all in
our towne or countie; And their is likewise new
supplyes made of Corne by such as doe often bringe
in more to this port by shippinge. For Brewers &

Victuallers within this towne, we have disallowed such
of theme as we thought unmete to contynue, And
have taken recognizances with sureties of the rest
for gyveing measure & kepinge the Assices, &
other good orders, accordinge to the trewe meanynge of the lawes and tenor of the said orders.
And it may further please your good LL*ᵖ* that we
have within this towne, no Maultsters, no Badgers,
brogers, or buyers of corne on the grounde; And for
the Bakers we shall endevoure (as we have don) to
cause them to kepe the Assice, and to restraine theme
frome hynderinge or abusinge the markett.   Of all
which we have undertaken heareby to gyve notice
unto your good LL*ᵖ* in discharge of our most bounden
duties.   And so craveinge pardon for this our boldnes
we humblie take our leaves.   Frome Kingston upon
Hull the 21st of February 1622-3.

"Your LL*ᵖ* humble at commaundement

"Jⁿ° Ramsden maior   Joseph Feild
Tho: Thackray   Tho: Swan
Nicholas Lyndley · Bernard Smyth
John Lister   Launcelott Roper
Edw. Richardsonn   Tho: Ferres
John Preston   Joe: Watkinson
Joseph Blaides, shirefe

"To the right Hoⁿ and oure verie good
Lords the LLˢ and others His Maˢ most
Hoⁿ pryvie Counsell." *

* Domestic—Charles I., Vol. CXXXVIII.

THE MAYOR, &c., OF YORK TO THE PRIVY COUNCIL.

" To the right Honorable the Lords of his Matie most
Honorable privy Counsell.

" The humble petition of the Maior and Citisens of
the Citie of Yorke as well for themselves as for
others of that Countrie praying relief against the
Grievances and wronges done unto them by the
Maior & Burgesses of the Towne of Kingstone
upon Hull.

" First, divers of that Corporation calling themselves contractors and combyning together have, for
their owne private Lucre and gayne, bought &
ingrossed all the Corne brought in by strangers, as
namely, this last yeare thirtie thousande quarters, &
have sold the same to countrie chapmen at 3, 4, & 5^{s}
profit in a quarter, not suffering the marchants of
Yorke to buy any part therof, contrary to a branche
of certaine Articles mutually agreed upon under the
Seales of both the said Corporations, and made by the
mediation of the right Honorable Henry, late Earle of
Huntingdon, Lord President of the North in June
1578, 20 Eliz. R. By which it was agreed that the
Maior and Citisens of Yorke might buy in Hull of all
forayners & strangers the moitie or under of all commodities brought thither to bee sold within the space
of ten daies after the shipp entred, and after ten daies
to buy all or part as the buyer & seller could agree,
cloth and lead onely excepted.

" Secondlie, it hath beene practised of late yeeres

by them of Hull (by way of forstallinge the markett)
that when they heare tell of any Corne brought in by
strangers & cominge up Humber, they send downe
Pilotts to meete the shipps tenn or twelve miles of,
with commission to buy their corne, and the M^r or
factor upon such invitation cominge to Hull before the
shipp, they doe usually bargaine for the corne before
the shipp be entred. By which meanes the marchants
of Yorke are prevented in their said priviledge, of buy-
inge; the strangers price is advaunced, and the countrie
iniured & damnified.

" Thirdlie, ye marchants of Yorke having within
13 monthes last past shipped out 50000 kaersies * and
above, & for the same bringing in great quantities of
Corne to their port of Hull, the late Maior Josua
Hall and divers others of that Corporation (to inforce
them to sell the said Corne unto them, that they might
vent it againe for their owne profit at higher prices
into the countrie) have not permitted the said Marchants of Yorke to sell the said Corne to the Countrie
chapmen of Yorkshire & Lincolneshire, who attended
the market there to transport the same by the Rivers
of Trent, Aire, Dun, and other Rivers into divers parts
of those Countries; But have against the lawe made
seisures of such Corne as they† sould to the said
Countrie Chapmen as forfeited‡ for foreyn bought and

---

* Kersey-cloths.   † *i.e.*, the York merchants.
‡ *i.e.*, to the Hull Corporation. The following remarks on
these disputes will be found in the Rev. John Tickell's *History*

sould, and have threatned the Contrey chapmen with
seizures and sute, contrary to the auncient priviledge
and right of the said Marchants of Yorke, who have
used time out of mind to sell great quantities of their
Corne so imported to the conntry chapmen attendinge
their marketts there, as by the Certificates of several
Townes & of the Justices of the peace of the Countie
of Yorke may appeare; To the great hinderance of the
vent of the Cloth of that Countrie, & thincouraging of
straungers to bringe in greater quantities of Corne, who
for the same export the moneyes out of the Realme; to
the utter decaye of navigation in those partes.

"Fourthlie, when they have bought divers shipps
lading of Corne as aforesaid, they by practise and
combynation & for their owne private lucre and gayne
(setting their servants aboord the shipps) sett a certaine rate & price upon their said Corne, with caution
that noe man sell under that stinted rate, nor any to
sell any Corne upon the shoare till those shipps load-
ings should bee sould. And so they force the Marchants

of Hull, referring to the year 1622:—"Notwithstanding the
agreement entered into, in the 28th year of Eliz., between the
inhabitants of York and Hull, fresh disputes about that ancient
custom of *foreign-bought* and *foreign-sold* soon arose between
these then rival towns, which was this year productive of another
law-suit. The immediate occasion of the present contest was a
seizure made by the magistrates of Hull of 50 quarters of rye
belonging to Mr. Barker, a citizen of York." We may here
remark that there is no date given to the above petition; but,
judging from this extract, coupled with the fact of Joshua Hall
having been Mayo: of Hull in 1622 (see p. 276), we may safely
assign it to the year 1623.

of Yorke (having such priviledge of buying a moitie
of Corne and other goodes as aforesaid) to buy Corne
of them to furnishe the Cittie of Yorke and the Countrie
thereabouts; By reason whereof the Countrie is in-
forced to pay dearer for their Corne, then otherwise
they should have done.

"Fifthly, whereas by a schedule annexed to the
Articles aforesaid the Marchants of Yorke are to pay
certayne rates to them of Hull for takinge up, weigh-
inge, houseroome, and strikinge of their Lead at Hull,
when there is occasion soe to take up the same, &c.
And whereas their Lead beinge weighed at Bawtry
and Yorke, & caried down in their Keeles and
Boates (the customers beinge agreed withall) is for
expedition and to save their marketts hoised out of the
keeles and boates into the shippes. Those of Hull by
color of the said Articles, but in truthe to hinder their
voyages & to lay a charge upon their Lead, to the
end they of Hull may undersell them at the Marketts,
doe inforce them to take up and weighe their said
Lead with them, & to pay the said rates, And (for
not doing the same in the case aforesaid) the Maior of
Hull about three yeeres sithence seised divers pigges
of Lead of the said Marchants of Yorke to the number
of 20 or 30 which they detayne or keepe from them till
this day.

"Sixtly. Some of their Aldermen by consent or
connyvence of the Maior have for these tenn yeeres
last past bought and ingrossed all the Herrings that

came into the port, sometimes five or sixe shippes loadinge at once, & would not permitt any marchant or fishmonger of Yorke to have any part of the said herrings unlesse they would buy of them. And further have and doe condition with the shippes, that what they buy not, shall bee caried away out of the port, that noe man els may buy any there, or that otherwise they will buy none at all themselves, and so the shippers loose some part of their markett. By reason whereof the prices of herrings have beene inhaunced from 15s. a barrel to 27s. to the great preiudice of the Countrie, especially the poorer sort of people.

"Seaventhlie, when the shipps laden with New-castle coales come to Hull to serve the countrie, those of Hull will not permitt either the marchants or mariners of Yorke to buy any coales out of the said shipps untill such tyme as they have bought for themselves and the parts of the country thereabouts, as many of the said coales as they thinke good, to the great preiudice of the said marchants and maryners whose keeles lie there at great charge, and sometimes loose their spring tides for their voyage to Yorke, & to the great damage and disappoyntinge of the Citie and Countrie about Yorke." *

THE MAYOR, &c., OF RIPON TO THE PRIVY COUNCIL.

"Right Hono^bls

"May it please your Lor^ps to be advertised, that accordinge to the tenor of the letters, which we received

---

* Domestic—James I., Vol. CXXXVIII.

from your Honors, we directed our precepts to the severall petty constables within this corporation and towne of Rippon, to have knowledge howe many severall Alehousekeepers were in the said towne, and fyndinge the number to be great, we have reduced them to halfe the number, and directed our further precepts to the said petty constables, to discharge such as we have disalowed for brewynge any Beere or Ale from that tyme, and we have likewise given direction to such Innes and Alehowses as are allowed and need-full for the entertayninge of strangers and such as come weekly to the Markitt, that they doe moderate the strengthe of Beere and Ale, accordinge to the rates ordeyned by the Statutes in that behalfe; and we doe intende from tyme to tyme to use our best indevours to see the same performed, for the helpe of the presente scarcety of grayne. A l which our proceedyngs herein, accordinge to our bounden duties and your Lor^{ps} speciall comaundemente we doe recomende to your Honors gravetyes and wisedomes. And soe humbly take our leaves from Rippon this twentie fifte day of February in the twentith yeare of the Kinges Maties most gracyous and happy reigne over us.

> " RAPHE WARWIKE Maior.
> WILLIAM BATTIE.
> EDWARD KIRKBYE."*

* Domestic—James I., Vol. CXXXVII.

Thᴇ Mᴀʏᴏʀ, &c., ᴏꜰ Hᴜʟʟ ᴛᴏ ᴛʜᴇ Pʀɪᴠʏ Cᴏᴜɴᴄɪʟ.

" Right hono^{ble}

" After presentment of our humble duties and service to your good Lo^{pps}, please to understand that wee laitly received your letters of the 31th December, and 26th January last, both importinge the makeing ready of two shipps of warr for his Ma^{ts} service formerly required from this Port, as likewise the sending upp of some sufficiently instructed to render an Accompt of our ·former proceedings in that busines, whereunto wee have carefully applyed ourselves with all possible dilligence, and thereof endeavoured to have given an Accompt unto your Lo^{pps} before this, but that wee could receive no full answer from those of the countie of yorke, concerning that parte of the charge, required from them by your Lo^{pps} towardes that service, untill the 16th daie of this instant Februarie. Att which tyme by direction from the right honorable the Lord Lieutenant of these north parts, two of our Aldermen attended his Lo^{pp} att Yorke, with two other Aldermen of that Citty where there was a generall meetinge of all or most of the deputie Lieutenants and Justices of peace, Commissioners for the loan mony in Yorkeshire, unto whome his Lo^{pp} made knowne againe the Contribution for setting out the said shipps required from the countie, as he had don formerly, and after conference returned us answere by those who attended him in that behalf, that he perceived that the county

would not be drawne to contribute to that charge, but
do absolutely denie it. As for the clotheinge Townes
of Hallifax, Leeds and Wakefeild, as also the other
Townes members of this Port, required likewise by
your Lo^{pps} to ioyne in Contribution to that charge, wee
can receive no satisfactorie answere nor hope of contribution from them at all, although wee have divers
tymes both by letters and messingers sollicited them
thereunto. (save only from the cittie of Yorke), who
alledge their inabilities, and have sent one of their
Aldermen in company with one of our Aldermen and
Towne Clarke, the bearers hereof, to give your Lo^{pps}
the better satisfaction to such particulers as shalbe
required, as likewise truly to enforme your Lo^{pps}, that
howbeit wee have imparted the contents of your Lo^{pps}
letters to our owne Inhabitants and enforced the same
to the uttermost of our powers, yet wee find them very
unwillinge, and in verie truth, altogether unable to
undergo so great a burthen, in respect of the stand,
both of forreyne and home trade, as also manie of them
haveing laitly paid mony upon privie seales, and now
at present, haveinge readily yeilded unto the loane
required by his Matie to shew their good affections to
all his Ma^{ts} Royall designes, to the uttermost of their
poore abilities, all which severall reasons they of Yorke
(amongst others) likewise alledge. In consideration
of which and for that our Inhabitants were at great
charge the last sommer, and still are forced to be at
greater, in necessary fortifications about our Towne,

they hope and pray that his Matie would be pleased to
ease them of this so great a charge as the shipps setting out, which they are altogether unable to undergoe,
being continually charged more then anie other parts
of the Kingdome, in maynteyninge of manie families of
decayed seamen and likewise with continuall watching, wardinge, and other needfull and unavoydeable
charges, in respect of the iminent danger threatned
by the visible preparations of the enimie, as wee
have cause to feare against this Towne, whereof wee
have had not only notice from your Lo^pps in Sommer
last, but also by a lait letter cast into the entrie of
the now Maior here, the originall whereof wee sent to
the said Lord Lieutenant in the north, for our discharge, of which wee hope your Lo^pps have had intelligence before this, and thereof thought it our duties to
put your Lo^pps in mynd, and also to become humble
petitioners to your Lo^pps to bee suters to his Mat^ie on
the behalf of this Towne, being a port of infinitt consequence to a great parte of the kingdome (a mapp
whereof wee have drawne for your Lo^pps viewe*) for
supplye of some great ordinance powther and shott &c.,
whereof there is too great need. All which wee leave
to your Honors grave wisdomes, and to the further relation of those whome wee send purposely to attend
your Lo^pps, haveing acquainted your Lo^pps with our
former proceedings about the setting out of the shipps,

* Now no longer attached to the letter.

by our letters of the 30ᵗʰ of October last past, And so humbly take our leaves and rest.

" Kingston-upon-Hull this
25ᵗʰ of February 1626-7.
" Your Honors in all humble dutie &
service to comaund,
" BERNARD SMYTH maior,

JOSEPH FIELD, ·	THO: SWAN,
THO: THACCRAY,	EDW: RICHARDSONN,
LAUNCELOTT ROPER,	JO: WATKINSON,
THO: FERRES,	JOHN PRESTON,
JNO: RAMSDEN.	

"To the Right Honorable the Lords and others of his Maᵗˢ most honorable privie Counsell, these." *

LORD SCROOPE TO THE DUKE OF BUCKINGHAM.

" Maye please your grace
to give mee leave by thease lynes to acquainte you how farre I have entered into this last servise, which I was commanded by his Maᵗⁱᵉ to imploye my best care, and dilligence to effect: (which was concearninge . . . . the loane monye).   Presentlye after my comminge to Yorke, I called the citisens and the . . . . belonginge to the same ; and theare wase not one mane, but hee did condiscend to give, as likewise to subscribe ; the like did Hull and the countye belonginge to itt.   Next I summoned all the Commissioners nominated for the

----

* Domestic—Charles I., Vol. LV. ·

countye, and theare wase nott anye that appeared,
towe excepted which did nott both give and subscribe:
I will crave pardone for not naminge them, in respect
rthey weare willinge to give. Since this theare hath
beene three meetings for the countrey, and they have
·come off verye freelye, and I dout nott but the rest
will doe the like; (iff wee succeede well in one place)
wheare as I am informed theare is some working un-
.derhande, but I doe nott much dout the people.

"I send your grace heare inclosed a letter* which
·wase sent mee by the maior off Hull; they likewise in-
forme mee, that iff they had some 12 peeces off ordinance to laye one a forte, which they have lately beene
att the charge to builde, itt would bee a greate meanes
tto secuer theare towne upon any occasione. What directions I shall receive either in this perticulaer, or any
·other, which maye anye waye conduce to the advancement of his Maties servise, I shall faithfullye see put in
·executione; till further occassione I will cease your
graces further trowble, and rest

"Your graces faithfull freend and servante

"EDM. SCROOPE.

"Yorke this

25th of Februarye 1626-7.

"To the duke of Buckingham his Grace this."

The following is the letter enclosed:—

"Sir, I doe hereby give you notice of an eminent
daunger your towne is to be beseiged this somer I

* The one mentioned in the letter preceding this.

knowe not howe soone it is thus agred by letters A great flete of small ships must come with everie one 40 land souldiers After some peales of ordinance half of them landed then the ships to bend there gunns against that side of your towne y^t lyeth on the water and when that wall is bett downe to enter in the smoke and the other to enter at another place they will nether hurt fort nor house yf they can gett them other ways for they meane to kepe it and to furnish it with vittale munision and amunision for two year kepe this to your selves secretly for it is come a greate way to you in love and play the wyse men for evell is intended the lord feight for this yoore land.

"To the lord mayor of Hull and his brethren this be delivered."

At the foot of this letter is the following note :—

"This letter was founde the 7th daye of Februarie laite at night, thrust under Mr Maiors foore doore, (the dore beinge shutt) or had ben otherwise scattered in his entrie neare the doresteade at evenynge, and so was taken upp laite, after the dore shutt in." *

THE INHABITANTS OF LEEDS AND HALIFAX TO THE PRIVY COUNCIL.

"To the Right Honble the Lords of his Maties most Honorable Privie Counsell at the Counsell Board.

"The humble petition of the Inhabitants of Leedes and Hallifax and their precincts.

"Maie it please your Honors, whereas wee have

* Domestic—Charles I., Vol. LV.

received lettres from this Board dated the 24ᵗʰ day
of March last past, to take speedy and effectuall
course to contribute with the Inhabitants of the Port
of Hull according to former Presidents rateably
towardes the charge of setting out three Shipps of
the Burthen of 200 Tunns a peece for his Maˡᵉ service
to be att Rendevous att Portsmouth the 20ᵗʰ daie of
Maie next furnished as men of Warre and victualled
for full foure monethes to be accounted from that
tyme forward. Albeit wee are readie & willing in all
humblenes & obedience to yeild and submitt to his
Maˡᵉ Royall pleasure and command, yet in regard of
the charges of moneyes which lately wee have under-
gone upon Privie seales, Loans of five Subsidies &
setting forth of Souldiers (all which wee have done
freely & chearefullie) as also the great stopp and staie
of Vent (vend) of Cloth by transportation thereof we
are att this present so much weakned as wee are no
wayes able (though willing) to make that supplie &
Aide which by your Honors' letters wee are enioyned,
And also wee doubt not but to give good satisfaction
to this Board both by presidents & reasons for our
discharge from contributing with the Port of Hull in
such manner as by your Honors lettres wee are required, Whereof wee doe most humblie intreate your
Honors consideration and that wee maie be admitted
to shewe and alleadge the same before your Honors,
Some of which reasons we have made bould to ex-
presse in this our petition.

" 1. That wee have no more particular priviledge or profitt by way of Traffique by the Port of Hull, then any other the remotest place in the Kingdome hath.

" 2. There is not that quantitie of Cloth made in these three * Townes and precincts as is made in the severall and dispersed Townes and Villages about us.

" 3. The Clothiers of the Countie Palatyne of Lancaster and the Myners of Darbyshire for Lead have greater Commerce & Traffique att the Port of Hull than wee have.

" 4. The vent of our Cloth is aswell from London Newcastle Westchester and other Ports as from the Port of Hull.

" 5. The most of the Inhabitants of these places that are of any abilitie are not Clothiers, but Gentlemen yeomen, Farmers and men of other Trades and professions.

" 6. The Inhabitants of these places are alwaies upon any service ioyned with, and are members of the rest of the Countrie and never severed from them in any service whatsoever, Whereas the Port of Hull is of it selfe onely charged with Sea service and not with land service nor ever ioyned in contribution with the Countrie.

" For which reasons together with others not herein

---

* Wakefield, Leeds, and Halifax stood in the original heading, but the first-named town appears to have been afterwards struck -out.

expressed but readie to be shewed when your Honors
shall appointe, We most humblie beseech your Honors
to take consideration of us, and that we may be freed
from Contribution with the Port of Hull in such
manner as by your Honors' lettres is required, and
that wee may contribute and be charged with the rest
of the Countrie rateably as formerly we have beene
accustomed to doe, And your petitioners as in duty
they are bound shall dalie pray for your Honors in all
health and happines long to contynue." *

THE INHABITANTS OF WAKEFIELD TO THE PRIVY COUNCIL.

"To the Right Honourable the Lords and others of
his Majesty's most honourable privie Councell.

"The humble petition of the Inhabitants of the Towne
of Wakefeild.

* To this petition are attached about 400 signatures, of which
the following are some of the most prominent :—
George Hurtley; John Crakanthorpe; Thomas Wither;
Gabriell Bristowe; William Marstonn; John Ambler; Chris-
topher Addison; Robert Clay, *Vicarius Halifax*; Nathaniell,
Isacke, Thomas, & John Waterhouse; John & Samuell Cloughe;
Richard Pighells; Richard Barrett; J. Haworthe; Edmund
Tetlow; Edmond Brearcliffe; John Farrar (mark); Abrah.
Sunderland; Mathew Suttliffe (mark); James Murgatroyd;
Richard Brooksbanke; Michaell Fawthropp (mark); Robert
Gledhill; Robert Lyall; Samuell Casson; Joseph Hillary;
George Killingbeck; James Levitt; William Massie; Richard
Aldred; John Burdsall; Ranfe Iles; Roger Millthorpe; James
Pinckney; William Fentonn; Francis Cloudsley; Joseph
Farbanke; William Earle; William Bloomer; William Powell;
Michaell Fawkiner; Thomas Woodrove; Nicholas Edmondson;
Abraham & Josias Jenkinson; Henry Roundell; Marmaduke
Lovell; Tho. Yowle; Will. Blande; Edmond Hinde; William
Curtis; John Thursby; Stephon Ramonson; Martin Milnes.

" Shewing : That, having receaved your honourable Lettres directed to y^m, and others to contribute with the Port of Hull towardes the setting forth of 3 Shipps for his Majesty's service, They doe most humblie crave your honourable consideration therein for theis reasons following—

" That there is not one person inhabiting in Wake-feild, or the precincts thereof that is a marchant, or that venteth any cloth at the Port of Hull, or any other comoditie there.

" That the Towne of Wakefeild is greatlie decaied, especyallie in the trade of Clothing And that, that smale quantitie of Cloth there made, is noe Sea ware, but sould to Drapers onlie.

" Which reasons the Petitioners doe most humblie submitt to your honourable considerations, and for the truth thereof, theie doubt not but the right honourable Sir John Savile k^t* can sufficientlie enforme your honourable Lords, and accordinglie doe crave to be freed by your honours from y^t contribution : For which the Petitioners shall (as dutie bindeth) dailie pray for your Honourable Lordships. &c." †

THE JUSTICES OF THE WEST RIDING TO THE PRIVY
COUNCIL.

" May itt please your Lordshipps
        "Accordinge to your Lordshipps directions by

* Of Howley.
† Domestic—Charles I., Vol. LXI. There are no names appended to this petition.

your Letters of the 29th of December last upon a petition
with reasons thereto annexed, exhibited to your Lordshipps by the Clothiers of the westridinge of Yorkeshire, for the continuance of the hott presse Boards
and papers as the same are nowe in use, which wee receaved togeather with the saide Letters. Our Quarter
Sessions fallinge out to be holden upon the 10th and
11th dayes of this Instant January at Wakefeilde,
which nowe is the greatest markett and principall place
of resorte of all sorts of Clothiers Drapers and other
Traffikers for Cloath in all theis parts.* Wee his
Majesty's Justices of peace of the saide westridd:
whose names are underwritten did cause generall and
publique notice to be given of the contents of the
saide Letters unto the saide persons, as well in theire
open Markett as att theire private houses and Lodgings. And therupon sundrie of them resortinge unto
us, wee have both by our selves aparte, and togeather
with them, considered, weighed and examined the saide
petition and Reasons, which for any thinge that hath
yett appeared unto us, are in all the parts thereof iust
and true as the saide Clothiers have informed your
Lordshipps. Butt for our further satisfaction and
better discharge of our dutyes and service to his
Majesty, your Lordshipps and the Countrie in this behalfe, Wee caused both the saide Letters Petition and

---

* This hardly accords with the statement of their affairs
made by the good people of Wakefield in the previous year,
when petitioning to be relieved from the payment of shipmoney.

Reasons to be publiquely and distinctly read in the
open Cort of the saide Sessions there beinge then present a very great concorse of people both Clothiers
drapers and others attendinge the same, requiringe
them to obiect what they or any of them coulde either
against the use of the hott presse Boards and papers
as they were then generally practised, or against the
saide Reasons and allegations made to your Lordshipps by the saide Clothiers. At which time wee did
nott finde any one man to oppose the same, but of
the contrary a generall acclamation and concurrence
of the voce of the whole Countrie with the said
petition. Neither hath any man sithence either in
publique or private offerred himselfe to any of us,
againste the same. And wee doe further upon Examination finde that the hott presse Boards and papers
have bene very muche in use from the time of the makinge of the Lawes against them. And that the same
albeit they add some glosse to the Cloath yet the saide
Cloath beinge withall well dressed is muche bettered
therby, as well by the dryeinge shrinkinge Thickninge
& fasteninge of the same, and layinge it even and
smooth from Cocklinge* as by the Triall and betteringe
of the dye therof. And we finde that by meanes of the
quicke and readie dispatche of the pressinge of
Cloathes with the said hott presse Boards and papers,
the poore Clothiers doe prepare and make readie theire

* Mr. Banks suggests that this is the same as our local word
cottering, that is, *knotting*.

And your [illegible] humbly take [illegible] Behing

About [illegible] Officers
[illegible] Refoilds 23 [illegible]

Atty's Copp't [illegible]

Cloathes much the sooner, Soe that thereby they double and treble theire returnes, And by occasion hereof Multitudes of families are sett on worke and manteyned, which if the same sholde be taken away should bee left without Imployment or meanes. The could presse nott beinge able in longe tyme to afford them that dis-patche which the hot presse will doe in short tyme, Lastly we finde the Information of the saide Clothiers against Wolridge to be true and therupon accordinge to your Lordshipps saide directions have given order for stay of his proceedings upon the saide Informations until we receave further directions from your Lordshipps. And soe wee humbly take our leaves   Restinge

> ¬Att your Lordshipps Comaundment

> "H. SAVILE*

> RIC. BEAU-MONT†

> ROBERT CLAY‡

> Jo: KAYE.§

"Att our Generall Sessions at Wakefeilde the xi^{th} of January 1627–8."‖

* Of Methley, of whom see the last chapter.

† Of Whitley ; see p. 200.

‡ Vicar of Halifax ; one of the Clay-house family.

§ Of Woodsome and Denby Grange. He escaped with a fine of 500*l.* for taking part with the King in the Civil Wars, "It appearinge that hee hath byn in Armes against the Parliament but for no long tyme. And that hee was one of the first Yorke-shire Gent. that came in : & hath taken the Covenant. And that his estate is no more then 500*l.* per ann. &. charged with above 3000*l.* debt." See Royalist Composition Papers, 1st Series, in the Record Office.

‖ Domestic—Charles I., Vol. XC.

"May itt please your good Lordshipps that we wear nott presente att this last Sessions by reason of our age and debillitye, butt we have conferred with some of the substantilists tradsmen; and they hould the reasons mentioned in the petion and exceedinge behooffull for the Cuntrye.

" JAS. BLYTHMAN*
RICHARD SUNDERLAND."†

THE CLOTHIERS OF LEEDS TO THE KING.

" To the King's most excellent Majesty.

" The humble petition of Robert Sympson and Christopher Jackson and many thousands of poore Clothiers of the Parish of Leeds in the County of York,

"Sheweth, That whereas it pleased your most excellent Majesty by your Letters patents dated the 12 day of July in the 2nd yeare of your Ma's most happy Raigne to incorporate the said towne nnd parrish for the better increase of the Trade of Cloathing. And your highnes said Letters patents did give liberty and power to all the said Parrishioners and inhabitants to distinguish and devide themselves

---

* Of Newlathes, near Barnsley, Esq., who married for his first wife, Margaret, daughter of Thomas Wentworth, of Wentworth Woodhouse, Esq. He was a Justice of the Peace and Treasurer for lame soldiers in the West Riding, 9 James I.

† Of Coley, and Highsunderland, near Halifax; was a Justice of the Peace and Treasurer for lame soldiers in the West Riding, 17 James I. His grandson Laugdale was captain of a troop of horse in the service of King Charles. Langdale sold all his lands near Halifax, and bought the manor of Ackton, near Pontefract.

into guilds and fraternityes, not giving authority to
the Aldermen and Assistants there to inforce or com-
pell any to bee Cympanyes unlesse they willingly submitted thereunto. Soe it is, may it please your most
excellent Ma^ty, that the present Alderman* (beeing
an Attorney at the Common Lawe) and a few of the
Cheife Burgesses for the increase of their own
authority and for their owne gaine (as the petitioners
conceave) and not for the good of Cloathing contrary
to the goodwill and liking of most and of the best of
the parrish (there beeing not the fortith part of the
Clothiers that doe consent thereunto as the petitioners
hope to make it appeare) endeavour to inforce the
petitioners to bee a company and to submitt themselves
to such Rules and constitutions as they shall please to

---

* Leeds was incorporated by Charles I. in 1626. Sir John
Savile, of Howley, was the first "Alderman," an office equiva-
lent to that of Mayor, and the Savile arms were adopted as the
arms of the town. Among the Harleian Manuscripts (No.
1,327) in the British Museum is a note of a petition presented
by the inhabitants of Leeds "for the staying of a corporation
procured by some of the inhabitants for their town of Leeds."
The petition sets forth that the inhabitants being many
hundreds of people desire a stay of the corporation lately
procured by some of the ablest men of Leeds, for their own
ends, in the name of the whole town, without the consent of
the greater number, and to their prejudice. A reference of the
matter is requested to Sir Thomas Wentworth, Sir Henry
Savile, and Sir John Wood to examine the conveniency or
inconveniency of the said grant. The 'Alderman' alluded to
in the text as an attorney of the common law was Robert
Benson, who was appointed clerk of the peace for the West
Riding about the year 1637. He was 'outed thereof' and fined
200l. for his activity against the parliamentarians.

make, to bee fined imprisoned and called from theire Labour at theire wills.

"Your petitioners shew that many of them dayly setting on worke above 40 poore people in theire trade, and that compelling them to come hither, dwelling 150 miles hence, tendeth much to theire impoverishing and overthrowe of theire trade.

"And therefore your petitioners humbly pray that your Ma⁷ would bee gratiously pleased to referre the examination as well of the consent and allowance of those whome this busines doth concerne as the consideration of the inconveniency of the thing that is desired by the said Alderman and a few burgesses unto such Lords Knights and Gentlemen of the County of York as shall seeme best to your Ma⁷ and whoe best understand the nature of Clothing.

"And your petitioners &c."

At the end of the petition is the following :—

"At the Court at Whitehall 21 March 1628-9.

"His Ma⁷ is gratiously pleased to referre this petition to the Lord President of the North and the Councell there togeather with Sʳ Henry Savile and Sʳ Richard Beaumont knights and Baronetts Sʳ John Ramsden knt.* Christopher Wainsford and John Keyes

---

* Son of William Ramsden, of Longley, Esq., of whom see p. 202. Some accounts of the Constable family which are preserved tell us that Marmaduke Constable, son of Michael Constable, a younger son of Sir Robert, of Everingham, married Anne, a natural daughter of Anthony Besson of Byrom, and that he sold Byrom to Sir John Ramsden. He was Justice of

Esquires or to any six, five or fower of them, whereof
the Lo. President to bee one ; whoe are to call the said
Alderman and such of the Burgesses togeather with
soe many of the poore petitioners as they shall thinke
meete in this cause before them and upon due consideration of the petition and the reasons annexed, to
settle some good course if they can for the remedying of
such inconveniences as they shall finde cause for or
otherwise to certefy his Ma^ty of the truth of the matter
togeather with theire opinions touching the same that
such further order may bee taken as to iustice shall
apperteyne.

"Ra: Freeman." *

Sir John Gibson to the Privy Council.

" Maie it please your Lo^pps

" Whereas you weare pleased by your Letters
dated the last of January 1630 (-1) to commaund me to
deliver unto the Justices of Peace of the severall
Divisions within Countie of Yorke, those books of
orders and directions which I received from your Lo^pps
concerning the same, and to appoint them severallie to
devide themselves and to certifie unto your Lo^pps such
theire Divisions. In obedience to your Lo^ps directions,
in the presence of both the Judges, in the Assize weeke
in March last past (as I conceived the fittest time for
discharge of that dutie) I read the Letters, and

the Peace and Treasurer for lame soldiers in the West Riding in
the 7th year of the reign of King Charles I., and High Sheriff
of Yorkshire in the 13th year of the said reign (remarkable for
that at the summer assizes at York no prisoner was executed).

delivered the Instructions unto them I had received
from your Lo^{p}. Att what time they undertooke to
devide themselves for the present execution of that
service. The names of which Justices according to
your commandment I present unto your Lo^{ps} in a noate
inclosed together with such letters and certificates, as I
have received from some of them in discharge of their
duties.

"I received likewise from your Lo^{ps} letters dated
the 2nd of Aprill 1631, referring to former letters
directed to my Predecessor (whereof I had a coppie)
comaunding the searching and certifying unto your Lo^{ps}
what provisions of Corne wee had within our Countie;
the seeing Marketts to be orderlie kept; and to
prevent forestallers, and excesse of makeing of Mault:
In performance of which comandment, I humblie
present unto your Lo^{ps} such certificates for Corne as
already I have received from the Justices of peace, and
such as hereafter I shall receave (which I daylie expect),
I will with all speede and care returne unto your Lo^{ps}.
And soe I humbly take my leave.

　　　　"Your Lo^{ps} most humble servant,

　　　　　　　　　　　　"Jo: GIBSON.

"April the 22th 1631."

The Justices of the Peace in the Westriding to
whom the books of orders and directions mentioned
in the above letter were given, were Sir Ferdinando
Fairfax, knt., Sir Edward Osborne, Bart., Sir Henry

"Gotherick, knt.,"* Robert Rockley, Esquire. With
this letter are enclosed the following reports :—

1. REPORT FROM HALIFAX.

" S^r

"Accordinge to his ma^{tie} late proclamation to us,
and other his ma^{tie} Justices of peace directed, for the
superfluage of Corne and graine, remaininge and lyinge
in the custodye and keepeinge of Riche men, and not
brought forth into the open markett, wheirby the
marketts is unfurnished, the rates of Corne raised and
exhoysted, and the poore theirby unreleived, And
alsoe the multiplicitie of Alhouses now aboundinge in
theise tymes beinge the greateste cause theirof. Soe
accordinge to the tenure of his ma^{tie} said proclamation
we haye mett monthly and weekly for the said service,
And for redresse theirof, we have cald the Constables
of every townshipp and hamlett within the vicarage of
Halifax before us, and apointed assistants with them
for that service, who att severall and all tymes hath
duely and respectively searchd & examined everye
man's barne, garner and stoore house for Corne, and they
have certifyed unto us, that ours beinge a mountenouss
Cuntry and hangs most by tradeinge and pore, that
not Twentye amongst Twentye thousand have Corne
more then is sufficient for sowinge of that litle ground
they have, and for maintenance of theire famileys

---

* Goodricke, of Ribston, knt., a Deputy-Lieutenant, Justice
of the Peace,and Treasurer for lame soldiers, 9 James 1.; married
Jane, daughter of Sir John Savile, of Methley.

which now they have remaineing in theire houses, And
as for the *Alehouskeepers we have supprest the greater
parte or number of them;* Thus in discharge of our
dutyes we thought good to Certifye thus much unto
you, And soe with our hartiest commendations; we
cease your further truble and ever rest,

"Your loveinge Frends
to be comanded

"J^{a.} BLYTHMAN,

RICHARD SUNDERLAND,

JO: FARRER.*

"Halifax this
16th of January 1630–1."

2. REPORT FROM DONCASTER.

"To the Right wor^{ll} Sir John Gibson, knighte high·
sheriffe of the County of Yorke.

"Wee whose names are subscribed the Maior and
Justices of peace within the Burrough & soake of Doncaster aforesaid according to his Ma^{ts} Comand in his
booke of Orders to us sent & delivered doe certefie as
followeth.

---

* John Farrer, who purchased Ewwood, in the vicarage of Halifax, of his elder brother Henry, was a Justice of the Peace
and Treasurer for lame soldiers in the West Riding of Yorkshire
in the 14th year of King Charles. He married first Dorothy,
daughter and heiress of Mr. Nicholas Hanson, of Eland, and
secondly, Susan, daughter of Mr. Anthony Waterhouse, widow
of Mr. William Fenay. Edward, one of his sons by the second
marriage, became Fellow, and afterwards Master, of University
College, Oxford. Henry Farrer, the uncle of John, purchased
Clubcliffe in Methley of Sir Edward Dimocke, knt., and built a
great part of that house.

"*First* wee have inquired what corne any man within our Libertie hath to spare over & above mentayninge of his familye & sowinge of his ground to bee sowne, and wee cause them to bringe weekly a proportionable rate therof to, our markett of Doncaster & some of us or all attend the markett every markett daie to see the markett supplied with Corne & the same to be sould in open markett by such quantitie, except in such cases as by his Matie booke of orders wee are directed, & the poore to bee first served.

" *Item.* Wee see that there be no ingrossers of Corne within our Libertie, nor that any buy Corne to sell againe without speciall licence.

" *Item.* Wee looke to the Assize and weight of bread, & that bakers deale well with the poore, & that the Bakers make but a measurable profitt, & wee sufferr noe bakers brewers or badgers to buy, but in open markett & by speciall licence, & that twoe howers after full markett.

" *Item.* Wee sufferr noe unlicensed brewers or ale-housekeepers, & wee have noe comon brewers within our libertie other then alehouse keepers, whoe sell ale to tipplers or poore people by twoe gallons at most, or by gallons or quarts, wee give strict chardge both to the alehousekeepers to sell, & to the Constables to look to yt, that they sell not above a penny a quart, & wee doe our indeavors ourselves to see this done.

" *Item.* Wee have restrayned divers in brueinge of mault & makeinge of malt.

"*Item.* Where wee have found any to have ingrossed into theire hands Corne, wee have caused them
to bringe a good proportion therof to the markett &
sell the same seaven shillings in a quarter under the
Markett to the poore by bushells & pecks & by noe
greater quantities.

"*Item.* We take a course to sett poore people on
worke that are able, & our impotent people wee releeve, & for that purpose wee have much inlarged our
weekly assessment.

"*Item.* Wee diligentlie ward for the Attachinge &
punishinge of Vagabounds & have sent of late divers
to the place of theire birth or habitation.

"*Item.* Wee have noe millers whoe are buyers or
sellers of Corne within our libertie, and wee see to the
millers that they use all sorts of people well in grynde-
inge of their Corne & takeinge of toll.

"*Item.* Our markett is sufficientlie supplied with
corne.

"*Item.* The prices of Corne in our markett are
these, viz.: Rye fyve shillings & fower pence the
bushell, wheat six shillings the bushell, Pease, fower
shillings & eight pence the bushell, Barley fower shillings & six pence the bushell, and malt fower shillings
& six pence the bushell.

"*Item.* Wee looke to yt according to our directions that alehouse keepers & tipplers doe nether suffer
those, whoe they ought not, to drinke in theire houses,
nor any at all on the saboath daie in tyme of dyvyne

service, & likewise that they observe all those Orders, which wee are enioyned to take care for that they bee observed by alehouse keepers & wee punish accordinge to the statute both the Alehouse keepers & tipplers & those persons that wee fynde offendinge and drinkeinge in theire houses.

" Dated at Doncaster
    5 martii 1630-1.

          " BRIAN COOKE,* maoir.
          WILLM. CARVER,
          WILLIAM GAMBLE."†

* Son of Brian Cooke, of Sandal juxta Doncaster. Both father and son were concerned for the King in the Civil Wars, as appears by the following extract from the Royalist Composition Papers : " Bryan Cooke yᵉ elder of Doncaster Alderman, & Bryan Cooke, his sonne. Their delinquency that they adhered unto and assisted yᵉ forces raised against yᵉ Parliament. Rendered in July 1644. Their estate in fee in possession 1088*l*. 2s. 2d., In good debts 1570*l*.; for which their fine at a tenth is 2333*l*. But if they settle 100*l*. per ann. for maintenance of a preaching Minister there for ever, that is 100*l*. per ann. with yᵉ 12*l*. which is already paid, then yᵉ fine remaines 1460*l*." A further statement of the Cookes' affairs, dated in October, 1646, describes the elder one as 72 years old, infirm in body, and not to travel in order to make the usual declarations. He died in December, 1653.

† " William Gamble, of Doncaster, alderman," was also fined by the Parliament on his submission in October, 1646. He is declared to have assisted the King's forces when they were at Doncaster, but never to have left his own house. His property consisted of a house in Doncaster valued at 4*l*. per annum, and a farm in " Longe Sandall," held for a term of years from the Corporation of Doncaster at 40s. rent and a " wayne Loade of Coales yeerely." The fine amounted to 25*l*.

3. Report from Bradford.

" S^{r.}

"Accordinge to the tennor of his Ma^{te} late seve-rall proclamations orders & directions, concerninge the surplusage of Corne & grayne remaineinge & beinge in the custodie and keepinge of riche men, & not brought forth into the open Markett, whereby the Marketts are unfurnished, the rates of Corne raised, & the poore thereby unreleived, for the suppressinge of the multiplicitie of Alehouses, and for the punishinge of rogues & vagabonds, & for the charitable releife of the aged and impotent poore, & puttinge forth of ap-prentices; wee have monethly mett for the said service, & have called before us the Constables, Churchwardens & overseers for the poore for everie the towneshipps & hamletts within the parishes of Bradforde & Ha-worth, have appointed assistants with the said Con-stables, who at severall & at all tymes have duely & respectively searched & examined everie man's barne, garner, & storehouse for Corne, who have certifyed unto us, that our country being mountenous & barren, & thinhabitants there of liveinge most by tradinge, have not corne more then is sufficient for soweinge that litle grownde they have, & for maintenance of their familyes, which nowe they have remaininge in there houses; And for the Alehousekeepers, wee have sup-pressed the greatest parte or number of them, have placed poore apprentices with all men of abillity within the severall towneshipps, taken order for the charitable

releife of the aged & impotent poore people, settinge of
worke Idle persones, & for keepinge watch & warde in
everie towne for apprehendinge of rogues & vaga-
bondes, & for good order, All which in discharge of
our duties we thought fitt to Certify unto you, so with
our harty Comendations, wee cease your further trouble
& shall ever rest

" Your loveing Frends,

" RICH. TEMPEST,*

RICHARD SUNDERLAND.

" Bradford this 14th of
March 1630-1."

4. REPORT FROM WAKEFIELD.

" Whereas by Order appointted by his Matie to bee
straitly observed for preventinge the dearthe of Corne
& graine, the Justices of peace are required to use all
good means that the markets bee well served & the
poore relieved: since which tyme wee have also received further Orders and directions concerninge a
monthely meeteing in our severall divisions — All
which takeing into due consideration, and myndinge
to give accompt accordingly; I doe certifie That Sr
Henrie Savile knt. & barronet, one of his Mats Justices
resiant within this weapontacke of Agbrigge was
troubled with ye Goute, Sr John Ramsden, knt., hath

---

* Of Bowling and Bracewell, Esq., son and heir of Sir
Richard; married Elizabeth, daughter of Sir Gervase Clifton, of
Clifton, county Notts. He was Colonel of a regiment of Horse
in the King's Service.

remained at Byrom, in another parte of the Westriding of this Countie; And that, takeing unto mee the
assistance of the high-constable, and Bayliffe of Wakefield, for viewinge & ordering the markets there, I
finde that the best wheat was the fourth daie of this
instante Marche, & for the space of one moneth before
hath beene, at 21ᵗᵉ shillings the load, Masslegen*
under 19ᵗᵉⁿᵉ shillings the load, cleane Rye about 18s.
the load, Oatmeale aboute 22s. the load, and the best
Beans above 17ᵗᵉⁿᵉ shillings the load. And that the
11ᵗʰ daie of this present moneth, was at 21ᵗᵉ shillings
the load, Oatmeale at 23ᵗᵉ shillings the load, Rye and
Masslegen at 19ᵗᵉⁿᵉ shillings 6d. the load; and Beans
and pease at 15ᵗᵉⁿᵉ shillings the load. And at two of
theise markets I found it necessarie That the poore
people should be provided for by pecks and stroaks
before the Badger, whoe bought whole loads together.

"Denby-grang, yᵉ 17ᵗʰ daie of Marche,
    "Anno Dm̄ 1630-1.
                            "Jo: KAYE."

"Mr. Sheriffe I certified the prices of corne in
Wakefield markett at the Assises. I was there againe
on Friday 15 Ap., where I found a load of wheat to be
at 21s., a load of Ry at 19s. 6d., a load of shillinge at
23s. 4d.

"Concerninge the orders & directions tendinge to the
releife of the poore etc., which his royall maiesty commanded to be published, These are to certify that Sʳ Ri.

* *i.e.*, Maslin—wheat and rye mixed.

Beamont, Sᵣ Jo. Ramsden & I have mett three times
allready, and doe effectually endeavour to relieve the
Impotent, to traine up youth in trades, and to reforme
disordered persons in nine parishes.

"Jo: KAYE.

"Denby Grange

"21 Ap. 1631."

5. REPORT FROM STAINCROSS, &c.

" To the Highe Sheriffe of the County of Yorke.

"The Certificate of Sᵣ Edward Osborne, Barronett,
& Robert Rockley, Esquire, two of his Majesties Jus-
tices of the peace within the Westrid. of the County of
Yorke.

" Theis are to certefy you that the division wherein
wee inhabit is the moste South-weste parte of the
Westriding of the County of Yorke; and for our
generall Sessions consisteth of the Weapontakes of
Tickhill and Strafforth, of Staincrosse and of Osgoldcrosse, All which devision wee together with the reste
of the Justices therin inhabitinge, have for the more
convenient accomplishinge the orders published by his
Maᵗⁱᵉ late proclamation for preventinge dearth of corne,
subdevided into the severall weapontakes above mentioned, allottinge the same to the Justices in every of
them personally inhabitinge, onely the Lordshipp of
Hattfield in the weapontake of Tickhill beinge allotted
to Sᵣ Thomas Wentworth & Mᵣ Portington* dwellinge

* Of Barnby on the Don; Roger Portington was a "delin-
quent" against the Parliament. He surrendered to Lord Fairfax in July, 1644, and was fined 350*l.*

within Osgoldcrosse as lyinge most convenient for
them. Wee doe further certefy that we have caused a
search to be made of all the corne in Staincrosse,
Tickhill and Strafforth except Hatfield afforsayd, and
in that search allowinge to every family possessed of
corne, sufficient for the mentainance thereof, and for
seede which they are to sowe, there was to spare to bee
sould in the markets *fourteene thousande quarters of*
corne, vizt., in Tickhill and Strafforth tenne thousand,
and in Staincrosse foure thousand, all which will
amounte to one thousand loades for every weeke to be
sould in the marketes.   There are within the said
weapontakes the market townes of Doncaster, Rotherham, Sheafield, and Barnsley, wherof Barnsley onely
lyeth within Staincrosse, Doncaster is within the jurisdiction of a corporation and not within oures, & we
conceive that the greate Lo^{pp} of Hatfield together with
the tradinge of the corne buyers dwellinge within that
towne, will, with a little helpe supply that market, &
then the corne to spare within the weapontakes as
afforsayd will suffice to provide the sayd severall marketes of Rotherham, Sheafield & Barnsley with three
hundred and thirty loades a piece weekely for about
thirty weekes from the firste of February, which upon
enquiry we fynde will sufficiently provide their marketes as they use to be provided in more plentifull
yeres.   Wee have severall tymes surveyed the markets
of Rotheram, Sheafield, and Barnsley afforsayd, and
have found Rotheram and Barnsley sufficiently supplyed

with Corne, but wee once fyndinge a defect of Corne in Sheafield, have caused it to be better furnished. Wee have caused that the poore have beene firste served, & by small quantityes in the markets afforsaid accordinge to their desyres. The price of corne is litle or nothinge increased in those markets since Christmas. The severall Statutes made for repressinge of disorder in alehouses, & drunkenesse, together with the statutes for reliefe of the poore, and for punishment of rogues, wee have used our beste endeavoures to put in execution, & caused forfeitures to be imposed upon the offenders to the benefit of the said poore, & to this ende, wee have observed speciall monethly meetinges. In witnesse wherof wee have hereto subscribed our surnames this 25th day of March in the sixt yere of our soveraigne Lord Charles, &c.

> " ED. OSBORNE[*]
> ROBERT ROCKLEY."[†]

SIR HENRY SAVILE TO SIR JOHN GIBSON.

" Mr. Sheriffe, In regard of the incertayntie of my health, I cannot give you soe exact an Account of y[e] service for y[e] poore & marketts as were to be desyred, for y[e] firste my selfe, Sir Ric: Beaumont, & M[r] Kay sate att Wakefeild yesterday where wee are in setlinge such a course for taykinge of stocks to sett y[e] people of able bodies on worke & to releeve y[e] impotent by way of assessment, as I hope in tyme shall serve to sup-

---

* Of Kiveton, see p. 234.   † Of Rockley, see p. 236.

presse y⁰ infinite number of beggars yᵗ swarme in these
partes. And for our markets, both these & in y⁰ rest
of y⁰ cuntryes about us, ytt ys hitherto soe farre from
want of corne, yᵗ ye fallinge daylie of these especially
of Barlye shewes our Cuntrye (thankes be to God) to
be plentifully stored besydes we border upon Lancashyre (a cuntry this yeare able to helpe theyre neighbours) yᵗ bringes downe y⁰ pryce of Oatemeale, which
ys y⁰ substance of y⁰ breade eaten in that Weapontacke
where wee lyve, as in y⁰ greatest part of y⁰ West-
rydinge; besydes my selfe am shortly for my healthes
sake to take a longe Jorney to y⁰ Bathe, soe as I shall
not be able to doe y⁰ further service to his Maᵗᵗⁱᵉ, and
ye cuntrie, which were to be wished, but must leave
y⁰ care thereof to others, who I doubte not will take
that reasonable Care which shalbe fittinge for soe
important a worke, holdinge ytt fitt in y⁰ meane tyme
to give you notice of this much, least by a totall
sylence, I might be censured of a Totall neglect, which
I commit to yʳ friendly consyderation restinge alwayes

> " Yʳ assured lovinge frende
>   to dispose of
>   " H. SAVILE.

" Metheley, 29 April
        " 1631."*

---

* The above reports are contained in Vol. CLXXXIX. Domestiq
—Charles I. In Vol. CCXXI. of the same series are preserved
some records of the small beginnings of tobacco consumption
in Yorkshire, of which some account here will not be devoid of
interest:—On the 26th of July, 1632, Sir John Ramsden and Mr.

An assessment made the 3rd of November 1635 : upon the County of York by Sir John Hotham, kt. and barronet high Sheriffe of the County by virtue of a writ to him directed for ye assessing of 12,000*l.* upon the sayd county as well clergie as layety for the furnishing and provideing of tow ships of 1200 tun for his Maties service.

Corporations :—	£
Upon the Citty of Yorke	520
Pontefrete	60
Headon	20
Kingston sup' Hull ·	140
Rippon	40
Richmond	50
Beverley	50
Doncaster	100
Leeds	200
Scarborough	30
Sum totall	1211

All the Mayors present and consenting but Doncaster who was absent.

John Kaye write to the Privy Council that, in accordance with the instructions given them, they had selected Wakefield, Almondbury, and Huddersfield, as the most convenient places within the wapentake of Agbrigg, at which tobacco should be sold ; and that they had communicated with the ' chief officers and governors ' of those towns, the certificates of whose doings they enclosed with their letter. The first certificate runs as follows :—

" To the righte wor^{ll} his Ma^{ts} Justices of Peace at the Sessions at Wakefeild assembled.

" Accordinge to your wor^{pe} directions these ar to certefye you

The remainder upon the county is 10,183*l.*

Westrideing:—

Upon the Westriding 4313*l.* 4s. 0d., where of upon the several divisions.

	£	s.	d.
Agbridge and Morley	1027	4	7
Stainecliffe and Ewcrosse	821	11	4
Strafford and Tickell	575	1	6
Osgacross and Staycrosse	390	4	8
Barston Ash	410	15	8
Skiracke	266	14	11
Claro	821	11	4

Northriding :—

Upon the Northriding	3594	6	8

Eastriding :—

Upon the Eastriding	2875	9	4

that these persons follcwinge viz: Willm. Brigs, Marie Preston, John Halliwell, grossers, and John Brigs maye be permitted in oure towne of Wakefeild to vente and sell Tobacco, bye retayle, for that they have usuallye and formerlie sould the same. And we allso think yt fitt and convenient for these personns followinge to vente and sell the saide Comodetye (yf so they please) for that formerlie as wee are enformed they have sould yt in theire howses : viz. Mr. Thomas Rustance, Mr. Robarte Burton, Inkepers: John Howldsworthe and Willm Schemell Alehowsekepers. And so we humblie take our leves, Ever restinge.

"Your wor*pps* in all service,

"EDWARD COPLAY, Bealle (?) of Wakefeild.
JOHN STORYE, one of the Cheife Constabells in Agbrigg and Morley.
RIC. GREATHED, Constable in Westgate."

Isaac Wormald, Deputy Bailiff, and John Kay, Constable of Almondbury, recommended Renne Trippier and John Kay, mercers, and Francis Horne, oil-drawer, to be retailers of tobacco in that place. At Huddersfield only one vender is recommended, John Stasye, mercer. John Hirst, and the Constable, Edward Cowper, report that one is quite enough, as very little tobacco is used in the town ; there had formerly been two other venders, but they had quite given it up.

On the 1st of August in the same year, Jasper Blythman, Richard Sunderland, and John Farrer, Justices, send similar Certificates to the Privy Council from Halifax, Bradford, and Eland. The Halifax certificate is signed by John Gibson, Bailiff, John Crosland and Richard Barraclough, Constables ; three retailers are recommended. Bradford would seem to contain a much larger number of lovers of the weed, for there no less than six dealers are mentioned. At Eland, Thomas Wilkinson, Constable, and John Nickolls, Churchwarden, think that Abraham Thomas alone will be sufficient to supply the wants of the population here.

CHAPTER VI.

TRAVELLERS' NOTES IN 1634 AND 1639.

At Norwich, in the year 1634, lived, according to their own description, a Captain, a Lieutenant, and an Ancient, all voluntary members of the "Noble Military Company" in that city. These gentlemen agreed at "an opportune and vacant leisure" to take a view of the Cities, Castles, and "chief situations" in the northern and other counties of England. To this end, all business set apart, they had a parley, and met on Monday, the 11th of August, 1634, and "mustring up their triple force from Norwich, with soldiers' journeying Ammunition they marcht that night to the Maritime Towne of Lyn."

They passed through Norfolk and Lincolnshire, and recorded in the manuscript from which we are quoting* many quaint notices of different places in those counties. At Lincoln they called a council of war, and debated which way was best for their speediest and safest march. They intended, say they, to have seen "that stately maritime town of Hull, and then that ancient privileged Corporation of Beverley, and the Minster in it; but that neither the day, nor way over Humber, would seasonably or safely admit;" so they bent their

* Lansdowne MS., 213.

course towards Newark. We take up the account of
their journey after their progress through Nottingham-
shire, and give it, as nearly as possible, in their own
words :—

"Near the Corporation of Retford, and a little on
our right hand we left Southwell, a house of the
Archbishops of York, where there is a fair Minster,
and at Scroby Park, also the Archbishops', we bade
the Town of Nottingham for this time adieu, and there
entered that large, rich, and famous Province-shire
of our Kingdom, and so made speedy haste through
wind and weather to old knitting Doncaster, and took
up our Lodging at the 3 Cranes, where we found a
grave and gentle Host (no less you can imagine him to
be, having so lately entertained, and lodged His Majesty
in his progress) for in that way his Majesties Gests
lay, and it fell out so fortunately for us, to march some
100 miles, from Newark to Newcastle.

"The Town consists for its Government of a Mayor,
12 Aldermen, 3 Justices, 2 Chamberlains, & a Recorder;† our Host was an Alderman, and in his
Worship's Inn, we were as soundly drenched at our
first entrance, as some Scotch Gentlemen were, whom
we fell upon by the way. We joined our forces,
English and Scottish together that night, and being
well aired and dried we had good free mirth, and made
it serve with ' yea forsooth,' and ' No forsooth' from
those young gallants.

* "Mr. Copley, Recorder"—*marginal note.*

" The next morning we arose to be gone, but these
Scotch Blades had so wearied themselves and their
' galloping galloways,' that forced they were to rest
there a day or two: so bidding them farewell, we
mounted and passed over the River that comes from
Sheffield, for to dine at Pomfret. In the midway (to
season our that morning's-purchased travelling plate)
being thirsty, we tasted a cup at Robin Hood's Well,
& there, according to the usual and ancient custom of
travellers, were in his rocky chair of ceremony, digni-
fied with the order of knighthood, and sworne to
observe his laws. After our oath we had no time to
stay to hear our charge, but discharged our due Feálty
Fee, 4ᵈ a piece to the Lady of the Fountain, and on we
spurred with our new dignity to Pomfret, that day
being Market-day.

" This Town of Pomfret is an ancient Corporation,
consisting of a Mayor, 12 Aldermen, & a Recorder ;*
and hath 2 churches therein; there to lighten ourselves, we lighted at the Star, & took a fair repast, to
enable us the better to scale that high, and stately,
famous and princely impregnable Castle, and Citadel,
built by a Norman upon a Rock: which for the
situation, strength, and largeness may compare with
any in this kingdom.

" In the circuit of this Castle there are 7 famous
Towers, of that amplitude, and receipt, as may entertain
as many Princes, as sometimes have commanded this

* " Mr. Copley, Recorder."—*marginal note.*

Island. The highest of them is called the Round Tower, in which that unfortunate Prince was enforced to flee round a post, till his barbarous Butchers inhumanly deprived him of life: upon that post the cruel hackings, and fierce blows do still remain: we viewed the spacious Hall, which the Giants kept, the large fair kitchen, which is long, with many wide chimneys in it: then went we up and saw the Chamber of Presence, the King's and Queen's Chambers, the Chapel and many other Rooms, all fit and suitable for Princes. As we walked on the leads which cover that famous Castle, we took a large and fair prospect of the Country 20 miles about. York we there easily saw, and plainly discovered, to which place (after we had pleased the She-Keeper our guide) we thought fit to hasten, for the day was so far spent, and the weather such, as brought us both late and wet into that other Metropolitan City of our famous Island.

"Here in this City it was that the great Emperor had his palace ;* it was built (as Tradition and Story tell) in the Reign of King David, by a British King,† and the City called after his name; in our way, as we travelled hither, we passed over 2 large rivers,‡ by 2 well-built and fair-arched bridges of stone, and had a cursory view *in transitu* of some gentlemen's seats of note.§ In this nocturnal travelling habit we entered

* " Constantius."   † " King Ebranke."
‡ " Still Aire and swift Wharfe."
§ " Mr. Hungate's, Mr. Hammond's."

late in the evening that place, not knowing where to
take our Sabbath day's rest, for here in this City was
the period of our first week's travel, resolved so
amongst us at the beginning thereof.   But for
strangers, we most happily and fortunately lodged
our colours in Coney Street and victualled the camp
at the house of a loving and gentle widow, who freely
and cheerfully extended her bounteous entertainment
to us ; for no sooner heard she of her wet, and weary,
benighted guests, but she came to us, and welcomed
us with a glass of good sack, and a dish of hot, fresh
salmon, she herself presenting both, in that kind and
modest family phrase of the Northern speech, 'May
God thank ye, for making my house your harbour ;'
and likewise took such care of us, both at board and
bed, as if she had been a mother, rather than a hostess.

" The next morning we prepared, and fitted ourselves for the Cathedral, which we found to be stately,
large, and ancient, richly adorned, and of an excellent
uniformity, with a rich, rare Library in it ; we heard
a 'domestical' chaplain of the Lord Archbishop preach,
the pulpit standing in the midst between the Quire,
high Altar, Archbishop's seat, and Organ, of which we
are able to give an account as we are bound.   There
we saw and heard a fair, large high Organ, newly
built, richly gilt, carved and painted, a deep and sweet
snowy Crew of Choristers, a Paul's Cross Auditory,
the Lord Mayor in his gold chain, with his 12 grave
brethren, 2 Sheriffs, 2 Esquires, viz., the Sword-

bearer, and his left-hand marcher with the great Mace,
he Recorder, many Serjeants with small Maces, &c.
The gentle Vice-President, with his grave and learned
Council, discreet Knights; his Mace, & Guard repre-
senting (next under the Lord President, now Lord
Lieutenant of Ireland) a Prince : many other worthy
Knights and gallant Ladies, that reside in that old
City, being mostly there present, with their handsome
retinue, did represent a second London.*

"After our forenoon's and afternoon's devotions
were finished, the remaining part of the day was
chiefly spent in the Cathedral, in viewing the many
rarities, Riches, and Monuments of that sacred Building,
the deceased Benefactors whereof, our day books make
mention of ; save those which are remarkable, of which
we took special notice ; The Santum Sanctorum beyond
the stately, rich, High Altar, and gilded Partition,
wherein St. William's shrine formerly was ; his Tombe
7 foot long, sometime covered all over with silver.
He was, as they say, cousin to King Stephen ; upon
the breaking up of the monument, King James commanded his bones, which are large and long, to be
kept as they are in the Vestry : but here I must not

* In the margin of the manuscript the following names are
given :—Sir Wm. Alanson, Mayor ; Sir Wm. Belt, Recorder ;
Sir Ed. Osborn, Vice-President ; Sir Wm. Ellis, Sir Th. Tilsley,
Sir Jo. Lowther, Sir Jo. Melton, Sen., Mr. Dyet, all of the
Learned Council ; Sir Arthur Ingram, Sen. ; Sir Arthur
Ingram, Jun. ; Sir Wm. Lister ; Sir Wm. Ingram ; Sir Hen.
Jenkins ; Sir Tho. Gower ; Sir Ed. Fleetwood ; Sir Th. Danby,
et aliis.

omit those living ' Studs ' and Pillars of this munificent
Cathedral, too many to be all inserted here, therefore I
refer the principal of them to the margin.*

" The sumptuous ornaments, & vestments belonging
to this Cathedral are carefully kept in the Vestry aforesaid, viz. : the gorgeous Canopy, the rich Communion
Table-Cloths, the Copes of embroidered velvet, Cloth
of gold, silver and tissue of great worth and value.
There Mr. Verger showed us St. Peter's Chair (which
we made bold to rest in) wherein all the Archbishops
are installed : two double gilt Coronets, the tops with
globes and crosses to set on either side of his Grace
upon the said Instalment ; when he takes his Oath
these are called his Dignities.   In this consecrated
place is a dainty sweet, clear well, called St. Peter's
Well, of which we tasted for the Saint's sake.

" But here I must not forget to tell you, what rich
Plate we saw, which is kept also in the Vestry and
was given by our most gracious Sovereign, in his
Progress into Scotland, worthy of a royal marginal
observation.   Then we saw Archbishop Hutton's fair

* " Archbishop Neale ; Dr. Scot, Dean ; Dr. Stanoy, Pre-
centor ; Dr. Hodshon, Church Chaplain ; Dr. Eashnall (?),
Bishop's Chaplain ; Dr. Wickham, Archdeacon of York ;
Dr. Cosens, Archdeacon of the East Riding ; Mr. Baily,
Archdeacon of Nottingham ; Mr. Thruffecrosse, Archdeacon of
Cleveland ; Prebends 36."

† " Two double-gilt flagons ; 2 double-gilt chalices, with covers ;
2 double-gilt candlesticks ; 1 large double-gilt basin ; 1 double-
gilt communion-plate ; a Bible and a Common Prayer Book,
covered with crimson velvet, clasped and embossed with silver
double-gilt."

tomb, on the south side of the Quire, lately built, and another still more lately built for Archbishop Toby Mathew, which is a stately rich Monument, seated under the east window; also Sr William Gee's, Sr William Ingram's, Sir Henry Bellasis', Dr Swinburne's, and the Friar's Monument in brass, who received his mortal wound at mass.

"To close up & amply to satisfy our thirsty desires, Mr Verger ushered us into that rich and rare model, and ' round Architect Master-piece of pieces,' the most stately Chapter-House; the magnificent rich and stately, & lofty winding entrance whereof did exactly promise, & curiously foretell us the worth within, which I am not able to express, to its worth; only this I remembered to commemorate. At the entrance over the door is curiously cut and framed the picture of Our Saviour in his Mother's arms, St Peter and St Paul on either side. The seven lofty stately rich windows, curiously painted with the story of the Book of Books; 8 high fair built squares, with 46 Prebends' seats, curiously cut in free stone, every one covered, wrought and gilded above, with divers works, and 300 knots of several rare forms and faces, not one like another; as also that strange miraculous roof, framed by geometrical art, which is most beautiful and rare to all that behold it, and is accounted one of the neatest, uniform, and most excellent small pieces in Christendom, by all travellers, foreign and domestic, insomuch as one, coming not long since into this kingdom, and viewing

with a considerate eye the rarity, and excellency of it,
did so approve, commend and admire, that he caused
this Latin verse in golden old Saxon letters to be
inserted in the wall, at the entrance thereof—

'Ut Rosa flos florum, sic est Domus ista Domorum.'

" After this we desired to see no other that night,
but gratified our Conductor, according to the place of
his trust; and the next morning, to begin our week's
travel, we thought it best to resort to the best place,
the Minster, and after our morning sacrifice therein
done, we tired our legs with an ascent of 270 stairs
march, to the top of the Minster, which we accounted
no task at all, his Majesty having lately taken the same.

" There we took view of the City, and Suburbs, which
are situated in a sweet and fertile soil, the Meadows,
Pastures, Cornfields, and Wolds, near 20 miles about.
It hath a large fair wall, with 8 gates, and many
towers and bulwarks, that fence it in ; and for the inhabitants 28 Churches to serve God in, and that famous
river which is navigable only for boats, and lighters
gliding through the City; which takes head from the
West Moors, where a 'messe' of brave rivers lovingly
springs near together ;* over which is built a fair long
arched Bridge, and amongst many other brave Houses
and Buildings in that spacious City, we beheld as it
were under us, adjoining to the Minster, as it were a
second Paradise, wherein liveth a generous, free, and

* "Eden, Lune, Swale, Eure."

grave old Knight* and of great revenue; we speedily descended to go thither, and had free passage to our own heart's desire.

" The first moiety of an hour, we spent in his rare Gardens, and curious long walks, which were adorned with many kind of Beasts to the life, with most lively statues in several shapes and forms. A pleasant fair Tennis-Court; a delightful large bowling ground, newly made; curiously contrived Fish-ponds; all which made up another sweet little City. A place it is so pleasant, to all the senses, as Nature and Art can make it.

" The other half-hour we spent in his rich Mansion, where we found so much contentive variety within, as before without, his store of massy Plate, rich Hangings, lively pictures, and statues rich, 150*l.* pearl Glasses, fair stately 500*l.* Organ, and other rich furniture in every room, Prince-like, his family and attendants Court-like, his free and generous entertainment Christmas-like; here we desired heartily (having such free liberty as was given us) to have spent another hour, but that time would not allow it.

" From thence with all due thanks, we marched to the Manor, sometime that famous Abbey called St. Mary's, now the Prince's and Lord President's Lodgings: There we viewed the ancient, and stately spacious demolished Buildings, and after a set at Tennis there, and

* " Sr Arthur Ingram."

a cup of Refreshment, we were enabled to enter the great Hall, situated close upon the banke of the River Ouse, where the Lord President and Council sit to determine all causes and controversies for the North parts, the Lord Mayor, Sheriffs and Justices for the Town.

"By this it was time to hasten to our good Hostess and her good Ordinary, which would not be forgot, for such in our Southern parts could not be afforded under three times the price. The Company and discourse was answerable to the cheer; well, for such an Ordinary, such Usage, such an Hostess, and such good Company, we shall hardly find the like in the whole Island.

"The next day the Lieutenant ventured to march alone to view the ruined Castle, which was built by William the Conqueror (and by it Clifford Tower) and so much thereof is yet standing as will lodge M^r 'Jaylor,' & his sojourners, the Prisoners; here no suspicion, no jealousy arose, for that his two comrades, Clerks of the Green-Cloth, did not there appear.*

"It's time for us to make ready to depart from this old City, though we would willingly have stayed longer, to have heard a famous Scholar tried for Blasphemy in the High Commission Court; but we had spun out our longest period of time, and so with many 'Marry God thank hers,' we bad our good cheap Hostess adieu;

* An allusion to some little unpleasantness which happened to the party when they visited Lincoln Castle.

and spurred on for Topliffe near 'Spur-Rippon,' by his Majesty's park, and forest, and some other Castles, and sweet 'situations' of Lords and Knights.* In this short way we twice crossed over by two fair Arched-Bridges that sacred River,† which 5 miles short of that days journey meets with another River,‡ and so together make that famous River Ouse : and although this town§ was small, yet had we good Lodging and Fare for a small matter.

"The next day we were to pass into another kingdom, the Bishóprick of Durham, for the Bishop is a Prince there ; as soon as we left our Inn, at the end of the Town appeared to us a fair, and neat Building, a Knight's House, most sweetly situated on the River Swale, and not far from thence another Knight's seat,¶ and by dinner time we got to booting Darlington."

Here we regret to have to part company with our entertaining friends.

We have been so fortunate as to find in another little manuscript ‖ a short account of a journey made along the same track some five years later. It is called "My journey to Yorke to attend the King (as a Privy Chamber-man Extraordinary) on the behalfe

---

* "New Park, Gaters forest, Sheriff-Hutton Castle, Crake, the Bp. of Durham's, Sʳ Thos. Hutton's, Popleton ; Mʳ Stapleton's, Miton ; Mʳ Cholmeley's, Bradford."

† "Swale."   ‡ "Lure."   § "Topliffe,"

¶ " Sir Wm. Robinson's.   Sir Arthur Ingram's."

‖ Add. MS., 28,566.

of my Brother. Anno 1639." We select the most
interesting portions :—

" Aprill 2. Lay y^t night at Mr Leavets ye White
Hart in Doncaster.

" 3. On Wednesday I baited at Ferry Brigg & lay
y^t night at Mr Taylors Poastm^r at ye Swanne in
Tadcaster.

" 4. On Thursday I came to Mr Pooles house in y^e
ould woorke Streete in Yorke, where I was billited myself & footman, & the rest of my men & horses at M^r
Atkinsons ye Elephant & Castle on Peasam Greene.

" DONCASTAR.

" A very spacious faire churche but few Monuments
or matter remarkeable in it.

" Onely this Inscription I noted for ye odd conceit,
written round about a faire plaine marble on ye north
side—' Howe, Howe, who is heere. I Robun of Doncaster. And Margaret my Pheere. That I spent,
that I had. That I gave, that I have. That I lent,
that I lost.' Quo'd Robertus Byrks : who in this
world did reigne threescore yeares and seaven, and
yet lived not one.

" YORKE.

" A faire lardge Cittie, 26 Churches in it. One
whereof ye Minster is a very goodly edifice & exceed-
ing lardge, & for lightsomnesse much excells Pauls.
The greatest blemish of ye building is y^t ye Roofe is of
wood. The Chapter House is a very faire. Round
Roome on the North side, wth faire painted glasse win-

dowes & portly fantastique woorke rounde y⁰ stone
seates, wᶜʰ seeme to be cut out in stone, but I beleive
are onely plaister woorke.

"Sʳ Arthur Ingrams house at y⁰ west end of y⁰
Minster the inhabitants beleive excells for a Garden,
being set out wᵗʰ images of Lyons Beares Apes & y⁰
like both beasts and birds, wᶜʰ from y⁰ Topp of y⁰
steeple please the eye, but otherwise are showes only
to delight chilldren, the cheifest pleasure of his
Gardens beeing the neare adjacency to y⁰ Towne
wall, wᶜʰ affoords him meanes to cast severall mounts &
degeees one above annother, y⁰ upmost veiwing the
whole countrey on yᵗ side, & is of a great liberty
extending half a qr. of a mile in length beyond Sʳ Tho.
Ingrams his next neighbour. His House is low, noe
extraordinary building, but very commodious & stately
& spacious enough though not suitable to his estate.
Yet hee showed himselfe an honourable Host by entertaining (during y⁰ time of y⁰ Kings abode there) the
Lo. Generall, the Lo. Chamberlaine, the Secretary of
Estate in his house, & the rest of y⁰ Lords (that attended
on the King) every day many of them at boord with
him beside gentlemen & others. The Cittie is abound-
antlie stored with provision, yet because of y⁰ Kings
presence & concourse wᵗʰ him, thinges were inhaunced
above yᵉ usuall price much. Neverthelesse there were
excellent ordinaries, 18d. y⁰ masters, & 6d. servants ;
As at y⁰ Talbot (a very faire Inne) especially. At
Ousemans y⁰ Poast mʳ y⁰ signe of the Dragon, for 12d.

z

and 8d. At y⁰ Bell in Thursday-markett, for 8d. and
6d. ; with many other places. The King hath a meane
Pallace here yet conveniently contriv'd affoording him
—An outer Coᵗ—A good square Base Coᵗ—A good
Guard Chamber, Privie Chamber & Presence wᵗʰ inner
Roomes befitting his state; & a small Garden. The
cheifest of ye Kings pleasure heere was to ride downe
into Clifton Ings (or meadowes) & have his Nobillitie
about him, & see his cavaliers on yᵉʳ brave horses, much
more like yᵉ recreation of Hide parke, than the fashion
of Campus Martius.

"To this Cittie I came yᵉ 4ᵗʰ of Aprill beeing Thursday & there remained till yᵉ 27ᵗʰ of yᵉ same moneth
beeing Saturday. The People are affable & free-
hearted, yet vaine glorious, & love to be praised, in
theire feasts they are very luxurious, & given to
excesse ; but it may bee yᵉ occasion now made them
to enlardge theire courtesies beyond yᵉʳ usuall bounds.
Otherwise they deserved the Kinges charactar of—Good
people who the longer hee stayed the better they
used him.

" The 25 June, Tuesday, I came to Rippon first, where
there is a Cathedrall Church subordinate to Durham,
and built very like it ; our countrey man Dʳ Dod is
deane thereof. This Towne is famous for spurrs ; the
best woorkeman now is one Harman, and 2 brothers
called Portars. One Warwick was accounted the best
woorkman, but hee is now remooved to Burrough
brigge.

"This night I lodged at Ripley.

"The 26 Wednesday I came to Bradford, a towne that makes great store of Turkey cushions & carpetts. Heere I lay all night in pravate man's house, a Tanner, who sometimes gave entertainment to travellers; the wett weather kept mee heere all this day and a good part of y° next.

"The 27 Thursday I came to Hallifax, a pretty well built towne of stone, and consists much of clothiers, to encourage whose trade, was graunted that priviledge of heading by y^er towne law any malefactor taken (as they say) hand-napping, back bearing, or confessing the felony. Theire heading block is a little out of towne westward; it is raised upon a little forc'd ascent of some halfe a dozen stepps, and is made in forme of a narrow gallowes, having 2 ribbs downe either side-post, and a great waightie block wth Riggalds for those ribbs to shoote in, in y° bottome of wch blocke is fastned a keene edged hatchet, then the Block is drawne up by a pulley and a cord to y° crosse on y° topp, and the malefactor layes his head on y° block below; then they let runne the stock wth y° hatchet in, and dispatch him immediately.

"Heere is one of y° fairest Innes in England call'd y° Crosse, because it stands right against y° Crosse, (I thinke) now kept by a widdow woeman."

FINIS.

APPENDICES.

APPENDIX A.

MISCELLANEOUS CORRESPONDENCE, &c.

SIR HENRY SAVILE, OF METHLEY, TO SIR RICHARD BEAUMONT.

(Add. MS. Brit. Mus. 24,475.)

S. Catherynes this Ashewensday, 1607.

. . . You may lett my cosen Ramsden knowe Mr. Kaye's
letter & his by my cosen Farrer came to my handes, & lett
him knowe I never expected any thinge in all my lyfe wherin
I was soe much deceyved, as in his refusall to acknowledge my
fyne. For other men's slownes in that busines I can say
notheinge, but I can not imagine nor ever could that my cosen
William Ramsden should not be as neare to me in curtesie and
love as either the Provost of Eton * or S^r. Jo. Jackson. I am
well assured I should not therby have wronged him more than
I have done them. But ytt ys a lamentable case and not
unworthie your observation to see howe frendes havinge the
trust of a yonge man's estate will tyranize over his fortune :
& I may speake ytt to you unfaynedly, yf God had not blest
me in myne owne cariage of my greatest busines beyond ordinary expectation, theire humorous cariage had made me worse
in my estate than the worst of them. But I thanke them I am
bound to, & I thanke God I am nowe so well settled, as I
have very ill fortune yf I need to them in the vallew of a hayre.
Fare you well.

Your assured lovinge cosen

H. SAVILE.

* His uncle, Sir Henry Savile, the distinguished scholar.

Sir Henry Savile to Sir Julius Cæsar.
(*Lansdowne MS. Brit. Mus.* 158.)

Right Honorable,—I have receyved y^r letters of the 28th of May by poste whereby I am sorie to understand of my uncle's sicknes and danger, prayeinge God (yf ytt be his heavenly will) to restore him to his former health, to the comfort of all his frendes. Yf I were perswaded he would not reçover I would leave all busynes to see him, but I trust in God to fynde him amended when my occasions drawe me upp. Concerninge the newe tytle I wyshe I might resolve ye beste for my selfe & posteritie,. *yf y^r Honor, my Lady, & Uncle Savile have thought ytt a thinge fitt for mee, there shall need noe other consents.* Howe farre soever y^r Honor shall engage y^r selfe for me I will make good. Only I will pray y^r Honors advertisement howe I must carrie my selfe for my personall attendance & att what tyme; yf there be no further cerimony but a patent, which may be dispatched in my absence, I pray y^r Honor to appointe the care of ytt to some such person as y^r Honor shall thinke fitt to make choyce of, & I wilbe thankfull to them. For such letters as my Lo : Stanhope shall hearafter sende by poste I would have them dyrected to John Hayford, postmaster of Ferribriggs, who ys ye next poste to my house att Metheley being but fyve myles of. I have wrytt answere to all my wyves letters y^t came to my handes with the advantage save only one sent by Sr Thom : Blande which miscaryed out of a great mischance. But of such as I have receyved there was not one concerned any busynes, therefore yf I may knowe her mynde in any thinge I shall presently give her satisfaction, soe with my humble dutie remembred to y^r Honor, & my Lady, with my kynde remembrance to my sister Vere my wyfe and Brothers I reste ever,

Y^r Honors moste bounden sonne in Lawe

H. Savile.

Metheley 1 June 1611.

To the Right Honorable Sr Julius Cæsar Chancelor of ye Exchequer and of his Ma^{ts} privie Counsell, with speede, Strand, London. *

* Sir Julius Cæsar was the son of Cæsar Adelmar, physician to Queen Mary and Queen Elizabeth, and was born at Tottenham in 1557. He was

The Same to the Same.

Right Honorable,—I have receyved y^r letters by poste of ye first of this Instant & the booke of ye Barronets enclosed, which havinge perused I fynde my presence not soe necessarily required in any one thinge as for entringe bonde for payment of ye severall sommes; for I fynde a speciall care taken in ye latter ende of ye booke for such as cannot conveyniently be present to take theire patents, y^t theire oathes may be taken by Commission, & soe I doubte not but in an ordinary Course my bonde may be taken heare by y^r honors warrants. Thus much I have thought fitt to deliver in excuse of my not comminge, beinge specially enforced to be of this opinion, presuminge y^r Honor will vouchsafe to be my meanes with their Lo^{pps}, which will give me a great deale more credit then yf I were myne owne immediate Instrument, in prosequtinge a newe dignitie. For my place amongst my Cuntriemen I desyre neither to be first nor laste; I can be content to followe Mr Wentworth & Sr Hen: Bellasis, for any other I yet heare of I may without any great incongruitye be rankt afore them. Howsoever ytt seemes y^t such as are allreadie created must hould theire rankes, yet for the reste I see noe entendment to martiall them till towardes ye 6^t of July, when the number shall grewe to be complete, but whatsoever theire Lo^{pps} shall resolve in y^t respect y^r Honor nowe knowes my resolution to perfourme whatsoever you shall please to undertake for me, aswell as yf I were present my selfe, which in all ye pore Judgment I have cannot soe well stande with my credit as to have ytt done by my honorable frendes, beinge desyrous ytt should appeare (accordinge to truith) to my much respected frendes in these partes, y^t ytt was ye good respect of my honorable frendes above, rather then any of my own ambitions y^t drewe me to ytt, insoemuch as I would scarce bee once seene

appointed Judge of the Admiralty Court and a Master in Chancery in 1588, Master of St. Catherine's near the Tower in 1596, and Master of the Rolls in 1614. He died in 1636, and was buried in St. Helen's, Bishopsgate-street, where he has a singular monument. Sir Henry Savile, of Methley, married the daughter of the wife of Sir Julius by her former husband, John Dent, of London, merchant; her second daughter, to whom allusion is made in these letters, was married to Sir Francis Vere.

yn ytt till ytt be dispatched. I humbly thanke y^r Honor for
y^r good newes of my uncle Savile; yf y^r Honor & my Ladie
shall notwithstandinge all my allegations reqnyre my cominge,
upon notice I will not fayle to repayre to accordingly upon 3
dayes warninge how soone soever; but I had rather ytt were
after ye creation ended a fortnight or three weekes then before.
Whensoever y^r Honor shall please to call mee I purpose to come
by Eaton to see my uncle, which shall only staye me a night.
And soe giving y^r Honor all humble & respective thankes, I
shall ever pray to God for ye contyneuance of y^r honourable
fortune & happines, & rest,

Y^r Honors most bounden
sonne in Lawe

Metheley 4to Junii 1611:   H. SAVILE.

I pray y^r Honor y^t ye partié appoynted to sue out the patent
see my name & place of dwellinge written—*Henrico Savile de
Metheley in Comitat Ebor., mil. &cet.*—as I wryte ytt my selfe.

THE SAME TO THE SAME.

May ytt please y^r Honor. I have answered both y^r letters
of ye 28th of May and 1^{rst} of this Instant which I doubte not but
you have safely receyved by way of poste. I have receyved
likewyse a letter from my Ladie yesternight about ye 400*l.* for
which wee have taken ye beste & speidiest course y^t may bee, soe
as I doubte not of ye payment thereof att ye daye. I
still hould my resolution not to come as every day fyndinge newe
reasons to strengthen y^t opinion; yf y^r Honor have made me
an undertaker for Ireland, I pray you move my Lo: Chancellor
for a Comission for takeinge my oath as soon as may be to
Sr George Savile ye elder, S^r Jo: Savile, S^r Jo: Jackson &
Sr Thom: Blande, kts., or any two of them. And for ye bondes
yf y^r Honor cannot staye ye entringe of them till my comminge
up, I would entreat y^r Honor to give my brother Jackson
authority to take them and returne y^{em} to ye Receyvor, but I
would have them drawen att London accordinge to the forme
allreadie used All which I presume to recommende to y^r Honors
trouble & rest y^r moste bounden sonne in law,

H. SAVILE.

Metheley, 8 Junii 1611, 12 a clock.

Right Honorable. . . . . I wonder much yt yr Honor hath
receyved noe answere from me touchinge yr proposition of the
newe dignitie, beinge I write ye first of this month in answere of
your Honors of ye 28th of ye last, I writt annother of ye 4th to
answere yr Honors of ye first & I have writt a 3d in answere of
my Ladies last of ye 8th of this month together with other
severall letters accordinge to my occasions ; all these letters
were sent by poste whatsoever is become of them. Leaste they
should all have miscaryed I hould ytt not unfitt to give some
short touche of ye moste essential parts thereof as farre as I can
remember. *For answere to ye proposition I referred my selfe to
what ye Honor, my Lady, and Uncle Savile should resolve of,* but
I considered ytt was a thinge rather to be done by ye motion of
yr Honor to my Lordes then that I should appeare in ytt
myselfe, to excuse me from *ambition amongst my better kyndred
and neighbors who will thinke much to see me leape before them, our
byrthes beinge equall & my state inferiour.* Upon perusall of ye
books besydes I fynde noe mannes personall apparance necessarie savinge for entringe bondes, which upon yr Honors letter to
some of my neighbors may I doubte not be taken heare and
safely returned accordinge as you shall please to appointe ; the
oath may be taken by *Comission,* which I would have dyrected
as I writt in my laste letter to Sir George Savile the elder, Sir
John Savile, Sir John Jackson, & Sir Thom: Blande, knightes,
or to any two of yem ; for any payments to be made I writt a
letter enclosed in yr Honors laste packett to Mr Eldred & Mr
Whitmore to paye upon ye 2d or 3d of July all or parte of 1500*l.*
in theire handes as yr Honor shall appointe, for though ye first
payment for ye newe busynes will requyre but 300 and odde
powndes, yet my Lady wrytinge shee had entred into a purchase, wherein shee sayde shee must disburse all her owne
moneyes & use her frendes, I thought fitt to offer all myne or
what yr Honor shall have occasion to use thereof, which I doubte
not but they will make readie upon notice from yr Honor
in case my letter be miscaryed. I pray yr Honor yt Mr Dod
or some other (as you shall thinke fittest) may sue out my

Patent, & I wilbe thankfull to them. There ys due from M^r
Eldred and Mr William Whitmore *fifteene hundred poundes* upon
a fortnightes warninge whensoever ytt shalbe called for, ye 2^d of
July they are to paye Interest after nyne in ye hundred for
3 monthes which cometh to 33*l*. 15*s*. over and above ye 1500*l.*
. . . . . And soe with my due remembrance respectively to my
Ladie and ye rest, I remayne

Y^r Honors most bounden sonne in Lawe

H. Savile.

Metheley 15 Junii 1611.

The Same to the Same.

Right Honorable,—I have receyved y^r 2 or 3 severall letters
with the liste of ye Baronetts as they are marshalled by his
Matie. The Comission & Bondes 1 returned with letters of
the 2^d of this instant, beinge ye same daye my othe was taken att
my house by my brother Jackson and Sr Tho. Blande. The
messinger promised me to deliver them safely to y^r Honor upon
Wensday night the 10th of this month, whereof I doubte not
but that they be delivered accordingly. And soe with humble
thankes for y^r Honors great & respective care of this troublesome affayre, with my remembrance of dutie to my Lady & love
to my wyfe and sister Vere not forgettinge my Brothers, I wishe
all happines may ever attende y^r Honor & all y^{rs}, Amongst
whom there ys none can be more obliged to y^r service then ys

Y^r Hon^{rs} most bounden
sonne in Lawe

Metheley this 14th   H. Savile.
of July 1611.

SIR HENRY SAVILE TO SIR DUDLEY CARLETON, AT VIENNA.
(*Domestic State Papers, James I., Vol.* 80.)

My lo: Ambassador. I have receyved y^r letter of ye 30th of
Decemb^r whereby I understand you have bene pleased to lende
my brother y^r creditt for 20*l.*, his owne moneyes faylinge him
through his neglect of givinge his frendes in England certayne
Advertisement of his remove from place to place, for which

-curtesye I give you many thankes havinge repayde y⁰ money to
Mʳ Burlamach accordinge to yʳ direction. I had sent sent my
brother to Geneva before Michaelmas laste a Bill of Exchange
for 50*l.* and a letter of creditt for 30*l.* more to make use of upon
any very urgent occasion in y⁰ rest of his travulls useing Mʳ
Burlamach's creditt only for his moneyes. The letters ·sent to
Geneva by y⁰ marchant yᵗ served him his money in France, we
sent me backe hither agayne synce Christmas soe there was noe
remedye for him but to have recourse to his frendes beinge soe
farre from home. Hereafter duringe his aboade in Italy or else
where he shall not fayle God willinge in this kynde so as he
exceede not his alloance of a 100*l.* per Ann. His frendes heare
must intreate yʳ Loᵖᵖ to have an eye to his government &
afforde him yʳ best advyse & dyrection in his courses for though
wee cannot expect much from his Education, whom nature did
more enclyne to make a ploddinge common lawyer then an
accomplisht traveller, yet synce he hath lefte his best element,
wee would be glad he should returne worthie his expence of
tyme & money yf ytt might be. I can wryte yʳ Loᵖᵖ noe
occurrents but yᵗ wee be all well heare att Eaton where I have
contynued & soe doe this wynter till sommer come yᵗ I goe
downe to settle myne aboade in my owne cuntrie. Wee often
remember you & my Ladie & as we have expected yʳ returne,
soe wee hope yᵗᵗ will not be long deferred before you exchange
for y⁰ better. Jn y⁰ meane tyme I recommende my best service
to yʳ Loᵖᵖ & my Lady & rest

Yʳ Loᵖᵖˢ ever to dispose of

H. Savile.

Eaton this 25ᵗʰ of January
    1614-5.

Thomas Savile to Sir Richard Beaumont.

(*Add. MS. Brit. Mus.* 24,475.)

Sʳ, though uninterested, I am bold to make this request
unto you for this Cock. I have been foiled as you know at
Leichfeild by my Lord of Dorcett, and my onelie meanes
of repaire is by this cockinge. I have with much adooe

borowed my father's cocks, to take my choice, and this is the onelie best I relie of. If either brothers or sisters of him will do you anie pleasure you shall commaund them in his roome. I go to-morrow post towardes London to get walkes for them some 15 miles of London, and if you would do us the pleasure to strenthen us with some of your Wheefers, it would make us the more confident. The time is verie shorte, therefore good S⁣ʳ make all the possible hast you may. I am persuaded you wish us strong, or els I should be ashamed to be so importunate with you, for I hope you know you may commaund both them and me who ever desires to be commaunded by you : and so I rest

　　　　　　　　　　　　Youres, assured Sir
　From Haigh Hall　　　　　　　　Thomas Savile.
　　29 of March 1615.
Pray Sʳ be at London as soon as you can.
To my honorable frend Sʳ Richard Beaumont at
　Longley these be dᵈ.

G. Cutler to the Privy Council.

(Domestic State Papers, Charles I., Vol. 26.)

Right Honorable,—May it please you that where I have received from Loᵖᵖˢ the twenty fourth of Aprill last, fiftie five severall privy Seales, for the delivery and collection thereof, These are therefore to certefie you, that most of the said privy Seales are already delivered : And that diverse of the Gentlemen whom the same doth concerne pretend to have formerly of late received privy Seales for the like Sommes from Sir Henry Savile, wherupon they conceive your Loᵖᵖˢ ententes are not to chardge them double : soe they desire respite for payment, untill such time as they may further knowe your Loᵖᵖˢ pleasures herein. And that Sir Francis Wortley, Sir John Jackson, Mʳ Copley of Skelburrough, Mʳ West and Mʳ Portington will answer the same upp above at London, soe I take it I shall not expecte any Receipt from them : For soe Sir Francis Wortley sayd (with much shéwe of discontente) that he would pay me none : And that for those whom already by their answers it may

bee coniectured will not pay at all, vizt Mr Anne, Mrs Anne,
Mr Bullocke, the Lady Foster, and Richard Nayler, I have herewith sent my servant that delivered their privy Seales, to make
oath thereof, if your Lo^pps soe bee pleased to require itt, for
Mr Annes servants (William Clayton and Lawrence Bayte)
threwe the privy Seale out of the dores after him : And M^ris
Anne and Mr Bullocke wilfully and peremptoryly avoydes the
same. And the Lady Foster & Richard Nayler, both of them
pleades sicknes, ould age, with much want and povertie. Soe
with all humblest due respectes, I crave leave to remayne at

Your Lo^pps comand

May 3 }
1626. }   G. CUTLER.*

Endorsed

May, 1626,

From Yorke about Privie Seales.

SIR RICHARD BEAUMONT TO THE DUKE OF BUCKINGHAM.

(*Domestic State Papers, Vol.* 32.)

My dearest Lord,—That this black Tempest and Confluence
of Confounding malice cast upon youe by the passions of some
people is past, I will ever thanke God, (Curst be the inventors)
and the same God grant the Kinge and youe a long life, who I
heare graple in the Ocean of affection, maye youe if it be his
will, never unclaspe but like two Ivies (Integritie beinge the
Oke) strive ever whoe shall hould hardest.

Maye itt please your grace that youe will pardone the bould-
nes of your servant who humblie sues for itt. And alsoe that
for my sake youe will cast your eye of Honor and favour of my
kinsman whoe carries my name, and is owner of the pretie neat
shippe called the Golden Cock of London : but my Lord my
humble suite is limited with this reservation noe further favour
then he shall merit bravely : thus intending to wait on your

---

* Probably Sir Gervase Cutler, of Stainborough, knt., who was a
treasurer for lame soldiers for the West Riding, 2 Chas. I., and lieu-
tenant-colonel of a regiment of foot there.

grace or it be longe, remembring my humblest and dearest
service to your grace I take leave restinge

Your Graces most humble and

most faithfull servaunt,

Whitley, in Yorkshire   Ric : Beau-mont.
27 Julii 1626.

Sir Thomas Savile to the Duke of Buckingham.

(Domestic State Papers, Charles I., Vol. 108.)

Most excellent Lord,—Although I do assure my selfe M^r
Nicholas hath made knowne unto your grace, y^t the reason of
my so rude departure out of towne was out of feare to approach
your graces presence from a house enfected wth the small pox,
and although I do well know, y^t the noble bosome of ye duke
of Buckingham is ever full of pardons to all such as erre,
through feare and reverence ; yet my most noble Lord, when I
came home I could not satisfie my selfe me thought wthout a
particular, humble and most thankefull augnowledgment of all
your graces bounties, showred uppon our house, but when I
came unto the particulers I found the bare catalogue of them
would fill so manie lines, as were not fitt for me to trouble your
grace wth all ; so I thought it more fitt to Caracter them in the
aptest place, wh^{ch} is the hartes of us and our posteritie, where,
whenever they shall meete a grave, may it from thenceforth
perish from this land, and be a house no more, but be turned to
a piller of unworthines, for all the wondering world to looke upon,
and in the meane space trulie my lord, I shall blush to owne that
fortune, bloud, or frend, wch should not live or die, to serve the
duke of Buckingham ; My lord I know these verball protesta-
tions are soone made, and are writt in such wth litle coat. But (as
I dare not wish for it) if a greater occasion of expression should
be offred, yet I certainlie know, y^t from our soules we should
then more willinglie signe this truth in crimson lines, then now
wth such, and wheresomever I shall have a being, I do beseech
your grace, to do me so much right as to believe, y^t there is not

another soule can live, and be more reallie devoted to your
graces service, then is

Your graces most humble most bounden
most affectionate servant

T. SAVILE.

Howley in Yorkshire
this 25 of June
1628.

Addressed—To the right excellent prince the duke
of Buckingham his grace, greate Admirall of
England, these at Court.

THOMAS, VISCOUNT SAVILE TO SIR RICHARD BEAUMONT.

(*Add. MS. Brit. Mus.* 24,475.)

H^d S^r,—I did thinke and impute it to be a great displeasure
unto me in that I could not enjoy your company the last weeke
at Pontefract, and were sorry to hear of your sickeness, but am
now glad to heare of your recovery. Upon Tuesdaie I entend to
kill a stagge in the Newe Parke, and am resolved to go to
Pontefract upon Wednesdaie, where I shall be for the most
parte of the weeke and would be glad to see you there. I have
sent a bucke to the Countess of Buckingham and shall at the
returne of the messenger know certainly whether shee will come
hither or noe. And as soone as I knowe it I will send you
word. In the meantime with remembrance of kind love to you,
I rest

Your verie loving and
Assured freind

SAVILE.

Howley, August 21th 1631.
To the right wor^ll his verie lovinge freind Sr Richard
Beau-mont, Knt. & Barronet, this ddd.

A A

APPENDIX B.

LIST OF PARLIAMENTARY REPRESENTATIVES, FROM 1542 TO 1640.

(Compiled from the Domestic State Papers, the Commons' Journals, and Willis's Notitia Parliamentaria.)

33 HENRY VIII.

County—Sir Ralph Ellerker, knt.
City—John Hogeston, gent., Geo. Gayle, alderman.
Scarborough—Sir Ralph Eure, knt, Sir Nich. Fairfax, knt.

1 EDWARD VI.

County—Sir Robt. Constable, knt., Will. Babthorpe, Esq.
City—Thomas Gargrave, Esq., Will. Holme, ald.
Hull—John Thacker, Walter Jobson.
Hedon—Edw. Elderton, Esq., Robt. Gouche, Esq.
Scarborough—Ric. Whaley, Esq., Reginald Beesley, Recorder.

7 EDWARD VI.

County—Sir Will. Babthorpe, knt., Sir Robt. Constable, knt.
City—Thos. Gargrave, Esq., ——
Hedon—John Constable, Robt. Shakerley.
Thirske—Thos. Legh, Esq., Reginald Beesley, Esq.
Scarborough—Thos. Eynns, Gen. Dakyns.
Hull—Alex. Stockdale, Wm. Johnson.

1 MARY—1st Parliament.

County—Sir Robt. Constable, knt., Sir Will. Vavasor, knt.
City—John North, Robt. Hall, gent.
Hull—John Thacker, Will. Johnson.

Ripon—Marmaduke Wyvill, Esq., Edw. Beesley, gent.
Scarborough—Sir John Tregonwell, knt., Leo. Chamberlain.
Thirsk—Thos. Eynns, Esq., John Gascoigne, gent.
Knaresborough—Reginald Beesley, Ralph Scrope.
Boroughbridge—Will. Tankard, Christ. Wray.
Hedon—Sir John Constable, knt., Robt. Shakerley, Esq.

1 MARY—2nd Parliament.

County—Sir Will. Babthorpe, knt., Sir Christ. Danby, knt.
City—John Beyne, Rich. White.
Hull—Alex. Stockdale, John Thacker.
Knaresborough—Edw. Napper, John Long.
Scarborough—Anthony Brann, Esq., Robt. Massey, Esq.
Ripon—Will. Rastall, John Temple.
Hedon—Sir Thos. Wharton, knt., Rich. Cuthbert, Esq.
Boroughbridge—Ralph Cholmley, Christ. Wray.
Thirsk—Thos. Waterton, Esq., Reginald Beesley, Esq.

1 AND 2 PHILIP AND MARY.

County—Sir Will. Babthorpe, knt., Sir Thos. Gargrave, knt.
City—
Hull—Francis Jobson, Thos. Dalton.
Scarborough—Reginald Beesley, Esq., Tristram Cook.
Knaresborough—
Hedon—Rich. Cuthbert, Esq., Sir John Constable, knt.
Ripon—

2 AND 3 PHILIP AND MARY.

County—Sir Robt. Constable, knt., Sir Thos. Gargrave, knt.
City—Will. Holme, Reginald Beesley, Esq.
Hull—Walter Jobson, John Thornton.
Hedon—Geo. Cobham, Rich. Cuthbert, Esq.
Boroughbridge—Christ. Wray, Robt. Kempe.
Knaresborough—Sir Humph. Fisher, knt., Sir Thos. Chaloner,
   knt.
Ripon—John Holmes, Thos. Pooley, Esq.
Thirsk—Christ. Lascelles, Esq., Robt. Rose, Esq.
Scarborough—Will. Hasey, Francis Ashley.

4 AND 5 PHILIP AND MARY.

County—Sir Thos. Wharton, knt., Sir Rich. Cholmeley, knt.
City—Will. Holme, John Peacock.
Hull—Walter Jobson, Thos. Alured.
Knaresborough—Henry Darcy, Esq , Thos. Ashill, Esq.
Scarborough—Rich. Joane, gent., Edw. Beesley.
Ripon—Will. Heythe, Esq., Thos. Lewknor, Esq.
Hedon—Sir John Constable, knt., John Goldwell, Esq.
Boroughbridge—Will. Fairfax, Esq., Christ. Wray, Esq.
Thirsk—Christ. Lascelles, Esq., Thos. Eynns, Esq.
Aldborough—John Gascoigne, John Browne, gent.

1 ELIZABETH.

County — SIR THOS. GARGRAVE, KNT., SPEAKER, Hen.
    Savile, Esq.
City—Will. Watson, Rich. Goldthorpe.
Hull—John Oversall, ——
Scarborough—Sir Henry Gate, knt., Will. Strickland, Esq.
The Sheriff returns that the bailiffs of Hedon, and the
burgesses of Thirsk, Ripon, Boroughbridge, Knaresborough, &
Aldborough, have given no answer.

5 ELIZABETH.

County—Sir Thos. Gargrave, knt., Sir Nich. Fairfax, knt.
City—Will. Watson, Ralph Hall, gent.
Hull—Christ. Eltofts, Esq., John Thornton, Esq.
Scarborough—Sir Hen. Gate, knt., Will. Strickland, Esq.
Knaresborough—Sir Hen. Gate, knt., Will. Strickland, Esq.
         (in whose places, as they were already re-
        turned for Scarborough.)
          Christ. Tamworth, Esq., Robt. Bowes, gent.
Ripon—Geo. Leigh, Rich. Pratt, gent.
Hedon—Sir John Constable, knt., Christ. Hillyard, Esq.
Boroughbridge—John Ashley, Esq., Thos. Disney, Esq.
Thirsk—Thos. Amys, Esq., Christ. Lascelles, Esq.
Aldborough—Will. Lambert, Anth. Talboys, gent.
Beverley—Nich. Bacon, Esq., Robt. Hall, Esq.

13 ELIZABETH.

County—Sir Thos. Gargrave, knt., Sir Hen. Gate, knt.

City—Ralph Hall, Hugh Graves, gent.

Hull—John Thornton, James Clarkson, gent.

Knaresborough—Sir Geo. Bowes, knt., James Cade, Esq.

Scarborough—Edw. Gate, Esq., Will. Strickland, Esq.

Ripon—Martin Birkhead, Anth. Roane, Esq.

Hedon—Christ. Hillyard, Esq., Will. Paler.

Boroughbridge—Cotton Gargrave, Esq., Thos. Boynton, Esq.

Thirsk—John Dawney, Esq., John Leighton, Esq.

Aldborough—Thos. Eynns, Esq., ——

Beverley—Edw. Ellerker, Esq., Thos. Leighton, Esq.

14 ELIZABETH.

County—Sir Thos. Gargrave, knt., Thos. Waterton, Esq.
(in whose place, deceased, Sir Robert Stapleton, knt.)

City—Gregory Peacock, Hugh Graves, aldermen (in Peacock's place, Roger Askwith).

Knaresborough—Francis Slingsby, Rich. Banks, Esq.

Hull—James Clarkson, Thos. Fleming.

Scarborough—Sir Henry Gate, knt., Edw. Carey, Esq.

Ripon—Martin Birkhead, John Scott, gent.

Hedon—Christ. Hillyard, Esq., John Moore, gent.

Boroughbridge—Thos. Eynns, Esq., Cotton Gargrave, Esq.

Thirsk—John Dawney, Esq., Edw. Gate, Esq.

Aldborough—Rich. Bunny, Esq., Thos. Tempest, Esq.

Beverley—Rich. Topcliff, Esq., Thos. Eglionby, Esq.

27 ELIZABETH.

County—Ralph Eure, Esq., Will. Mallory, Esq.

City—Will. Robinson, alderman, Robt. Brooke, ald.

Hull—John Thornton, ald., John Alured, Esq.

Knaresborough—Edward Pooley of Gray's Inn, Fran. Slingsby, Esq.

Scarborough—John Hotham, Esq., Will. Strickland, Esq.

Ripon—Will. Spencer, Esq., Gervase Lee, Esq.

Richmond—John Pepper, Esq., Marmaduke Wyvill, Esq.

Hedon—Henry Constable, Esq., Fulk Grevill, Esq.

Boroughbridge—Hen. Cheke, Esq., Nich. Font, Esq.

Thirsk—Sir John Dawney, knt., Robt. Bowes, Esq.
Aldborough—Will. Wade, Esq., Robt. Waterhouse, Esq.
Beverley—John Stanhope, Esq., Robt. Wrote, Esq.

28 ELIZABETH.

County—Sir Henry Gate, knt., Sir Thos. Fairfax, knt.
City—Will. Hillyard, Esq., Robert Brooke, ald.
Hull—Edw. Wakefield, ald., John Alured, Esq.
Knaresborough—Francis Palmes, Esq., William Davison,
    Principal Secretary.
Scarborough—Sir Ralph Bourchier, knt., Edw. Hutchison,
    Esq.
Ripon—Will. Spencer, Esq., Sam. Sands, Esq.
Richmond—Robt. Bowes, jun., Esq., Sam. Cox of London,
    Esq.
Hedon—Sir Henry Constable, knt., John Hotham, Esq.
Boroughbridge—Geo. Savile, Esq., Robt. Briggs, gent.
Thirsk—Sir John Dawney, knt., Hen. Bellasis, Esq.
Aldborough—George Horsey, Esq., Raynold Harleston, Esq.
Beverley—Geo. Purefoy, jun., Esq., Mich. Wharton, Esq.

31 ELIZABETH.

County—Sir Hen. Constable, knt., Sir Ralph Bourchier, knt.
City—Robert Askwith, ald., Will. Robinson, ald.
Hull—Leonard Willan, ald., Will. Gee, jun., gent.
Knaresborough—Thos. Preston, Francis Harvey, gent.
Scarborough—Edw. Gate, Esq., Will. Fishe.
Ripon—Peter York, Will. Smith of Essex, Esq.
Richmond—James Dale, John Smith, gent.
Hedon—John Alford, Esq., Christ. Hillyard, Esq.
Boroughbridge—Sir Edw. Fitton, knt., Francis Moore, of the
    Middle Temple.
Thirsk—Sir John Dawney, knt., Henry Bellasis, Esq.
Aldborough—Thos. Fairfax, Esq., David Waterhouse, gent.
Beverley—Launcelot Alford, Esq., John Truslowe, Esq.

35 ELIZABETH.

County—Sir George Savile, knt., John Askew, Esq.
City—Andrew Trewe, alderman, James Birkby, alderman.

Hull—Leonard Willan, alderman, Peter Probe, gent.
Knaresborough—Samuel Fox, gent., Simon Willis, gent.
Scarborough—Edw. Gate, Esq., Roger Dalton.
Ripon—Anthony Wingfield, Esq., Will. Bennet, Student in
Gray's Inn.
Richmond—Talbot Bowes, Esq., John Pepper, gent.
Hedon—Hen. Brooke, Esq., Christ. Hillyard, gent.
Boroughbridge—John Brograve of Braughing, co. Hertford,
Esq., Vincent Skinner, Esq.
Thirsk—Sir John Dawney, knt., Hen. Bellasis, Esq.
Aldborough—Anth. Fisher, Esq., Edw. Hamock, Esq.
Beverley—Edw. Alford, Esq., John Mansfield, Esq.

39 ELIZABETH.

County—Sir John Savile, knt., Sir Will. Fairfax, knt.
City—James Birkby, Thos. Moseley.
Hull—Leonard Willan, Anthony Cole.
Scarborough—Sir Thos. Hoby, knt., Walter Pye, Esq.
Knaresborough—Hugh Beeston, Will. Slingsby.
Ripon—John Bennet, LL.D., John Perkins, Dean of Ripon.
Richmond—Marmaduke Wyvill, Esq., Cuthbert Pepper, Esq.
Hedon—Thos. Selwyn, Christ. Hillyard, Esq.
Boroughbridge—Henry Fanshaw, Esq., Thos. Crompton,
LL.D.
Thirsk—Geo. Lister, Esq., Thomas Bellasis, Esq.
Aldborough—Hen. Bellasis, Esq., Rich. Gargrave, Esq.
Beverley—Thos. Crompton, Esq., Edw. Alford (?).

43 ELIZABETH.

County—Sir Thos. Fairfax, knt., Sir Edw. Stanhope, knt.
City—John Bennet, LL.D., Hen. Hall, gent.
Hull—John Lister, merchant, John Graves, merchant.
Scarborough—Will. Eure, Esq., Edw. Stanhope, Esq.
Knaresborough—Hen. Slingsby, Esq., Will. Slingsby, Esq.
Ripon—Christ. Parkins, LL.D., John Thornborough, Esq.
Richmond—Cuthbert Pepper, Esq., Talbot Bowes, Esq.
Hedon—Matth. Pattison, Esq., Christ. Hillyard, Esq.
Boroughbridge—Thos. Fairfax, Esq., Richard Whalley, Esq.
Thirsk—Henry Bellasis, Esq., John Mallory, Esq.

Aldborough—Sir Edw. Cecil, knt., Rich. Thrackeston, Esq.
Beverley—Ralph Swaine, gent., Edw. Francis, Esq.

1 JAMES I.

County—Sir Francis Clifford, knt., Sir John Savile of Howley, knt.

City—Robert Askwith, alderman, Chr. Brooke.

Hull—Anth. Cooke, alderman, John Edmonds, alderman.

Aldborough—Sir Henry Savile, knt., Sir Edm. Sheffield, knt.

Beverley—Alan Piercy, Esq., Will. Gee, Esq.

Hedon—Sir Hen. Constable, knt., Sir Christ. Hillyard, knt. (in Constable's place, Sir John Digby, knt.)

Boroughbridge—John Ferne, Esq., Sir Hen. Jenkins, knt. (in Ferne's place, deceased, Sir Rich. Gargrave, knt., and in Gargrave's place, Thos. Vavasour, Esq.)

Richmond—Talbot Bowes, Esq., Rich. Percivall, Esq.

Knaresborough—Sir Hen. Slingsby, knt., Sir Will. Slingsby, knt.

Ripon—Sir John Mallory, knt., Sir John Bennet, knt.

Thirsk—Sir Edw. Swift, knt., Timothy Whittingham, Esq.

Scarborough—Francis Eure, Esq., Sir Thomas Posthumus Hoby, knt.

12 JAMES I.

County—Sir John Savile, knt., Sir Thos. Wentworth, knt. and bart.

City—Roger Askwith, Christ. Brooke.

Hull—

Knaresborough—Sir Henry Slingsby, knt.

Scarborough—Sir Thos. Posthumus Hoby, knt.

Ripon—Sir Thos. Vavasour, knt., Will. Mallory, Esq. (?)

Richmond—Talbot Bowes, Esq., Will. Bowes, Esq. (?)

Beverley—Sir Walter Covert, knt. (?)

Hedon—Sir Christ. Hillyard, knt., Clem. Coke, Esq.

Thirsk—John Gibb, Esq., Sir Henry Bellasis, knt. (?)

Aldborough—Sir Henry Savile, knt., Edm. Scot. (?)

Boroughbridge—Sir John Ferne, knt , John Bingley. (?)

18 JAMES I.

County—Sir Geo. Calvert, knt., Sir Thos. Wentworth, knt. and bart.

City—Sir Roger Askwith, knt., Christ. Brooke.

Hull—John Lister, Esq., Maurice Abbot, Esq.

Scarborough—Sir Richard Cholmley, knt., Will. Conyers, Esq.

Knaresborough—Sir Henry Slingsby, knt., Richard Hutton, Esq.

Richmond—Sir Talbot Bowes, knt., Will. Bowes, Esq.

Beverley—Sir Christ. Hillyard, knt., Edm. Scot, Esq. (?)

Boroughbridge—Sir Ferdinando Fairfax, Geo. Wethered, Esq.

Aldborough—Christ. Wandesford, Esq., John Carsvill, Counsellor at Law.

Thirsk—Sir Thos. Bellasis, knt., Sir John Bellasis, knt.

Hedon—Sir Matt. Boynton, knt., and bart., Sir Thomas Fairfax, knt.

Ripon—Sir Thomas Posthumus Hoby, knt., Will. Mallory, Esq.

Pontefract—Geo. Shilletoe, Esq., Edm. Sandys, jun., Esq.

21 JAMES I.

County—Sir John Savile, knt., Sir Thos. Savile, knt.

City—Sir Arthur Ingram, knt., Christ. Brooke, Esq.

Hull—John Lister, Esq., Maurice Abbot, Esq. (in Sir John Suckling's place, chosen for Middlesex.)

Knaresborough—Sir Henry Slingsby, knt., Rich. Hutton, Esq.

Scarborough—Hugh Cholmley, Esq., Will. Conyers, Esq.

Ripon—Sir Thomas Posthumus Hoby, knt., Will. Mallory, Esq.

Richmond—Christ. Pepper, Esq., Recorder, John Wandesford, Esq.

Hedon—Sir Thos. Fairfax, knt., Sir Christ. Hillyard, knt.

Boroughbridge—Sir Ferdinando Fairfax, knt., Philip Mainwaring, Esq.

Thirsk—Sir Thos. Bellasis, knt., Sir Will. Sheffield, knt.

Aldborough—Chr. Wandesford, Esq., John Carvill, Esq.

Beverley—Edm. Scot, Esq., Sir Hen. Cary, knt.

Pontefract—Sir Thos. Wentworth, knt. & bart., Sir John Jackson, knt.

1 CHARLES I.

County—Sir Thos. Wentworth, bart., Sir Thos. Fairfax, knt.

City—Sir Arthur Ingram, knt., Christ. Brooke, Esq.

Hull—John Lister, Esq., Sir Maurice Abbott, knt.

Knaresborough—Sir Rich. Hutton, knt., Sir Henry Slingsby, knt.

Scarborough—Hugh Cholmondeley, Esq., Will. Thompson, Esq.

Ripon—Sir Thos. Posthumus Hoby, knt., Will Mallory, Esq.

Richmond—Christ. Wandesford, Esq., Sir Talbot Bowes, knt.

Boroughbridge—Sir Ferdinando Fairfax, knt., Will. Mainwaring, Esq.

Thirsk—Hen. Bellasis, Esq., Hen. Stanley, Esq.

Aldborough--Rich. Aldborough, Esq., John Carvill, Esq.

Beverley—Sir John Hotham, Bart., Will. Alford, Esq.

Pontefract—Sir John Jackson, knt., Sir Rich. Beaumont, knt.

Hedon—Sir Thomas Fairfax, of Walton, knt., Sir Christ. Hillyard, knt.

1 Charles I.—2nd Parliament.

County—Sir John Savile, knt., Sir Will. Constable, knt.

City—Sir Arthur Ingram, knt., Christ. Brook, Esq.

Hull--John Lister, Esq., Lancelot Roper, gent.

Knaresborough—Sir Rich. Hutton, knt., Hen. Benson, gent.

Scarborough—Hugh Cholmondeley, Esq., Stephen Hutchinson, Esq.

Ripon—Sir Thos. Posthumus Hoby, knt., Thos. Best, Esq.

Richmond—Christopher Wandesford, Esq., Matt. Hutton, Esq.

Boroughbridge—Sir Ferdinando Fairfax, knt., Will. Mainwaring, Esq.

Thirske—Henry Bellasis, Esq., Will. Cholmley, Esq.

Aldborough—Rich. Aldborough, Esq., John Carvill, Esq.

Beverley—Sir John Hotham, bart., Will. Alford, Esq.

Pontefract—Sir John Jackson, knt., Sir Franc. Foljambe, bart.

Hedon—Sir Thos. Fairfax, knt., Sir Chr. Hillyard, knt.

3 Charles I.

County—Henry Bellasis, Esq., Sir Thos. Wentworth, knt. and bart.

City—Sir Arthur Ingram, knt., Thos. Hoyle, alderman.

Hull—John Lister, Esq., James Watkinson, Esq.

Knaresborough—Sir Rich. Hutton, jun., knt., Hen. Benson, Esq.

Scarborough—Sir Will. Constable, knt. and bart., John Harrison, Esq.

Ripon—Sir Thos. Posthumus Hoby, knt., Will. Mallory, Esq.

Richmond—Sir Talbot Bowes, knt., James Howell, Esq.

Hedon—Sir Christ. Hillyard, knt., Thos. Alured, Esq.

Boroughbridge—Sir Ferdinando Fairfax, knt., Francis Nevill, Esq.

Thirsk—Christ. Wandesford, Esq., Will. Frankland, Esq.

Aldborough—Hen. Darley, Esq., Rob. Stapleton, Esq.

Beverley—Sir John Hotham, knt. and bart., Sir Will. Alford, knt.

Pontefract—Sir John Jackson, knt., Sir John Ramsden, knt.

15 Chas. I.

County—Hen. Bellasis, Esq., Sir Will. Savile, bart.

City—Sir Edw. Osborne, bart., Sir Roger Jaques, knt.

Hull—Sir John Lister, knt., Henry Vane, Esq.

Scarborough—Sir Hugh Cholmeley, knt., John Hotham, Esq.

Knaresborough—Sir Hen. Slingsby, bart., Hen. Benson, Esq.

Ripon—Will. Mallory, Esq., Sir Paul Neille, knt.

Richmond—Sir Will. Pennington, bart., Maj. Norton, Esq.

Hedon—Sir Philip Stapleton, knt., John Alured, Esq.

Boroughbridge—Sir Ferdinando Fairfax, knt., Francis Nevill, Esq.

Thirsk—Hen. Bellasis, Esq., Will. Frankland, Esq.

Aldborough—Rich. Aldborough, Esq., Brian Palmes, Esq.

Beverley—Sir John Hotham, knt. and bart., Michael Warten, Esq.

Pontefract—Sir John Ramsden, knt., Sir Geo. Wentworth, knt.

APPENDIX C.

DODSWORTH'S ACCOUNT OF THE CALDER.

(From Harleian MS. 803, written probably between the years 1620 and 1630.)

Kelder taketh his name of 2 springs ariseing at o^r Appoinne, the one in Kell hill, th'other at Dearestones in the forrest of Sowerby, and so taketh his name at the meeting of the foresaid springs.

Under Sandal Castle Kelder augmenteth his streame with a Rivulet called Staynbrigbeck, which hath his head in Rihill near Havercroft, and boundeth Walton the seate of Watterton, (whose Ancestor married the da: and heire of Burgh, Lo: of Walton, Brearley, Shafton, Calthorne &c., their lands, who had 3 daughters, married to Watterton, who had Walton, another to (blank) who had Brearley, the third died *sans* issue and gave Calthorne to Watterton, and Shafton to Brearley (*sic.*), then keepeth on his course by Cold Henley, the ancient possession of Hoptons knyghts, thence between Cheet and Woolley where Nevell and Wooderow have long tyme lived in good repute, and so by Stainbrigg into Kelder.

At a place called Thornell Leas, the house of Mr Nettleton, a little brook called aunciently Ravensbrook falleth into Kelder wch hath his head about Shibden, beeing increased with many small brooks cometh bye long Liversedge ye seat of the Nevills for a long time, which he had by mariage of the daughter and heire of Liversedge the Ancient owner thereof, where hath been a parke disparked in our memory; the last of Nevells was Charles, who when he fled for sideing with the rebellious Earles,

Q. Eliz. gave it to Sir (Edward) Carrey —— then goeth to Burstall.

At Dewsbury a litle Rivulet called Wookirke becke falleth into Kelder beginning above Batley, cometh by Howley not far from Woodkirke, a cell belonging to St. Oswald, by Sir John Savile Smithies and by Sotehill hall and parke nere Dewsbury church.

APPENDIX D.

BY WM. VAVASOUR OF HAZELWOOD, ESQ., OBSERVED.

(*Lansdowne MS.*, 900.)

In the 38th year of King Henry the Eighth, his Majesty made his progress to the City of York. And among his nobles and honorable retainers, one Dr. Tunstall attended, who was a famous and learned man, and then Bishop of Durham, one of the greatest travellers into foreign Nations of that time. When the King was come some miles on the north of Doncaster this Bishop took upon him about Scaursby Leazes, to show his Majesty one of the greatest & richest valleys that ever he found in all his travels through Europe, and moved the King to look about him and behold the great mountains and great hills on the East side of the said valley, being called York wolds and Blackamoor, and upon the west hand the high fells of Craven, and all within the County of York, the breadth about 40 miles, and the length of the valley about 50 miles, wherein betwixt Doncaster, which is the South point, and the confines of the Bishoprick of Durham, which is the north point thereof, you pass in a direct line northward within the compass of Yorkshire 7 great rivers, and all navigable to the place you pass over or very near, viz.: the river Dun at Doncaster, which hath there two streams, the river Aire at Ferrybridge, the Wharfe at Wetherby, the Nidd at Walshford, the "Your" at Baroughbridge, the Swale at Topcliffe, Teage at Nesham, all on the road between London and Berwick.

Upon the west hand not far from the street or road you leave the river Calder and not 5 miles on the East hand the river Ouse, which bring ships of great burthen.

Very near the centre of this valley is seated upon the rising of a hill the manor house of Hazelwood where the ancient name and family of Vavasour has continued and dwelt there ever since the time of William the Conqueror as by good record appeareth. And within eight miles of this house (or little more) are all these prospects and pleasures which are not to be found in so plentiful a manner in so small a compass within all England, that is to say 165 manor-houses, the dwellings of Lords, Knights, and Gentlemen of the best qualities inhabited at this present or within this few years last past, by the gentle-men whose names are set down hereafter; 275 several woods whereof some of them contain 500 acres of wood, 32 parks, 2 chaces of deer, 12 rivers and brooks whereof 5 are navigable upon which are 76 water-mills for corn and stored with exceed-ing many salmon and other fishes, 25 coalmines which yield abundance of coal for the whole country; 6 market towns and but ten miles distant from York, where there are 3 market days every week, and every Tuesday, Friday, and Saturday great store of sea-fish new and fresh from the sea; three forges for making of iron,* and stone for making the same, great store of corne and cattle, yielding that which is sufficient for the benefit of the Counties adjoining, and for the sustenance of men and beasts; within the said limits there wanteth nothing that any other county hath, flesh, fish, fowl, great store of meadow and pasture, and excellent air.

And for pleasures which recreate the minds and bodies of men there are within these limits as much sport and pleasure as in any place of England, in the arts of hunting, shooting, fishing and fowling. There is within this limit one thing which must not be forgotten, which is, that there may be found more excel-lent free stone, lime and plaster than would build as many churches, cities and castles as are at this day in all Yorkshire; In probability whereof, there is good evidence in the hands of Vavasour. Out of a little piece of a quarry within the manor of Haslewood have been taken the Cathedral Church of York, the Minsters of Howden, Selby and Beverley, the Abbey of

---

* Kirkstall, Folly-foot, and Rothwell Haigh.

St Mary's in York, Thornton College in Lincolnshire and divers other churches.

The Manors with some additions of the now or late Honors within 10 miles compass of Haslewood.

The Manor of York—The King's House.
The Honor of Pontefract—The same.
Knaresbrough Castle—The Queen's jointure.
Cawood Castle—The Lord Archbp. of York.
Bishopthorpe—The same.
Spofford Manor—The Earl of Northumberland.
Heaghley Manor—Lord Wharton.
Harwood Castle—The Earl of Strafford.
Gawthrop Hall—The same.
Pontefract, the New Hall—The Earl of Shrewsbury.
Swillington—The Lord Darcy and Menill.
Eskirk—Lord Howard.
Walton—Lord Fairfax *vise* Emeley.
Nun Appleton—Lord Fairfax.
Bilbrough—The same.
Hamilton—Sir Thos. Widdrington.
Helthwate Hill—The same.
Aldwalley (?)—Sir Jervis Clifton, knt.
Nostall Abby—Sir John Worsenam (Wolstenholme).
Kippax—Sir William Slingsby.
Kippax-park—Sir Thos. Bland, Bart.
Grimston—Sir Edward Stanhope, Knt.
Haslewood—Sir Walter Vavasour, Bart.
Headley—Sir John Hewett, Bart.
Steeton by Sherburne—Sir Fran. Fulgeamb.
Toulston—Sir Robert Barwick.
Barley—Sir Geo. Twisleton, Bart.
Methley—Sir Henry Savill, knt. and Bart.
Temple Newsam—Sir Arthur Ingram.
Seacroft—Sir Ralfe Hansby.
Burne—Sir Andru Younge.
South Milford—Sir Fran. Bailden.
North Milford—Sir John Leeds.

Byram—Sir John Ramsden.
Wheele Hall—Sir William Gascoyne.
Mooreby—Sir William Acklam.
Naburne—Sir George Palmer.
Woodhall—Sir Walter Vavasour, Bart.
Kirsksgill—Sir Geo. Wentworth of Wolley.
Bramhope—Sir Robert Dineley.
Swinden—Sir Benjamin Thornebrough.
Cayley—Sir William Dalton.
Farneley—Sir Thos. Danby.
Plumpton Tower—Sir Edward Plompton.
Stockhill—Sir Peter Middleton.
Gouldsbrough—Sir Rich. Hutton.
Allerton Malere—Sir Tho. Maleverer, Bart.
Ribston—Sir John Goodrick, Bart.
Scriven—Sir Hen. Slingsby, Bart.
Redhouse—The same.
Middleton—Sir Ferdi. Lees.
Barnebow—Sir Tho. Gascoyne, Bart.
Parlington—The same.
Saxton—Sir William Hungate.
Huddleston—Sir Phil. Hungate, Bart.
Whixley—Sir Rich. Tankred.
North Dighton—Sir William Ingleby, Bart.
Lindley—Sir Guy Palmes.
Leathley—Sir Ing. Hopton.
Bardsey Manor—
Nidd—Sir Francis Trapps Bernand.
Copgrave—Sir Tho. Harrison.
Steeton—Sir William Fairfax.
Temple Copenthorpe—Sir William Vavasour.
Popleton—Sir Tho. Hutton.
Coulthrop—Sir Tho. Walmesley.
Colton—Sir Geo. Ratcliffe.
Bramham biging—Sir Fran. Armitage.
Beeston—Sir John Wood.
Cattall—Sir William Ingram.

B B

Overton—Sir William Belts.
Beningbrough—Sir John Bourchier.
Heathhall—The Lady Bowls, Baronetesse.

———

Wighill—Mr. Stapleton.
..asedike—The same.
Scardingwell—Mr. Hammond.
..oulton—Mr. Anlabie.
Lead—Mr. Vavasour.
Smawes—Mr. Foster.
Wothersom—Mr. Maliverer of Arneclif.
Oglethorpe—Mr. Oglethorpe.
Berkin—Mr. Cressy.
Brotherton—Mr. Tindall.
Scarcroft—Mr. Rither.
Ledston—Mr. Witham.
Leadsham—Mr. Harebred.
(Win)strop—Mr. Moore.
(Ake)ton—Mr. Beckwith.
Gateforth—Mr. Brooke.
Munkfriston—Mr. Wilson.
Sharleston—Mr. Slingers (*sic* Stringer ?).
Credling Stubbs—Mr. Percy.
Thorpe Hall—Mr. Clough.
Roundhay—Mr. Oglethorpe of Roundhay.
Kiddall—Mr. Ellis.
Sturton—Mr. Gascoyne.
Munk...—Mr. Killingbeck.
Walton-head—Mr. Johnson.
Arthington—Mr. Arthington.
Casley—Mr. Arthington of Casley.
Burrougbridg—Mr. Tankred.
Aldbrough—Mr. Aldbrough.
Scotton—Mr. Pullon.
Breame—Mr. Cholmeley.
Rither—Mr. Robinson.
Cawood—Mr. Lister.

Barkston—Mr. Barkston.
Beckay—Mr. White.
Micklethwate Grange—Mr. Bilby.
(*Query*, Beilby Grange—Mr. Micklethwaite.)
Marston—Mr. Thwates.
Appleton Northall—Mr. Moyser.
Acaster Selby—Mr. Harrison.
Stillingfleet—Mr. Ellerkar.
Kelfeild—Mr. Stillington.
Uskelfe—Mr. Persons.
Horneington—Mr. Topham.
Pallethorpe—Mr. Inglebye.
Acham—Mr. Newarke.
Acham Grange—Mr. Gayle.
Askham parva—Mr. Swales.
Askham magna—Mr. Geldard, Alderman of York.
Bilton in the Ainsty—Mr. Snawsell.
Bilton parke—Mr. Stockdall.
Acworth—Mr. Pickering.
Monkroyds—Mr. Hammerton.
Calverley—Mr. Calverley.
Nunmonkton—Mr. Payler.
Horsforth—Mr. Stanhope.
Tong—Mr. Tempest.
Chevit—Mr. Nevill.

APPENDIX E.

CONTRIBUTORS TO THE QUEEN'S LOAN, 1590.

CITY OF YORK.

Thomas Moaley, of Walmegate ward, gent.		.	.	.	50l.
Thomas Apleyarde, of the same, alderman		.	.	.	20l.
Marmaduke Southbie,	,,	.	.	.	20l.
Thomas Mason,	,,	.	.	.	20l.
Robert Asquythe, of Crux parish, alderman		.	.	.	30l.
William Robinson,	,,	,,	.	.	50l.
Robert Walter,	,,	,,	.	.	50l.
William Gibson,	,,	,,	.	.	20l.
Alice Beckwith,	,,	widow	.	.	20l.
Leonard Beckwith,	,,	.	.	.	20l.
William Woode,	,,	.	.	.	20l.
Thomas Harbart,	,,	.	.	.	20l.
Harbart,	,,	widow	.	.	20l.
Robert Myres,	,,	.	.	.	20l.
William Grenbery,	,,	.	.	.	20l.
John Watson,	,,	.	.	.	30l.
Robert Broke, of All Hallows upon the Pavement, alderman					30l.
Andrew Trew, of the same, alderman		.	.	.	20l.
Richard Murton,	,,	.	.	.	20l.
Percivall Broke,	,,	.	.	.	20l.
Henry Hall,	,,	.	.	.	20l.
Percivall Levet,	,,	.	.	.	20l.
Bryan Brickhead	,,	.	.	.	20l.
John Waddesworth	,,	.	.	.	20l.
John Gibson, of St. Peter the little .		.	.	.	20l.

John Plomer, of St. Peter the little . . . . 20*l.*
Christopher Turner, of St. Mary in Castlegate . . . 20*l.*
John Yowdale,   ,,   ,,   . . . 20*l.*
Roger Lee, doctor of Phisick of St. Dennys parish . . 20*l.*
Dorothy Cartmell, of the same . . . . . 20*l.*
James Birkeby, Alderman of Christ's parish in Munckwarde 20*l.*
Thomas Wanton, of the same . . . . . . 20*l.*
John Weddell,   ,, ... 20*l.*
William Paicock,   ,, ... 20*l.*
James Mudd,   ,, ... 20*l.*
Thomas Wilson, of Trinities in Groodrongate . . . 20*l.*
William Richardson, of St. Sampson's parish . . . 20*l.*
John Robinson,   ,,   ,, . . . 20*l.*
Laurance Meres, of St. Dell Pike . . . . . 20*l.*
Jane Younge, of the same, widow . . . . . 50*l.*
Raphe Rokebye,   ,,   esquire . . . . . 20*l.*
William Smythe, of St. Morrice parish . . . . 20*l.*
Thomas Elwood,   ,,   ,, ... 20*l.*
Robert Criplinge, of St. Mary in Lathropp . . .20*l.*
George Munford, of St. Androwes . . . . 20*l.*
Ryc. Smythe, of Alhallowes in Peysholme . . . 20*l.*
Edward Stanhope, of Bowthom warde, esquire . . 30*l.*
John Bennett, doctor of law, of the same . . . 20*l.*
Edward Fawcett, of the same . . . . . . 20*l.*
Henry Swinborne,   ,, ... 20*l.*
William Allan,   ,, ... 20*l.*
William Calme,   ,, ... 20*l.*
James Stock,   ,, ... 20*l.*
John Standeven,   ,, ... 20*l.*
Frauncis Killingbeck,   ,, ... 20*l.*
George Watson,   ,, ... 20*l.*
William Fethergill,   ,, ... 20*l.*
William Hyldyarde, of St. Wilfrid's, esquire . . . 30*l.*
John More, the younger,   ,,   ,, . . . 30*l.*
James Cotterell,   ,, ... 20*l.*
Anthony Teale,   ,, ... 20*l.*
Henry Procter,   ,, ... 20*l.*

John Loskay, of St. Wilfrid's	20*l.*
Robert Man, ,, ...	20*l.*
Rowland Fawcett, of St. Ellins in Staniegate . . .	20*l.*
Oswolde Dente, ,, ,, . . .	20*l.*
John Stevenson, ,, ,, . . .	20*l.*
Tho. Jackson, Alderman of St. Olyves parish . . .	30*l.*
Tho. Buskell, of St. Martens in Coni Streete . . .	20*l.*
Katherine Colthrist, ,, ,, widow . .	20*l.*
John Darley, ,, ,, ...	20*l.*
George Kitchinge, ,, ,, ...	20*l.*
Henry Pulleyne, ,, ,, ...	20*l.*
Michael Pickeringe, ,, ,, ...	20*l.*
John Bilbowe, ,, ,, ...	20*l.*
Guy Netham, ,, ,, ...	20*l.*
Ambrose Awne, ,, ,, ...	20*l.*
Thomas Harrison, of Mickleth Warde, alderman . .	100*l.*
Raphe Richardson, alderman of the same . . .	20*l.*
George Terry, of the same	20*l.*
Christopher Beckwith, of St. Johns at Owsebridgend .	20*l.*
Frauncys Bayne, ,, ,, . .	30*l.*
Raphe Harte, ,, ,, . .	20*l.*
John Bewe, ,, ,, . .	20*l.*
Frauncys Wayde, ,, ,, . .	20*l.*
Henry Banister, ,, ...	20*l.*
John Race, of Bishopshill, thelder	20*l.*
Thomas Walter, of Trinities in Micklegate . . .	20*l.*
Henry Wilkinson, ,, . . .	20*l.*
Henry Holdesworth, of Alhalowes in North-street . .	20*l.*
Robert Dawson, ,, . .	20*l.*
William Fayrefax, of Bolton Percy, esquire . . .	50*l.*
Robert Snawsell, of Bilton, esquire	20*l.*
George Twaythes, of Marston, esquire	30*l.*
Henry Fayrefax, of Bilborough	50*l.*
Peter Newarke, of Acombe	20*l.*

KINGSTON UPON HULL.

Richard Reade, of Humber Warde	20*l.*
Stephen Prestwood, ,, ...	20*l.*
Edward Preston, ,, ...	20*l.*

John Perse, Archbishop of York	200*l.*
Thorneboroughe, Dean of York . . .	50*l.*
Ramsden, Archdeacon of York . . .	50*l.*
Richard Remington, Archdeacon of the East Riding	50*l.*
Birde, Archdeacon of Cleveland. . .	30*l.*
Louthe, Archdeacon of Nottingham . .	40*l.*
Christopher Gregory, Prebendary of Amplefrd .	30*l.*
James Cock, Prebendary of Langtoft . . .	30*l.*
William Power, Prebendary of Ricall . . .	30*l.*
James Willford, Prebendary of Stillington . .	30*l.*
William Wilkinson, Prebendary of Fridaythorpe .	20*l.*
Edwyn Sandes, Prebendary of Wetwange . .	30*l.*
Lyndlay, Prebendary of Hustwayte . .	20*l.*
Prebendary of Bugthorpe . .	20*l.*
Miles Sandes, Prebendary of Wighton . . .	20*l.*
Reginald Tunstall, Prebendary of Knaresborough .	50*l.*
Griffin Biskyn, Prebendary of Osbaldwick . .	
(In first fruits and a poor man.)	
Edmond Bunny, Prebendary of Wistowe . .	30*l.*
Binge, doctor, Prebendary of Strenshall . .	20*l.*
(A poor man.)	
Williams, Prebendary of Fenton . . .	20*l.*
Richard Remington, Prebendary of Northnewbolde, quia antea.	
Bulleyn, doctor, Prebendary of Ulleskelfe, ,, .	
Gibson, doctor, Precentor in the Church of York	40*l.*
William Palmer, Chancellor in the Church of York .	50*l.*
Henry Wright, Subdean of York	30*l.*
Edmond Bonney, parson of Bolton Percy, nihil quia antea.	
Richard Batsone, parson of Birken . . .	20*l.*
Ramsden, parson of Spofourth, nihil quia antea.	
Alexander Fasett, vicar of Leeds, poor.	
William Power, parson of Elmett in Barwicke, nihil quia antea.	
Arthur Kaye, vicar of Doncaster, poor.	
parson of Sprotburghe . . .	30*l.*
parson of Baddesworth . . .	20*l.*
parson of the moiety of the Church of Darfield	30*l.*

Leesam, doctor, vicar of Hallyfax . . . . . 20*l.*
Edward Whitakers, parson of Thornehill . . . 20*l.*
William Lawson, vicar of Rudby . . . . .
     parson of Stokesley . . . . 20*l.*
     parson of Lythe . . . . . 20*l.*
Tompson, doctor, parson of Settrington . . . .
John Barnes, parson of Siglesthorne . . . . 20*l.*
     parson of Baynton . . . . . 20*l.*
William Goodwyn, parson of Stangrave . . . . 20*l.*

INDEX.

C C

Smithson, Trynion, 167.
Smyth, Richard, 167, 373 ; William, 373 ; Bernard, 284, 294.
Snaith, 68, 108.
Snape, 67.
'Snapethorpe, 1.
Snawsell, Robert, 371, 374.
Soothill, 365.
Sotheby, Robert, 70 ; Marmaduke, 372.
Southwell, 139, 235.
Spencer, William, 357-8.
Spofforth, 368, 374.
Sprotborough, 154, 236, 375.
Sproxton, Richard, 129.
Stable, William, 237.
Stainton, 235.
Standeven, Mr., 95 ; John, 373.
Stangrave, 375.
Stanhope, Sir Edward, 233, 238, 359, 368 ; John, 358 ; Edward, 359, 373 ; Mr., 371.
Stanley, 71, 82, 234.
Stanley, Pierce, 72 ; Henry, 362.
Stanoy, Dr., 330.
Stapleton, Brian, 69 ; Sir Richard, 68 ; Sir Robert, 71, 137, 139, 357 ; Robert, 35, 363 ; Sir Philip, 363 ; Mr., 370.
Steel, Edward, 153.
Steeton, 71, 368-9.
Stevenson, Francis, 236 ; Geoffrey, 150 ; John, 374.
Stillingfleet, 371.
Stillington, Mr., 371.
Stillington, 375.
Stittenham, 68, 154.
Stock, James, 373.
Stockdale, Alexander, 354-5 ; Mr., 371.
Stockeld, 369.
Stokesley, 70, 171, 375.
Storey, John, 322.
Storthes, Thomas, 84.
Strensall, 375.
Strickland, William, 70, 356-7.
Stringer, Mr., 370.

Studley, 68.
Sturton, 370.
Sunderland, Abraham, 299 ; Richard, 304, 310, 315, 323.
Sutcliffe, Matthew, 299.
Sutton upon Derwent, 19, 25, 67.
Sutton in Galtres, 154.
Sutton, Thomas, 9 ; Katherine, 181.
Swaine, Ralph, 360.
Swales, Mr., 371.
Swan, Thomas, 276, 284, 294.
Swift, Sir Edward, 360.
Swillington, 40, 69, 368.
Swinborne, Henry, 373.
Swindon, 369.
Swine, 277.

Tadcaster, 16, 27, 32, 42, 153, 208, 226, 238, 336.
Talbot, John, 180 ; Richard, 180.
Talboys, Anthony, 356.
Tamworth, Christopher, 356.
Tankard, Richard, 170-3 ; William, 19, 63, 69, 355 ; Sir Richard, 369 ; Mr., 370.
Tattersall, Edmund, 54.
Taylford, Richard, 167 ; Giles, 153.
Taylor, Agnes and John, 151 ; Margaret, 151, 153 ; Thomas, 83, 151, 153 ; William, 129, 266 ; Giles, 153.
Teale, Anthony, 373.
Tempest, Henry, 71 ; Sir John, 15 ; Sir Richard, 15, 233 ; Thomas, 84, 357 ; Richard, 68, 84, 315; Mr., 371.
Temple, John, 355.
Temple, Newsome, 194.
Tenny, Robert and Janet, 153.
Terry, Michael, 150 ; George, 374.
Teske, Edward and Anne, 151.
Tessymond, William, 150-1.
Tetlow, Edmund, 299.
Thacker, John, 354-5.
Thackeray, —, 154 ; Thomas, 284, 294.

CPSIA information can be obtained
at www.ICGtesting.com
Printed in the USA
BVHW092347020922
646137BV00002B/21